ST TERESA OF AVILA

ST TERESA OF AVILA

Stephen Clissold

THE SEABURY PRESS · NEW YORK

1982
The Seabury Press
815 Second Avenue
New York, N.Y. 10017

Printed in the United States of America

First published in Great Britain in 1979 by Sheldon Press,
Marylebone Road, London NW1 4DU

Library of Congress Cataloging in Publication Data

Clissold, Stephen.
St Teresa of Avila.
Includes index.
1. Teresa, of Avila, Saint, 1515-1582.
2. Christian saints—Spain—Biography. I. Title.
BX4700.T4C55 1982   282'.092'4 [B]   81-9304
ISBN 0-8164-2621-X (pbk.)   AACR2

Contents

The Author

Stephen Clissold, O.B.E., was born in 1913 and attended Salisbury Cathedral Choir School. He won an open scholarship to read Modern Languages at Oriel College, Oxford, where he first became interested in the writings of the Spanish mystics. He made his career in the British Council, serving in Denmark, Chile and Turkey, and with the Foreign Office. He is now retired and lives in Bayswater, London.

He is the author of many books including *Latin America—A Cultural Outline; Latin America—New World, Third World; The Saints of South America; In Search of the Cid; Spain; The Wisdom of the Spanish Mystics* and *The Wisdom of St Francis and his Companions*. He is married with one daughter.

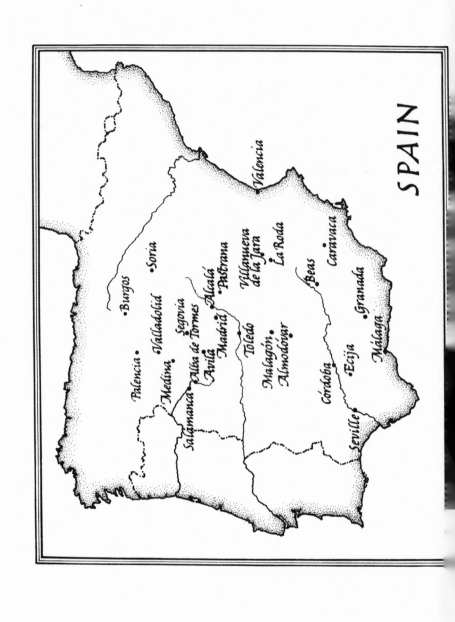

Main Characters

Teresa de Cepeda y Ahumada; also known as Teresa de Jesús or St Teresa of Avila.

Alonso (Sánchez) de Cepeda; her father.

María (married to Martín Guzmán); her elder half-sister.

Juana (married to Juan de Ovalle); her younger sister.

Lorenzo; a brother who made his fortune in the New World.

Teresita; Lorenzo's daughter.

Duke and Duchess of Alba; friends and patrons of St Teresa.

Alvaro de Mendoza; Bishop of Avila, and firm friend and supporter of St Teresa.

Ana de Jesús (Lobera); Prioress in Beas and St Teresa's successor as head of the Reform.

Ana de San Bartolomé (García); Discalced Carmelite lay-sister and nurse-companion to St Teresa in her later years.

Angel de Salazar; Carmelite Provincial, ambiguous in his attitude towards the Reform.

Antonio de Jesús; one of the first Carmelite friars to join the Reform, in which he became a leading figure.

Baltasar Alvarez; St Teresa's Jesuit confessor in Avila.

Baltasar de Jesús (Nieto); turbulent Carmelite friar.

Catalina de Cardona; eccentric hermit and foundress revered by the Discalced Carmelites.

Domingo Báñez; Dominican theologian and supporter of St Teresa.

Princess of Eboli; wife of the King's favourite Ruy Gómez, at first a patron and later an opponent of St Teresa.

Filippo Sega; papal nuncio hostile to the Reform.

Francisco de Salcedo; a devout layman of Avila and friend of St Teresa, also known as the *Caballero santo*.

Gaspar Daza; a priest of Avila, at first a critic and later a friend of St Teresa.

Gaspar de Quiroga; Cardinal Archbishop of Toledo and Grand Inquisitor.

Giovanni Battista Rossi (or Rubeo); General of the Carmelite Order, supporter and later critic of the Discalced Carmelites.

Guiomar de Ulloa; friend and collaborator of St Teresa in the early days of the Reform.

Isabel de Santo Domingo (Ortega); prioress at Pastrana, noted for her tact and firmness during the difficulties with the Princess of Eboli.

Jerónimo Gracián; close friend of St Teresa and a leading figure in the Carmelite Reform.

St John of Avila; 'Apostle of Andalusia', noted for his 'discernment of spirits'.

St John of the Cross; poet and mystic, the first friar to join the Carmelite Reform, and St Teresa's chaplain at the convent of the Incarnation.

Juan de la Miseria; Italian friar and artist.

Juan de Ovalle; husband of Teresa's sister, Juana.

Julián de Avila; chaplain of St Teresa's first reformed convent and later her biographer.

Luisa de la Cerda; wealthy noblewoman of Toledo whom St Teresa was sent to console in her bereavement.

María Bautista (Cepeda y Ocampo); daughter of a cousin of St Teresa and prioress at Valladolid.

María de San José (Salazar); maid-in-waiting to Luisa de la Cerda, later prioress at Seville and a friend and correspondent of St Teresa.

Main Characters

Mariano de San Benito (Azzaro); Italian courtier, soldier and inventor, who became a leading figure in the Reform.

Nicolás Doria; former Genoese banker, who ousted Gracián as leader of the Reform.

Nicolás Ormaneto; papal nuncio and supporter of the Reform.

Pedro Fernández; Dominican Provincial sympathetic to the Reform.

St Peter of Alcántara; Franciscan ascetic, mystic and reformer who encouraged St Teresa to embark on her Reform.

Chronology

1554	A vision of the wounded Christ marks the beginning of Teresa's mystical life.
1556	She experiences the 'Mystical Betrothal'.
1558	Her friends pronounce her to be possessed.
September 1558	First projects for the reform of the Carmelite Order.
Early 1562	Teresa is sent to console a rich widow in Toledo; she starts to write her *Life*.
24 August 1562	Foundation in Avila of St Joseph's, the first reformed Carmelite convent; Teresa begins to write *The Way of Perfection*.
Early 1567	The General of the Carmelite Order visits Avila and approves the Reform.
August 1567	Teresa's second convent founded at Medina del Campo where she secures the collaboration of St John of the Cross.
1568	Foundation of convents at Malagón and Pastrana, and of the first reformed priory at Duruelo.
1569	Teresa founds a convent at Toledo; visits the Princess of Eboli at Pastrana, where a convent and priory are founded.
1570	Convent founded at Salamanca.
1571	Teresa, with the help of St John of the Cross, founds a convent at Alba de Tormes; she reluctantly accepts nomination as Prioress at the Incarnation.

1573   Teresa begins to write the *Book of the Foundations*.

1574   Convent founded at Segovia; the nuns leave Pastrana on account of difficulties raised by the Princess, who denounces Teresa's *Life* to the Inquisition.

1575   Teresa founds a convent at Beas and meets Father Gracián who persuades her to found another at Seville; an aggrieved novice delates her to the Inquisition. The General disapproves the Reform and orders Teresa back to Castile.

1577   Teresa writes *The Interior Castle*. She petitions King Philip to order the release of St John of the Cross, abducted by hostile friars ('The Calced').

1578   Dispute between Calced and Discalced reaches its height; Father Gracián and Teresa in disfavour.

1579   Teresa permitted to resume her travels.

1580   She founds convents at Villanueva de la Jara and Palencia.

1581   Convent founded at Soria.

1582   Teresa founds her last convent at Burgos and dies at Alba de Tormes (4 October).

1622   Teresa canonized by Pope Gregory XV.

1

Don Alonso

Consternation reigned in the noble city of Toledo. It was the month of May 1485, in the eleventh year of the reign of the Catholic Monarchs, Isabella of Castile and Ferdinand of Aragon. Five years before, with inexorable severity, the Inquisition had begun to extirpate all New Christians – converts to the Catholic Church and their descendants – suspected of 'judaizing'. On charges of reverting to their ancestral faith or secretly continuing its practices, 298 had been sent to the stake in Seville and 79 sentenced to life imprisonment; in Ciudad Real, the toll was 52 executed and 183 penanced. Now the Inquisitors had come to Toledo.

The city, towering over the curving gorge of the Tagus and the bleak Castilian plateau, stood at the geographical centre of Spain. The Visigoths had made it their capital, and after them it had continued to flourish for nearly four centuries under the Moors. Christians, Moslems and Jews had lived together behind its walls for the most part in tolerance if not in amity, and the rulers of Castile were once proud to style themselves Kings of the Three Religions. The Jews formed a particularly powerful and thriving community. Their skill in trade and finance had won them the protection of the monarchs, whom they served as bankers, surgeons, secretaries and tax-gatherers, but it had also earned them the rancorous envy of the populace which periodically found vent, as elsewhere in Europe, in fearsome pogroms. Following a savage outbreak of violence at the end of the fourteenth century, many had sought safety in baptism. As slaughter and defections thinned the ranks of the Jews, the *conversos* or New Christians took over more and more of their functions and reaped the same consequences. Many embraced the new faith with sincerity; others, Christians through expediency but still Jews at heart, retained links with their co-religionists and continued, either from conviction or habit, to practise many of the observances enjoined by Mosaic law.

The events which occurred in Toledo have been recorded in detail, and with evident approval, by an eye-witness and resident of that city called the Licentiate Sebastián de Orozco. The proceedings opened on 24 May with a sermon in the Cathedral in which the purpose of the Inquisitors' visit was explained and the obedient co-operation of the faithful enjoined. Officials and leading citizens took oaths pledging support. An Edict of Grace was then published calling on the guilty to come forward and confess, and promising pardon and lenient penances for such 'self-delators'. For two weeks the summons met with no response. Even the 'leniency' of the Inquisitors was known to bring ignominy and ruin on the offenders, the boldest of whom resolved on a desperate bid to avert the blow. They plotted to seize control of the city's strong-points and to hold out until the royal promise was given for the withdrawal of the Inquisition. So crack-brained a scheme might well appear a mere fabrication of their enemies did we not know that the *conversos* of Seville had also planned something of the sort and that the chief Inquisitor of Aragon would shortly be struck down by assassins in the cathedral of Zaragoza. The Toledan conspirators planned their coup for 2 June, and prepared to fall on the Inquisitors whilst they were walking in the Corpus Christi procession. The plot was discovered on the eve of that feast-day, and the ring-leaders were arrested. Some were hanged and others heavily fined. No further resistance was attempted by the *conversos*, and the first self-delators began to come forward.

Amongst them was Juan Sánchez, son of Alonso and Teresa of that name, who had made a fortune in the wool and silk trade, tax-collecting, and the management of ecclesiastical finances. Some said that he had even been secretary to King Enrique IV, who made much use of able Jews and *conversos*. Juan Sánchez was married to Doña Inés, of the noble Cepeda family, and had several children, one of them called Alonso after the boy's grandfather. Of what he saw fit to accuse himself before the Inquisitors we do not know. The notary's record merely states that 'he confessed to having committed many grave crimes and offences against our Holy Catholic faith'. He might have been guilty of donning a clean shirt on Fridays, the Jewish Sabbath, or been careful to strip away fat from his meat. Perhaps he refused to touch pork, but ate other meat in Lent, or was wont to hold the traditional valedictory supper before setting out on his frequent journeys. He may have recited one of the psalms without adding the Gloria obligatory for good Christians, or washed and shaved the corpses of deceased relatives according to Mosaic custom. These, or other equally heinous signs of 'judaizing', would be enough to incur the direst penalties.

So great was the number of New Christians coming forward to confess to such trivial but savagely punishable crimes that the period of grace had to be extended from its initial forty days whilst the Inquisitors pressed on with their examinations. It was not until 12 February of the following year that they were ready to stage their first *auto de fe*. A second followed on 2 April and a third on 11 June, involving a total of 2,400 men and women 'reconciled' to the Church. The victims were paraded through the streets, naked to the waist and barefoot, though permitted to wear sandals on account of the intense cold. They carried unlit candles of green wax to signify that the light of salvation had been extinguished in their souls. On reaching the Cathedral, they mounted a large scaffold where they remained standing whilst Mass was celebrated, a sermon preached, and the offences attributed to each one of them read out in turn. Then sentence was passed. The offenders were graciously reconciled to Mother Church, but required to parade again on six successive Fridays, half naked as before, and to be whipped as they went from church to church. For the rest of their lives they were disqualified from wearing ornaments and fine apparel or holding honourable offices or employment. They were warned that should they fail to carry out any part of their penance, or lapse again into error, they would be sent to the stake. In addition, they were made to forfeit one fifth of all their possessions to help finance the crusade which the Catholic Monarchs were preparing against the last Moorish kingdom of Granada.

In which of these degrading charades Juan Sánchez, like many other respected citizens, was forced to appear we do not know. The Licentiate Orozco states that in one of the *autos*, in addition to the scourgings and penances, 200 of the victims were sentenced to wear the *sambenito* – a yellow tunic with large green crosses at back and front, which was later hung up in the culprit's parish church with an inscription recording his name and offences. More than twenty years later, a witness in a suit involving the sons of Juan Sánchez recalled seeing their father clad in this garment of shame and taking his place in the penitential processions. The witness added that with Juan Sánchez went his sons, sharing in their father's guilt and degradation, despite their tender years. One of them was a lad about five years old called Alonso.

For the next few years we have no further word of Juan Sánchez. Shock and humiliation, and the need to salvage what he could of his shattered fortune, must have kept him to his house. His ordeal was but the prelude to the terror unleashed in Toledo against his still more unfortunate fellow *conversos*. The period of grace having expired, suspects now pounced upon were treated as obdurate heretics. By August the burnings were in full swing; two priests were unfrocked and sent to the stake, whilst twenty-five other men and women, including a *regidor* and a Knight of

4

Santiago, suffered the same fate. The purge showed no sign of abating as the years went by. The Licentiate Orozco records that in February 1501 no fewer than sixty-three women perished in one holocaust. These unfortunates had been bewitched, it appears, by the messianic ravings of a girl who claimed to have been caught up into heaven where she saw those martyred by the Holy Office seated on golden thrones together with the Messiah who would shortly descend to liberate and avenge his people. Orozco adds that one result of the Inquisition's persecutions was to cause many of the victims' dependants to change their family names. Juan Sánchez began to style himself Sánchez de Cepeda, whilst his sons tended to avoid the tainted patronymic altogether. His eldest son Hernando, who seems to have been studying at Salamanca and to have escaped involvement in his father's disgrace, called himself Fernando de Santa Catalina. Alonso took the name of Piña for a time, and later, like his other brothers, that of Cepeda. It was a prudent precaution. Sánchez is not only a common name in Spain, but its associations could be unfortunate. We find a certain 'Juan Sánchez, notary' recorded in the Inquisition archives as having been burned in Avila for judaizing in 1496 – a year or so after the arrival in that city of the eponymous *converso*'s sons.

Juan Sánchez de Cepeda showed exceptional resilience and resourcefulness in rebuilding his family's fortunes and reputation. The expulsion from Spain of all Jews in 1492 left the field clear for the *conversos* in the traditional spheres of rent- and revenue-collecting, and set a higher premium on their financial and commercial abilities. Toledo, with its bitter memories and tell-tale *sambenitos*, was not a suitable place for *reconciliados* to make a new start. The merchant looked round for a fresh opening for his sons and found it at Avila, where a kinsman carried on a flourishing trade in silk and woollen cloth. When Alonso was about fourteen years old he and other brothers joined their relative and started a new life there. Their father followed them a year or two later. 'The Toledan', as he was often called, does not seem to have spent much time in Avila. He had by now triumphantly lived down his disgrace and won the confidence of such dignitaries as the Bishops of Salamanca, Plasencia and Santiago, whom he probably assisted in the management of their finances. Wealthy *reconciliados* could purchase immunity from the penalties which disqualified them from living in honourable style and holding desirable offices, and Juan Sánchez was no doubt amongst their number. In 1500 he even secured a certificate attesting his noble rank and ascribing to him a lineage as illustrious as it was fictitious. A document of this sort could be acquired at a price and the *reconciliado* was once again a rich man. He needed it less out of wounded vanity than because only hidalgos were entitled to handle certain crown revenues. He was resolved too that his sons, on whom he had bestowed an impeccably Catholic education, should be accorded an honourable place in society.

The father's next step was to enhance his children's status through advantageous matches. In Spain, antipathy to the Jews stemmed more from religious than from racial grounds, and inter-marriage between Old and New Christians was common. Jewish blood flowed through the veins of many of the noblest families, even of King Ferdinand the Catholic himself. Catholic society, to its undoubted intellectual, artistic and spiritual enrichment, thus acquired a strong Semitic strain. There was therefore nothing unusual in the ambition of Juan Sánchez de Cepeda (whose own wife probably came of Old Christian stock) to complete the rehabilitation of his family by means of matrimonial alliances. Before the indomitable old man died, he had the satisfaction of seeing Alonso, now in his early twenties, married to the well-born lady, Catalina del Peso y Henao. His bride bore two children, María and Juan, before dying prematurely only two years after the marriage.

The widower was left well provided for, but he lacked his father's drive and business flair. The family trade in silks and cloth had been abandoned in favour of the *conversos'* traditional pursuits of tax-farming and financial administration, into which Don Juan had initiated his sons. If Alonso continued these activities after his father's death, it was with indifferent success and a half-heartedness stemming from the assumption that in reality they were little suited to a man of his standing. Don Alonso had grown into a dignified, serious-minded man, conscientious and circumspect to a fault. The trauma of his childhood shame made him sensitive and punctilious in everything touching his personal honour and dignity. The affectionate portrait drawn of him in later life by his daughter stresses the fervour of his religious faith, his fondness for books of devotion, his charity to the poor and compassion for the sick, and a tender-heartedness which kept him from owning Moslem slaves, as gentlemen of his condition still often did. Measured and careful in speech, he was never heard to swear or to speak ill of anyone. He was renowned for his uncompromising probity and strict morality. We also know that he had another, seemingly paradoxical, side to his character. Don Alonso loved jewels and fine clothes and was much given to outward display and lordly living. Perhaps the memory of his family's humiliation led him to set excessive store by the respect accorded to the outward trappings of rank and wealth. In later years, when his fortune was much diminished, he could still not bring himself to moderate his expenditure, and he contracted debts which he must have known he could hardly hope to repay. Only towards the very end of his life, when he had withdrawn altogether into the inner world of the spirit, did he adopt a correspondingly simple style of living.

Within two years of his wife's death, Don Alonso secured the hand of another bride – Doña Beatriz de Ahumada, daughter of a family reputed to have won fame and name from an exploit of the Reconquest when father and sons, after heroically defending a tower, fought their way to safety through the smoke (*humo*) of its burning. Doña Beatriz was only fourteen and, moreover, a cousin of her betrothed's first wife. Dispensation had to be obtained (at an appropriate price) from the Church before the marriage could take

place. It was celebrated amidst rustic festivities at Gotarrendura, a
village some four leagues north of Avila, where the Ahumadas had
extensive estates. In addition to much land, the bride brought with
her a dowry of 600,000 *maravedís* – no mean sum at a time when a
farm labourer could expect no more than 15–20 *maravedís* for his
daily wage.

Doña Beatriz had not long settled into her new home in Avila –
a large, rambling mansion known as the Casa de la Moneda since it
had once done service as a mint – and given birth to Hernando, her
eldest son, before events of state interrupted the rhythm of their
domestic life. King Ferdinand cherished the ambition of
conquering Navarre, the small Pyrenean kingdom which
maintained a precarious independence against rival pressures from
France and Spain. His chance came in 1512. The Duke of Alba
assembled his forces for the invasion of Navarre, and royal *cédulas*
were dispatched to the hidalgos of Avila and other cities bidding
them muster for the enterprise. Don Alonso, as was required of
him, accoutred himself and rode off to the wars. The campaign
proved short and his young wife's prayers evidently efficacious,
for it was not long before he was back home again safe and
sound, with the satisfaction of knowing that he had honour-
ably fulfilled the duties, as well as enjoyed the privileges, of a true
hidalgo.

Three decades had passed since Juan Sánchez and his infant
sons had appeared before the Inquisitors and confessed to 'many
grave crimes of heresy and apostasy'. The respect of his neighbours
and his own clear conscience had done much to efface Don
Alonso's shameful memories of the *sambenito* and the penitential
processions. For thirty years his conduct had been irreproachable,
his orthodoxy unquestioned. He had become rich, respected and
well-connected, losing his tainted Sánchez identity in the lustre of
the Cepeda and Ahumada lineage. He was the head of a rapidly
growing family. Soon Doña Beatriz gave birth to their second son
Rodrigo, and then to a daughter. Don Antonio opened the book in

which he meticulously recorded such matters and added a fresh entry: 'On Wednesday, the twenty-eighth of March 1515, at five o'clock in the morning within half an hour or so of daybreak, my daughter Teresa was born.'

2

Avila of the Knights

Rising above a valley in the austere uplands of New Castile, more than three thousand feet above sea-level, stands the walled city of Avila. To the south-east, the road winds through a gap in the Gredos mountains towards Toledo; to the west lie the university city of Salamanca, the rolling Estremadura steppes, Portugal and the Atlantic. The plateau is scarred by stony river-beds and strewn with gigantic boulders which give it a grim, primeval look, whilst the fourscore towers and the ramparts of the city itself seem like outcrops of the same rocky landscape. The apse of the Cathedral forms one bastion of the girdling walls, whilst the city's other churches, no less than the houses and the nobles' palaces, retain something of their ancient, fortress-like character behind the baroque façades which some of them acquired as Spain entered her Golden Age.

Don Alonso and his wife worshipped in the church of San Juan, where the massive stone font at which their daughter was baptized may still be seen. They called her Teresa after her maternal grandmother Doña Teresa de las Cuevas, and perhaps too after that other Teresa, mother of Juan Sánchez, whose origins were commonly the object of a prudent reticence. The child's godparents were María de Aguila, who was probably also of *converso* stock, and their neighbour, Francisco Núñez Vela. The latter's brother, Don Blasco, became the first Viceroy of Peru, where several of Alonso's sons were to join him, one of them falling at his side when the ill-fated viceroy perished at the hands of Gonzalo Pizarro's rebel forces on the field of Añaquito.

To serve God by the sword or in the cloister was held to be equally meritorious, and Avila – proudly known as the City of Knights and Liegemen – had often chosen the way of arms. Not that there was any lack of religious vocations, for in Teresa's childhood the city supported half a dozen nunneries as well as monasteries for Benedictines, Carmelites, Franciscans and Dominicans. The latter boasted an imposing edifice dedicated to St Thomas and built largely out of the spoils confiscated from Jews and *conversos*. There the Holy Office for a time had its headquarters and held its prisoners, and there Torquemada, the first Inquisitor-General, had died and lay buried.

But Avila was pre-eminently a city of martial traditions. Little remained of its Roman, Visigothic or Moslem past, for it stood in the ancient no-man's-land between Christian and Moor and suffered such devastation that, after King Alfonso VI had won back Toledo and all New Castile for the Cross, Avila needed to be totally refounded. The task was entrusted to the King's French son-in-law, Count Raymond, who gave the city its un-Spanish rectangular form and allowed the nobles to build fortified mansions which gave them direct and rapid access to the great walls. It was in Avila that Alfonso VIII mustered his troops before sallying out to win the great victory of Las Navas de Tolosa against the Moslems. Here too the stout-hearted Jimena Blázquez mobilized the women of the city when their menfolk were away campaigning, and sent them up to the ramparts disguised with false beards and broad hats to frighten off a Moslem raiding party. Though the Moors had been driven from the peninsula, Spain was constantly at war during Teresa's lifetime, and Avila continued to furnish contingents and captains for the battlefields of Italy, France, Germany, the Netherlands, North Africa and the New World.

When Teresa was five years old, Avila was caught up in the turmoil of the *Comuneros* revolt. The youthful king, later to be known as the Emperor Charles V, angered nobles and burghers alike by his inexperience and tactlessness, the arrogant presumption of his Flemish favourites, and the insatiable financial demands made on his new subjects. Avila, whilst still protesting loyalty to the Crown, became a centre of this dissidence, and envoys from the aggrieved cities held their deliberations inside her Cathedral. Don Alonso, with characteristic prudence, refrained from taking sides and spent much time on his estates at Gotarrendura. Besides, he had important battles of his own to fight. A year before the *Comuneros* rebellion, zealous local tax officials laid claims against him and his brothers on the ground that they were not true hidalgos and so were as liable as other commoners to pay the dues from which only those of noble blood were exempt. Many witnesses were called, some of whom declared that in Avila the Cepedas were accounted hidalgos, and had always conducted themselves as such; but others, including a brother-in-law of his first wife, recalled the tainted origins of the Sánchez family and the infamy at Toledo. The case was carried to an appeal court in Valladolid which, after the delays caused by the *Comuneros* upheaval, found in the defendants' favour. Honour was satisfied and Don Alonso's social status vindicated. But the affair had reopened old wounds.

It seems improbable that a girl as sensitive and alert as Teresa could have been unaware of her family history. In the opening chapters of her *Life* she extols her parents not on the then standard grounds that they were Old Christians of noble descent, but because they were 'virtuous and God-fearing'. The discretion she showed in the questions of lineage which so obsessed her contemporaries is remarkable, and hardly to be attributed to Christian humility alone. She chides a brother who had made good in the New World for thinking too highly of his 'honour', living ostentatiously, and insisting on having himself and his sons formally addressed as 'Don'. And when a friend confided his well-intentioned desire to chronicle her illustrious ancestry, she tartly observed that it was enough for her to be counted a faithful daughter of the Church, and that it would grieve her more to commit one venial sin than to be descended from the meanest of forebears.

Yet Teresa was a daughter too of that Avila of the Knights whose martial atmosphere left a deep imprint on her character and imagination. The contemplative vocation to which she gradually felt called was never escapism, but rather the summons to a combat in which prayer and virtue were the arms, and courage, discipline and sacrifice just as necessary as to the soldier on his battlefield. The sublimest of her mystical writings, which treats of the 'many mansions' prepared by God for the human soul, is entitled *The Mansions of the Interior Castle*. Teresa was constantly exhorting her nuns to bear themselves, not as weak women, but as valiant men; to show 'holy boldness, for God helps the strong', and 'to strive like strong men until you die in the attempt, for you are here for nothing else but to strive'. We seem to be listening again to the stirring words of the heroic Jimena Blázquez. Both came of a race of which the women as well as the men were born to a hard lot in a hard world. For Avila, as the saying went, had nothing but stones and saints — *En Avila, cantos y santos.*

The saints of Avila! To the child Teresa they were no less real for being legendary figures round whom the popular imagination had woven its colourful fantasies. There was Santa Barbada, the beautiful shepherdess saved from dishonour at the hands of a young nobleman by the sudden sprouting of a beard. There was St Segundo, said by tradition to have come to Spain with St James and to have brought the gospel to Avila. Teresa, then four years old, may even have shared in the excitement caused by the reported discovery of the saint's remains in a little chapel just outside the city walls. Most dear to her of all were the child martyrs St Vincent and his sisters Cristeta and Sabina, who had suffered atrocious deaths for their faith in Roman times. A fine basilica, which Teresa knew well, was dedicated to their memory.

It was said to have been built by a Jew who had been attacked by a huge snake as he was gloating over their mutilated corpses, but had been saved and converted after he had called on the God of the martyred children.

When Teresa grew old enough to read, she found many such stories in the Lives of the Saints with which the library of her pious father was well stocked. She and Rodrigo, the brother who was nearest to her in age and shared her childish enthusiasms and plans, devoured them avidly.

> When I read of the martyrdoms they suffered for the love of God [she recalls] I used to think it a very cheap price to pay for their entry into God's presence. Then I fervently longed to die like them, not from any conscious love for him, but so that I might come to enjoy as quickly as they those great joys which I had read are laid up in heaven. And with this brother of mine I used to discuss the ways and means of doing this. So we agreed to go off to the land of the Moors, begging our way for the love of God, so that they might behead us there.

Such is Teresa's own account of her first great adventure. The would-be martyrs did not go far. As soon as their flight was discovered, their uncle Don Francisco Alvarez de Cepeda, who had come to live in a house opposite Don Alonso's, mounted his horse and galloped off in pursuit. Tradition has it that he came up with them on the road to Salamanca at the spot marked by a monument known as the Four Posts. But contemporary accounts make it clear that he overtook them nearer home, before they had got much further than the bridge over the Adaja river or had time to eat the crusts of bread which Teresa, with characteristic good sense, had brought with her. The escapade earned the children a good scolding from their anxious mother. Rodrigo, though the elder of the two, put the blame on his sister, who had talked him into the adventure. Teresa forgave this unmanly behaviour, for she loved her brother dearly. Many years later she was to shed bitter tears on learning that he had fallen fighting against the pagan Araucanians in distant Chile. She found solace in the thought that he had assuredly now won the crown of martyrdom which they had once set out together to find in the land of the Moors.

The austere, boulder-studded Castilian landscape, rimmed by the blue line of the Gredos mountains, held a powerful fascination for Teresa. When she turned her back on Avila there was nothing but earth and sky – a vast emptiness of space and time through which it seemed she might go on walking for ever. For ever! The thought lingered in her imagination with a strange sensation of awe and delight. That was how they said the saints lived in heaven, and the wicked, too, in the flames of hell. 'We were amazed to learn from what we read that pain and bliss last for ever, and we often loved to talk about this together and to go on repeating "For ever, for ever and ever!"' From this spark of childish wonder was to spring the dazzling radiance of Teresa's mystical life.

Don Alonso was now the head of a large family. Teresa's half-sister María, a serious-minded girl in her teens, would soon need to be found a husband. Her half-brother, who styled himself Juan Vásquez de Cepeda, was nearly old enough to enlist for service in Africa or Italy and to be the first to fall on the battlefield. From Don Alonso's second marriage there was Hernando, who sought his fortune in the New World, and another Juan, who may have died young or perhaps become a monk; he does not seem to have figured largely in Teresa's life. Next to Rodrigo, and after the latter's death the closest to his sister, was Lorenzo. Then followed Antonio, the difficult and troublesome Pedro, Jerónimo – another favourite of Teresa's – and Agustín, the youngest of the brothers. Last of all came Juana, thirteen years younger than herself, on whom Teresa was to lavish a mother's care. 'We were three sisters and nine brothers', she tells us. 'I was very attached to them all, and they to me.' With her winsome ways, her warm nature and ready sympathy, her talent for leading without domineering, Teresa was a universal favourite and the darling of her grave father.

Of Doña Beatriz, the mother of this large family, we know little more than what Teresa has to say about her. She was gentle, submissive and deeply religious. Her early life in the hilltop town of Olmedo, where the Ahumadas lived, had been shadowed by tragedy. Two of her brothers had been killed in the Italian wars, and her two sisters had also died; only she and one brother survived. Teresa describes her as a woman of quiet disposition, good understanding and exceptional beauty – 'yet she never gave the slightest sign of setting any store by it, and she dressed like a matron of mature years, though she was only thirty-three when she died'. Doña Beatriz brought up her children as devout Catholics. Teresa learned from her to say her prayers and tell the beads of her rosary. She even imitated her mother's charity by giving away what little pocket money she had as 'alms'. With Rodrigo's help Teresa also devised an absorbing new game – playing at hermits in the orchard of their country house at Gotarrendura where the family spent much of the summer. They would pile up stones to build little huts which, for Teresa at least, meant more than the dolls' houses and cubby-holes dear to children everywhere. The small girl who was so lively and gay in company was also strangely fond of being alone. She loved to find some quiet corner where she could repeat her mother's prayers and savour the strange sensation which would steal over her mind when she tried to grasp the meaning of the words 'For ever and ever and ever'. That was how the nuns must pass their lives, she reflected, behind the blank walls of their convents in Avila. Teresa half thought she would like to become a nun herself when she grew up, but there were so many other things she wanted to do too. Her enthusiasm cooled a little when the experiment of being a hermit proved no more successful than the quest for martyrdom. The piles of stones kept tumbling down, 'and so we found no way of achieving our desires'.

There was one of her mother's habits which, as she grew older, Teresa imitated too, though Don Alonso strongly disapproved.

Whilst he pored over edifying tomes like *The Consolations of Philosophy* by Boethius or *The Treatise on the Mass*, Doña Beatriz devoured the fashionable books of chivalry. In a Spain which had but lately emerged from the Middle Ages, the adventures of Amadís de Gaul and other fabulous knights enjoyed an immense vogue. St Ignatius of Loyola was much addicted to them, before embarking on his own adventure as a soldier of Christ, and many other estimable Spaniards had the same weakness until Cervantes laughed them out of court with his Don Quixote. Teresa is quick to excuse her mother's passion for this dubious literature. Doña Beatriz never neglected her domestic duties on its account, and she read only, her daughter declares, 'to distract her mind from her great sufferings, or perhaps simply in order to amuse her children and keep them out of greater mischief'.

Far more blameworthy, it seemed to her in retrospect, was Teresa's own liking for such books. She was never happy unless absorbed in some marvellous new tale, which she took care not to let her father catch her reading. Very different from the holy martyrs and chaste maidens of the *Flos Sanctorum* were the amoral heroes of these romances and the high-born damsels who abandoned themselves so readily to their guilty amours. Teresa tells us that she wasted much time and came to great harm through reading such pernicious fantasies. She and Rodrigo even composed one of their own, which was much praised by those privileged to read it. A century later, when the festivities for Teresa's canonization were being celebrated, there appeared a book recounting the adventures of a knight of Avila which purported to come from the saint's pen. But we may be sure that its alleged author would have taken good care long before to consign such impious juvenilia to the flames.

Teresa was now entering her teens, and what she later regarded as the wickedest and most worldly period of her life. After the early death of Doña Beatriz, worn out by illness and constant confinements, she tearfully implored the Blessed Virgin to become her true mother, but soon she was beguiled by the fantasy world of the romances and a flattering awareness of her personal attractions. Teresa, like other girls of her age, began to take an interest in fine clothes; one old nun, still alive at the time of her beatification, recalls her resplendent in an orange skirt with black velvet cross-bands. Teresa lavished care on her lustrous black hair and dainty hands. Perfumes and gems delighted her. Years later, on seeing a richly bejewelled Virgin, she humorously observed how envious she would have been of the image in the days when she cared for such things. Her half-sister Doña María, earnest, conventionally pious and now engaged to be married, was the mistress of the mourning household and did what she could to exclude from it all contaminating influences. But Don Alonso had a sister Elvira, a wealthy widow and the mother of several children of about Teresa's age whose upbringing was a good deal less strict than their cousins'. Soon they were her inseparable companions, confiding to her 'their affections and their follies, which were far from edifying' and exerting an influence over their impressionable and lively young cousin which Doña Beatriz had recognized as undesirable and tried in vain to discourage. Don Alonso was bound to his sister not only by family affection but by gratitude for the financial help she had given him, and it was impossible to slam the door in her children's face.

One of the relations, whom Teresa charitably refrains from naming but who was probably a daughter of Doña Elvira, was chiefly to blame for leading her astray. Some of Teresa's biographers have also surmised an affair with a male cousin. There is nothing however to support this in the account given by Teresa, who was never one to miss an opportunity for self-reproach. The Castilian code of honour was strict and included not only a vigilant defence of female chastity but a jealous concern for the family's good name as well. When not carried to the excess of vengeful touchiness, pride and vanity, it was no poor substitute for Christian virtue. Teresa herself says that even when her 'wickedness' led to her losing the fear of offending God, she still retained a natural repugnance for anything immodest and a lively concern for her reputation. Even a cousin might not presume too far. Concealing her undesirable friendship as best she could from her father and brothers, she never went so far as to expose them or herself to serious disgrace. Don Alonso's anxieties were nevertheless aroused. Something clearly had to be done. His eldest daughter was about to be married, and a maiden as young and attractive as Teresa could not be left unchaperoned at home.

Teresa had grown into a beautiful girl. The only authentic portrait we have of her is from the brush of an Italian friar, painted in her later years and so crudely done that the saint could not help exclaiming: 'God forgive you, Fray Juan – you have made me ugly and blear-eyed!' Descriptions of her as a young woman stress her regular features and fresh complexion, her well-proportioned and graceful figure, the dark, expressive eyes beneath thick, slightly arched eyebrows, now sparkling with merriment, now glowing with an intense earnestness, the extraordinary distinction and charm of manner, to which all bore witness but which none could quite define. 'The Lord gave me the grace of pleasing', was her own simple summing-up. Those who knew her did not find themselves merely in the presence of a woman whose beauty was enhanced by her ready sympathy, humour, quick understanding and delightful conversation; they were left with a sense of something beyond and above those qualities, something akin to genius. Yet Teresa had no intellectual pretensions and her artistic talents were but modest. It was not genius, but something no less rare: the mysterious resonance of the call, as yet but half heard and heeded, to holiness.

The climax to Teresa's worldly phase came in the spring of 1531, when she was in the full bloom of her sixteen years; her mother, at that age, had already married and given birth to her first child. The City of Knights and Liegemen was *en fête* for the visit of the Empress Isabella, accompanied by a magnificent retinue of courtiers. People danced in the streets, and there were receptions and ceremonies of every kind, including the formal presentation of the four-year-old boy who was to become Philip II, attired for the first time in a manly pair of breeches. Before the public rejoicings were over, Teresa's life had undergone a sudden change. The marriage and departure of his eldest daughter provided Don Alonso with his opportunity. Teresa was packed off to the Augustinian convent of Our Lady of Grace, which eked out its modest revenues by taking a few boarders.

For the first week Teresa was miserable – more, she declares, because of the shame she felt lest others should see this sudden relegation as punishment for her recent frivolities than from any intrinsic dislike of convent life. She soon indeed began to settle down and even to feel happier than she had been at home. Life was spartan, but Teresa quickly became a favourite with the nuns, and she in turn took a great liking to them, particularly to the virtuous novice-mistress, Doña María Briceño, who slept in the same dormitory as the girls, accompanied them when they received visits, and became the recipient of their intimate confidences. This new friendship quickly effaced the memory of the mondaine cousin, and reminders of her former life, in the shape of messages and notes which her friends tried to smuggle in to her, were intercepted or had little effect. The novice-mistress spoke eloquently of spiritual things, of the joy and peace of detachment from the world, and of how she had been led to a religious vocation. Teresa listened eagerly. She came to love and admire Doña María and other simple, dedicated souls like her. 'I was weary now of wrongdoing', she wrote, and there revived within her that inclination for the cloistered life she had begun to feel as a child, and once again an awareness that the things of this world, however desirable they might be, would soon pass away and could never satisfy. But as yet she felt no call to become a nun herself.

After a year and a half at the convent of Our Lady of Grace,

Teresa fell ill and had to be sent back to her father's house. We do not know the nature of her complaint, but she writes of fainting fits and high fever. Most probably it was brought about by the strain of having to reach a decision regarding her future. Convent or marriage? There were only those stark alternatives, for no other career was open to a woman of her rank. She felt torn between two worlds, reluctant to take the veil without any sure vocation, yet fearing marriage. 'Teresa de Ahumada may marry whomsoever she chooses', folk would say, mindful of her attractions and the dowry which Don Alonso was expected to provide. But although more fortunate than many others in those respects, she could not forget her mother's joyless lot – the incessant round of childbearing, the absolute submission to a husband's will. Her half-sister's life seemed likely to follow the same pattern, though María's husband Martín Guzmán was a worthy if somewhat improvident man. He and María were solicitous about Teresa's health and invited her to convalesce in their country home at Castellanos. On the way there she broke her journey at the hamlet of Hortigosa, where one of her father's brothers led the life of a country hidalgo.

Don Pedro Sánchez de Cepeda had been left a widower. He was an intensely religious man who spent much of his time perusing books of devotion and was only waiting for his children to grow up to become a Jeronimite friar. The few days which his seventeen-year-old niece spent in his company seem to have proved decisive for the future course of her life. Don Pedro asked her to read aloud to him, and although his books were not much to her taste she readily complied. Her reading, and Don Pedro's grave discourse, harping constantly on the vanity of the world from which he was determined to cut himself off, moved her greatly. 'The truths dimly sensed when a child', she writes, 'were once more borne in upon me – that all things are nothing, that the world's vanities would soon pass away, and that if I were to die I feared I should go straight to hell.'

Teresa's mind was in turmoil, but gradually she found herself moving towards a decision. Haunted by 'servile fear' rather than drawn by love, it seemed to her that a bleak life spent behind cloistered walls would at least be preferable to an eternity of damnation. But could she stand the hardships and privations? The Devil, conjuring up the austerities practised by Doña María de Briceño, did his utmost to persuade her that she could not. Then she reflected on the passion of Christ, his patience under suffering and his promise to help all who followed him to bear their cross, and she grew comforted and confident. But still she compromised. There were other nunneries in Avila where life was less rigorous than at the convent of Our Lady of Grace: the large and rather easy-going Carmelite convent of the Incarnation, for example, where a close friend of hers, María Suárez, had taken the veil. If she became a nun – and her mind was now almost made up – Teresa would go there.

Teresa spent only two weeks with her sister and brother-in-law at Castellanos. Though the fits of fainting and fever had not left her, she was impatient to return to Avila and break the news to her father. The letters of St Jerome, which were amongst her uncle's favourite reading, had left a deep impression. The fiery old ascetic, who had yet proved a sensitive spiritual director of the high-born women whom he encouraged to follow a strictly religious life, seemed to have a message for her too. His words stung her conscience like a lash: 'Say, craven knight, what dost thou lingering there in thy father's house?' For men, the call and the response were clear enough. Her elder brother Juan had left for the wars in which he was soon to lose his life. Hernando, the oldest of Doña Beatriz's sons, was already impatient to set out for Peru. Her beloved Rodrigo, Lorenzo, Jerónimo and the others would all follow in their turn. For Teresa, the combat had to be fought behind convent walls and the conquest to be over herself. But first must come the encounter with her father – an encounter bound to prove painful for both, but in which, once her decision had been taken, she was resolved not to retreat an inch. She, too, had been nurtured in the City of the Knights.

Don Alonso was overwhelmed on learning his daughter's decision. Widowed now for the second time, and with María no longer at home to take care of the smaller children, he really could not accept this fresh sacrifice. Besides, Teresa had ever been his favourite. Fervent Catholic though he was, he could not bear the thought of losing her. The only concession she could wring from him was that she might take the veil after his death. Teresa saw that such delay would prove fatal. Her good desires might evaporate and the world and its vanities reclaim her after all. She fell silent and let the matter drop. But a new plan was already taking shape in her mind.

In the *Book of the Foundations* which she was to write many years later, Teresa suddenly digresses to tell the story of a certain very young girl of noble birth called Casilda who, in the teeth of strong opposition from her family and her betrothed, ran away from home to become a nun. She tells it with immense relish and vividness of detail, for in reality she is reliving her own escape into the life which she had finally chosen for herself. Accompanied by one brother – probably young Juan de Ahumada, whom she had roused to a similar vocation to become a Dominican friar – she stole away from the Casa de la Moneda and presented herself at the Convent of the Incarnation. The nuns were expecting her and at once accepted her as a postulant. Don Alonso was faced with a *fait accompli*. His pain, and perhaps his first angry reaction, must be left to our imagination. For herself, Teresa says that the anguish of that joyless spiritual elopement was such that she felt as if her very bones were being wrenched apart. She was still acting largely out of 'servile fear'. Her love of God was not yet strong enough to transcend the love she felt for the father and family she was forcing herself to leave behind.

3

The Convent of the Incarnation

It was a cold November morning when Teresa and her brother tiptoed from their father's house and hurried through the deserted streets. Beyond the city walls a track led northwards, dropping across a gulley to a long, low pile of buildings on the bleak slope beyond. There the Jews had once brought their dead for burial, and a year or two before Teresa's birth a convent had been erected on the site of their old cemetery. The nuns belonged to the Order of Carmel which claimed descent from Elijah and 'the sons of the prophets', and from the early Christian hermits who had lived out their austere lives on the sacred mountain. The friars, and the Carmelite sisters who were added to the Order in the fifteenth century, now lived under a 'Mitigated Rule' which dispensed them from the harshest of the pristine severities. The convent was an unpretentious, dilapidated building which had the air more of a large farmhouse than of a religious institution.

Once within the friendly, honey-coloured walls of her new home, Teresa felt an immense sense of relief. María Suárez was there to give her an affectionate welcome. The other nuns eyed her with benevolent curiosity. There were few who had not heard something of her family and her own reputation, and fewer still who were not quickly charmed by the grace and eager sincerity with which the postulant sought to make their mode of life her own. They were of all ages and conditions. The poorer ones slept in a communal dormitory; those who, like Teresa, were better off had rooms or simple apartments of their own. Besides her cell,

Teresa was given a guest-room (to be occupied, after her father's death, by her younger sister Juana), a little kitchen, and an oratory which she could adorn with sacred pictures of her choice. One of these, which used to hang in her bedroom at home, depicted Christ and the woman of Samaria at the well, and bore the legend *Da mihi hanc aquam* (Give me this water).

The transition to her new mode of life was eased for Teresa by the good grace with which her father, who had set his face so sternly against her going, came to accept the situation. Don Alonso well knew the steely temper beneath his daughter's charm and warmth. She had inherited all the indomitable spirit of her grandfather Juan Sánchez. He resigned himself to the inevitable and told himself that it must be the will of God. Besides, would he after all see very much less of his beloved child than if she had married and left home to live in distant parts? The *locutorio*, or convent parlour, was a sociable place, and though the grille was interposed between them, father and daughter could still meet and talk. She might even from time to time return home and stay beneath his roof, for the rule of enclosure was not strictly enforced. The convent was so poor that the prioress was often glad to have one less mouth to feed.

For the first year Teresa had to serve her apprenticeship as a postulant. Only then would she qualify for the habit and the white veil of the novice. After a further year and a day, as the Rule prescribed, she would be allowed to make her profession as a nun. In the meantime, details of her dowry would be worked out and the necessary legal documents prepared. On 31 October 1536, as her postulancy drew to its close, Don Alonso presented himself at the *locutorio* and signed the covenant in the presence of a notary. The nuns, from the other side of their grille, pledged themselves 'to accept Doña Teresa de Ahumada and to give her board and lodging all the days of her life'. In return, Don Alonso undertook to supply every year twenty-five measures of grain, half in wheat and half in barley, from his Gotarrendura estates, or two hundred gold ducats instead. He also promised to provide a bed and bedclothes for his daughter, the clothing she would need as novice and nun, and such books as were customarily used. In addition, he would bestow on every nun a new coif, or its equivalent in cash, and bear the cost of a collation and a supper for the whole community on the day Teresa made her profession. Two days after the signing of this contract, Teresa was given the habit and status of a novice.

From that moment, Teresa recalls, 'I was granted a happiness so great that it has never failed me to this day, and God transformed the dryness of my soul into a very great tenderness.' It was no longer a matter of forcing herself forward by sheer willpower; love was beginning to cast out fear and draw her gently on. The nuns sometimes caught her weeping, shook their heads, and murmured that she was discontented and most likely hankering after her old life. But they were tears of compunction, of remorse for her past hardness of heart, her worldliness, her 'wickedness', that the novice was shedding. Sometimes, indeed, her proud spirit was irked by the humiliation of being censured for something which was not her fault. She hated to look small or to risk losing her reputation in the eyes of others. It went against the grain to admit she was sometimes at sea over the singing in the chapel, and needed to ask for guidance. These were trifles which sometimes loomed disproportionately large and made her despondent. But never for a moment did she regret her decision to become a nun. 'I found delight in everything to do with the religious life', she writes. 'Sometimes, indeed, when I was busy with the housework at hours which I had used to spend adorning and indulging myself, the thought that I was now free from such things brought me a fresh joy which astonished me, for I could not understand whence it came.'

The novices were instructed in the history of their Order and the austere Rule which was prescribed for it but far from strictly observed. The celebration of an elaborate liturgy took up much of the nuns' time, and the practice of mental prayer and contemplation to which their Order was pledged was much neglected. Teresa devoted herself to the demands of her new calling with characteristic ardour. She followed the current practice of 'taking the discipline', scourging herself with nettles in the privacy of her cell, eating sparingly of the plain food provided, and schooling herself to speak little and then only with downcast eyes in the demure manner befitting nuns. If she happened to offend one of them, she learned to prostrate herself at the feet of the injured sister until the offence was pardoned. Not content with such externals of self-abasement, Teresa volunteered to nurse a nun who was suffering from a loathsome disease. The sufferer's stomach had become an ulcerous sore exuding pus, blood and excrement, the stench of which caused repulsion and nausea. Teresa tended the sick woman devotedly until she died, seeing only the Christian patience with which she bore her sufferings and praying that it might be given her to acquire virtue in the same way.

Her prayer was soon to be answered in full measure. Teresa herself merely records: 'The change in my life and diet had a bad effect on my health.' Almost certainly the severity of the penances she inflicted upon herself and the effect on her proud and high-spirited nature of the constant striving after perfection, with its accompanying remorse for a 'worldly' past from whose ties she could not at once detach herself, brought about a deterioration which seriously alarmed her father. There was no mistaking the growing pallor of the face which smiled wanly through the grille. The best doctors which Avila could boast accompanied Don Alonso to the convent parlour. They talked vaguely of *mal de corazón* – heart disease – and later of *perlesía* – palsy – and her biographers were subsequently to ascribe the trouble to every variety of ills from tuberculosis to malaria. The fainting fits and fever seemed to be a recurrence of the ailment she had suffered whilst at the convent of Our Lady of Grace, only more severe.

When they seemed to have brought her to the brink of total breakdown, Don Alonso removed her from the Incarnation and arranged for the invalid to make the journey to Becedas, a small town in the foothills of the Gredos mountains, where her half-sister María sang the praises of a local *curandera* or healer.

Teresa had no wish to leave the convent. Hardly a year had passed since the day when she had made her solemn profession as a nun – the day both of her nuptials and of her death to this world, whose bitter-sweet memory was to last to the end of her life. In the presence of the whole community and a great concourse of friends and relations, Teresa de Ahumada had become the Bride of Christ. To the strains of the *Veni, Creator Spiritus* she had moved through the throng of nuns arrayed in their new white coifs presented by Don Alonso, to the sanctuary steps where, prostrate upon the ground, she had craved the privilege of perpetual enclosure with her sisters and God's grace to observe the Rule. Now, through the weakness of the flesh rather than any faltering of the spirit, she was being returned to the world and the fearsome ministrations of a country quack.

The *curandera* concocted her physic from herbs which must be gathered in the spring. As the autumn was only just setting in, Teresa had to spend the whole winter in the care of her sister and of María Suárez, who had accompanied her from the Incarnation. Though her health showed no improvement during this long period of waiting, Teresa felt that God was turning it to account for her spiritual progress. Despite the pain and the prostration, she had the solitude in which to devote herself to 'recollection' – the contemplative calm in which the soul gathers or 're-collects' itself into a prayerful waiting upon God. It was the first stage of the journey which was to lead to the mystic heights. She had, indeed, been accustomed since childhood to say her prayers. But now she was starting to experience something new. 'The Lord began to raise me sometimes to the Prayer of Quiet', she writes, 'and occasionally to that of Union.' What she sought to convey by these terms we shall try to understand later. At the time she scarcely knew herself, except that 'I seemed to feel the world was far beneath me, and I remember pitying those who followed its ways, even on their lawful pursuits.'

What had brought about this change? Partly it may have been the endurance of physical pain which, as she had prayed, was purging away her remaining attachments to earthly things and was teaching her to enter into the sufferings of Christ. Partly it was the guidance she had sought in vain – and was to continue for another twenty years to seek – from confessors of real spiritual insight, but had begun to find in the pages of a book. On the way to Becedas the cavalcade had stopped briefly at the house of her pious uncle Don Pedro who had given her a volume from his library – the quaintly entitled *Third Spiritual Alphabet* published not many years before by a Franciscan friar, Francisco de Osuna. This rather rambling and confused treatise is generally regarded as the first attempt in Spanish to describe the successive stages in the practice of contemplative prayer which had recently been gaining more and more adherents. It did not meet with unreserved approval. Personal piety was one thing, innovation in matters of religion quite another. Unwise zeal had spawned the Lutheran heretics in Germany and the Inquisition was busily rooting out their sympathizers in Spain. Almost as pernicious, and having something in common with them, were the *alumbrados*, who also practised a form of mental prayer, believed themselves to be under the direct guidance of the Holy Spirit, studied the Scriptures on their own and were suspected of setting little store by the sacraments and established usages of the Church. The prudent St John of Avila, whose apostolic ardour had changed the whole spiritual climate of Andalusia and who was regarded as the foremost spiritual director in the country, cautioned that the *Third Spiritual Alphabet* had to be read with circumspection and should not be put into the hands of everyone. But for Teresa it proved a boon. 'I was delighted with the book', she wrote, 'and determined to follow its directions with all my strength.' Her treasured copy of Osuna's work, its yellow pages scored with hearts, crosses and hands pointing to those passages which seemed to correspond most closely to her own experiences, may still be seen in Avila today.

But worldly perils were soon to intrude upon the solitude and meditations of the sickroom. They took the unexpected form of visits, too frequent and too prolonged, by the local priest who came to hear her confessions. With her usual blend of generosity and shrewdness, Teresa describes him as 'a priest of very good birth and understanding, and also of some learning – though only a little'. Father Pedro Hernández quickly fell beneath the spell of those dark eyes aglow with a more than human fire behind the nun's veil, and the quiet voice speaking so fervently of spiritual things beyond the ken of his own sensual nature – 'My thoughts were then so taken up with God', she tells us, 'that my greatest delight was to speak of him.' Searching her conscience many years later, she could find 'nothing bad in itself in the affection he felt for me, but because it grew excessive it ceased to be good . . . He realized that there was nothing on earth that would make me consent to anything I knew to be a mortal sin, and he assured me of the same thing for himself.' The young invalid, physically prostrate but spiritually so compellingly alive, was clearly no ordinary penitent. As they talked together their roles became imperceptibly reversed. Such was her transparent purity of soul that, as she had to admit herself, 'I had little at that time to confess.' Not so the priest, who was living in mortal sin. Like many others in those times, he had taken a woman to live with him as a concubine. He confessed as much to the invalid, who soon learned the full story from other members of the household. It was said, in mitigation of his guilt, that the woman had cast a spell over him by means of a copper amulet which she gave him to wear round his neck. 'I do not altogether believe this tale about the spell', Teresa observes, but such was the influence she came to acquire over the erring confessor that she was able to induce him to hand over the charm which she forthwith had thrown into the river.

> As soon as he parted with it [she writes] he became like one roused from a long sleep and began to call to mind everything he had done all those years, and filled with amazement at himself and with remorse for his fall, he started to loathe that woman . . . He finished by giving up seeing her altogether, and could never thank God enough for granting him light.

The following year Teresa learned that Father Hernández had died. She was filled with astonishment and humble gratitude that God had deigned to use such a vile and worthless instrument as herself for saving a soul from eternal perdition.

Spring came, and the wise woman began her cure – purges administered daily for four weeks and concoctions so potent that after two months the patient was left almost lifeless. Instead of being relieved, the pains in her heart grew worse, 'as if sharp teeth were being plunged into it'. Her nerves 'started to contract, causing such unbearable pain that I could get no rest either by day or by night'. Such was her agony that it was feared she might go out of her mind. Teresa ran a high temperature and could take nothing but a few drops of liquid. Her condition became so wretched that her father, in desperation, decided to take her home.

The Avila doctors now pronounced the invalid to be suffering from consumption. Teresa has left us a harrowing description of how she felt. She was racked with pain from head to foot; all her nerves were contracting, and it seemed impossible that anyone could endure such torments for long. Yet she still found the strength to pray, and God rewarded her with the gift of resignation and comforted her with the thought of Job exclaiming in the midst of his tribulation: 'What? Shall we receive good at the hand of God, and shall we not receive evil?'

In August Teresa appears to have suffered a syncope and did not regain consciousness until four days later. Her family recited the creed over her, and a priest administered Extreme Unction. Don Alonso's grief was heightened by bitter self-reproach. A few days before she had asked for confession, but he had not allowed it, as he feared it would only sap her will and hasten the end. The thought that his daughter had now passed away unshriven so appalled him that he cast it from him, kneeling beside the motionless body and repeating obstinately, 'The girl is not dead! The girl is not dead!' But in the Incarnation the bell was tolled and a grave dug for her.

On the fourth day following the attack Teresa began to recover consciousness. She opened her eyes with difficulty, for the lids were heavy with the wax already smeared on them in accordance with the practice customary when preparing a body for burial. It seemed to her that the Lord had raised the sinner Teresa from the dead, and long afterwards, whenever the thought came to her, her soul was filled with wonder and gratitude. But her body continued to be racked with torments:

> My tongue had been bitten to pieces, my throat was so swollen through my not having eaten anything and through my great weakness that I could not even swallow a sip of water, my bones seemed to have been all wrenched from their sockets, and my head was spinning. My body was so shrivelled and knotted up as a result of the tortures I had been suffering all those days, that I could no more move arm, foot, hand or head without somebody's help than if I had been dead. All I could do, I believe, was to wiggle one of the fingers of my right hand.

In this pitiable condition the young nun was carried back to the convent she had never wished to leave. They had to lift her in a sheet held at either end, for she could not bear the pain of being touched. Instead of a corpse the sisters received a living body, but a body only just alive, reduced to skin and bones, and unbelievably frail.

The acute state of paralysis lasted for eight months and then gradually relaxed. It was three years, however, before the invalid could leave her bed, 'and when I started to crawl about on all fours I praised God for it'. She attributed her recovery largely to the intercession of St Joseph who, having been the paternal guardian of his Divine Son on earth, was now the most powerful of advocates in heaven. It was therefore in gratitude to 'the glorious St Joseph', the saint who had given her back her health, that Teresa was later to dedicate her first convent.

4

Between Earth and Heaven

Teresa's recovery, after almost all had given her up for dead, was accounted a miracle. During the years in the infirmary she bore her sufferings with heroic fortitude and with a joyful serenity which seemed not of this world. A curious legend had long been current that the convent of the Incarnation would some day produce a saint called Teresa. The name was not uncommon; but was it not rare indeed to find one who, while yet so young, had passed through such a purgatory of suffering and emerged crowned with every grace and virtue, and with that mysterious power to charm and find favour in human eyes actually enhanced?

Teresa was now twenty-eight and already something of a celebrity. Her fellow nuns came to her for advice on both spiritual and practical matters. A group of younger nuns gathered round her admiringly; she referred to them as her friends, but they were in reality more like disciples. She spoke to them of Recollection, and how she had found in constant mental prayer the strength to endure tribulations. Her conversation was so natural, so vivid, so spiced with wit; she spoke of holy things with an authority and lack of sanctimonious jargon which captivated her listeners. Friends and kinsfolk came to the convent to congratulate Teresa on her recovery, and they too fell under the spell. They came again and again. The parlour of the Incarnation became a salon presided over by the veiled enchantress behind the grille. Privileged ladies had the entry to her apartment and joined the pious circle of her intimates. In affectionate gratitude to the father who had watched over her with such solicitude, she took his spiritual welfare in hand, initiating him into the methods of contemplative prayer which had proved of such benefit to herself, lending him the books she thought suitable, and even receiving from him regular reports of his progress with the authority of a true spiritual director.

Teresa was inspired with the best of intentions. She did not see the perils inherent in the new role which seemed to have been assigned her by divine providence, rather than through any deliberate seeking on her part. Later, when she sat down at the behest of her confessor to write an account of her life, this period seemed to her to have been one of wanton blindness and vainglory. Those around her would have found any such self-condemnation astonishing. The Rule, at least in its Mitigated form then practised, was not broken. Her confessors saw nothing wrong in Teresa's multifarious social contacts. Neither did the nuns. To all concerned, they seemed indeed to be bringing nothing but good. For the lay folk of Avila to frequent the convent in order to consort with one known to be so chaste and devout as Teresa de Ahumada must surely be edifying. Moreover, they showed their appreciation by bringing alms. And the convent, with its 180 inmates, was insufficiently endowed and in constant want of money. There could be no possible reason to discourage the increasing flow of visitors.

Yet Teresa's conscience grew uneasy. The desire to help others – 'a very common temptation with beginners' – was absorbing so much of her time that it left her little for the one thing which she knew was the pre-condition for any help – a deep and regular prayer life, and the seclusion necessary for it. In her autobiography she passes the severest strictures on herself for consenting to these distractions and speaks of 'vanity after vanity', 'amusement after amusement' and 'one occasion for sin after another'. With human affections and interests now crowding her mind, she felt ashamed to seek the intimacy with God which she had experienced in contemplative prayer. The Devil tempted her with false humility, urging her to be satisfied, like most of those around her, with the common observances of religion and nothing more. Her sisters noticed that she still liked to withdraw to her oratory and was no less fond than before of reading pious books and speaking readily of heavenly things, and that she scrupulously eschewed all convent gossip or any conduct that could be considered the least reprehensible. The high regard they continued to have for her caused her pain, 'since I knew what I was really like'. She eventually ceased to practise Recollection altogether, and had to admit as much to Don Alonso, alleging the poor state of her health as an excuse. His visits grew shorter and less frequent, probably out of consideration for her still frail condition. Teresa took this to denote that he had made such excellent progress himself that she was no longer needed as a mentor and so he felt his calls were now a waste of time. 'As I was wasting mine on other vanities,' she comments, 'I paid little heed to this.'

There was one person whose frequent visits had a particularly disturbing effect on Teresa. Her references to the anonymous visitor are extremely guarded, and we cannot tell from them whether the 'person' was man or woman. Some biographers have surmised a romantic attachment, but the undesirable intimacy might equally well have been with some female friend, such as the cousin who had frequented her home a dozen years before. An elderly relative who was a nun at the Incarnation scented danger and cautioned her against the association, but Teresa, telling herself that it was entirely harmless, brushed aside her objections. The episode seems significant chiefly for giving rise to what appears to be the first recorded irruption of the supernatural into Teresa's life in the form of a vision. Here are the words in which she describes it:

Christ appeared before me, looking very stern and giving me to understand that there was something about this [friendship] displeasing to him. I saw him with the eyes of the soul more clearly than I could have seen him with those of the body; and so great was the impression left on me that, although this happened more than twenty years ago, I seem to see him even now. I was greatly astonished and perturbed and wanted never to see that person again.

It was the first of the mystical experiences which were later to assume such varied and vivid forms. For nearly thirty years Teresa had lived a life of generally intense religious piety, and had started along the uncharted paths of contemplative prayer, without the impact of any such disturbing phenomenon. She tells us that in consequence she at first put it down to the imagination, or perhaps to the work of the Devil. The message it sought to convey was not at all to her liking, and she tried to dismiss it as mere illusion. And yet she could not escape the conviction that 'it was of God, and not of the imagination'. She did not then know, she tells us, that 'one can see things with eyes other than those of the body', and that she had experienced what is generally termed an 'imaginary' vision – imaginary, not in the sense of being the product of pure fantasy, but because it takes the form of a visual image, as distinct from the sudden nonrepresentational awareness of an 'intellectual vision'. Teresa was, in any case, too alarmed to confide to anyone what she had experienced, and knew no one to whom she could turn for guidance. Not only did she try to dismiss the whole matter from her mind, but she let herself be persuaded that there was really no harm in continuing to see the person whose presence had occasioned the vision of Christ's wrath.

A second warning soon came to her. This time it took the repulsive shape of a great toad which suddenly appeared from nowhere in broad daylight. It happened when she was in the company of the dangerous visitor, and she tells us that it was seen by others too. It seemed to her the very symbol of loathsome sin and, whether a real creature or an apparition, to have been sent as yet one more token of divine displeasure and admonition.

For a dozen years or so after her recovery, Teresa continued to lead a life which seemed to others exemplary, but to herself culpably short of that perfection to which she believed God was calling her. A priest who visited the Incarnation on an official inspection in 1552, when she was in her thirty-seventh year, gives a revealing picture of the impression she left on her contemporaries:

> She was a woman of admirable parts [he writes], being of good lineage, talents and abilities. She was still quite young, I should say about thirty [*sic*] or so. She was dark and well-built, with a round face, very cheerful and gay, and most ready and pleasant in conversation. They told me she had quite a following in the Order . . . though I never heard that her behaviour exceeded the limits proper to a nun.

Teresa's own judgement on herself was very different:

> My life was one of great tribulation, for when I prayed my faults became more obvious to me. On the one side God was calling; on the other I followed the world. I took pleasure in all divine things, but worldly affairs still held me captive. It seemed that I wanted to blend together two things as contrary and hostile to one another as are the life and joys of the spirit and the tastes and pleasures of the senses. I found it very hard to pray, for the spirit was not the master but the slave. I took no joy in God, and no pleasure in the world. In the midst of worldly satisfactions the thought of what I owed to God distressed me, and my worldly affections made me restless when I was with God.

It needed all the efforts of her strong will to enter her oratory and pray, and even then she would find herself listening impatiently for the clock to strike and her prayer-time to end.

But at least, after giving it up altogether for a short time, she *had* resumed the practice of mental prayer, however half-heartedly. It was, she believed, her father's parting blessing on her. At Christmastide 1543, Don Alonso passed peacefully away after a short illness in which she tended him as devotedly as he had once tended her. Her grief, which she sternly repressed, was intense. Father and daughter, despite their differences in temperament, had been at one in their fervent piety and they were very close together. 'In losing him,' she wrote, 'I was losing all the good and comfort of my life – for he was all that to me . . . I felt as if my soul was being torn from my body when I saw him nearing his end, for I loved him very dearly.'

Amongst those who stood around Don Alonso's deathbed was his confessor, Fray Vicente Barrón, from the monastery of Santo Tomás. He comforted Teresa with the assurance that her father's soul would go straight to heaven, so clear and Christian a conscience did the old hidalgo have. The friar was one of the few Dominicans who looked with approval on the growing vogue for mental prayer. When Teresa confided to him the troubled state of her own soul, he urged her fervently to turn back to the practice of Recollection. She would have liked to take this learned and perceptive man for her confessor, but the Carmelite friars claimed a monopoly of spiritual authority over the nuns of their Order and would have resented the intrusion of an outsider, however eminent. She nevertheless did her best to follow Fray Vicente's advice.

Don Alonso's death involved Teresa in fresh mundane distractions. Her father had nominated her an executrix, and all her powers of tact and cajolery were needed to curb the fierce quarrels which at once broke out over what remained of his estate. For all his moral integrity, the hidalgo had died heavily in debt. Fifty creditors clamoured for their due. Thanks to Teresa's persuasions, her brothers Pedro and Antonio renounced their claims in favour of their half-sister María. Martín de Guzmán, the latter's husband and also an executor, nevertheless contested the will. The case was carried to court and lawyers consumed most of the little that was left of the inheritance. Teresa took her younger sister Juana to live with her in the Incarnation and tenderly devoted herself to the orphan's material and spiritual welfare. The dissensions amongst those she loved deepened Teresa's sense of the vanity of worldly ambitions and affections.

Early in 1554 a publisher in Salamanca issued a Spanish translation of St Augustine's *Confessions*, a copy of which came into Teresa's hands. She had already conceived a special devotion for this saint from the days she had spent with the nuns of his Order in the convent of Our Lady of Grace. It comforted her to think that at one time he had been as great a sinner as she believed herself to be.

> When I began to read the *Confessions* [she relates] I seemed to see myself there too, and when I came to his conversion and read how he heard the voice in the garden I felt in my heart that it was just as if the Lord was speaking to me. For a long time I dissolved into tears, absorbed in great inner anguish and distress.

The crisis followed soon after the emotional shock of seeing an image of Christ with horribly bleeding wounds – probably one of those lifelike Spanish polychrome sculptures whose stark realism can indeed be deeply moving, though some say it was in fact a painting showing Mary Magdalene at the Saviour's feet. This image, or picture, had been brought into the convent and kept in an oratory in preparation for use on a feast-day. 'The thought of everything he had suffered for us,' Teresa recalls, 'and of the wretched return we had made for all those wounds, so touched me that I threw myself on the ground before him shedding floods of tears and imploring him to give me strength once and for all never to offend him again.' She vowed she would not rise to her feet until this prayer had been granted.

Such is Teresa's account of what is sometimes called her 'second conversion'. Perhaps it was not as sudden as the term implies, nor the long phase of preparation which preceded it so wicked – at least by any yardstick but a saint's – as she believed. But the bleeding figure of the Christ and the burning words of the contrite sinner struck her imagination with a force which left no room for earthly things. Her allegiance was from now on absolute and uncontested.

> It seemed that my soul derived great strength from the Divine Majesty [she wrote] and that he must have heard my lamentation and taken pity on my tears. There began to grow in me a desire to spend more time with him and to turn away my eyes from all occasions for sin, and once they had gone, I would forthwith return to loving him again.

She could no longer doubt that she loved her Lord, and belonged only to him. But with what awesome and overwhelming graces the Beloved would requite her love she had yet to learn.

5

Voices and Visions

The woman who was to be accounted the greatest mystic of her day had lived to be nearly forty with almost no experience of those phenomena commonly held to be associated with the mystical life. The stern Christ-figure which Teresa believed she saw reproaching her for being too friendly with the undesirable visitor she dismissed as an effect of the imagination. The wounded Christ who had released the flood of tears and led to her 'conversion' was no vision but the work of some artist's brush or chisel. Yet Teresa's fervent and hypersensitive nature clearly had some latent disposition for the mystical graces, and she hints at earlier experiences which seem to foreshadow those to come.

> This is how I used to pray [she wrote]. Since I could not meditate intellectually, I would try to imagine Christ within me, and I found myself the better, I believed, for dwelling on those times in his life when he was most lonely. It seemed to me that when he was alone and in affliction, he must, like anyone in trouble, admit me. . . . For those who would quickly enter into Recollection a book is useful. I also found gazing at fields, water, or flowers a great help, for they spoke to me of the Creator, and served as a book in bringing me to a state of Recollection. . . . I used at times to feel — though it passed very quickly — the beginning of something which I will now describe. It used to happen that whilst I was imagining myself at Christ's side in the way I have said, or sometimes simply reading, there would

unaccountably come over me such a feeling of the presence of God that made it impossible for me to doubt that he was indeed within me and that I was wholly engulfed in him. This was no sort of vision; I believe they call it Mystical Theology. The soul is then caught up and as it were carried outside itself. The will loves; the memory is, I think, almost lost, and the understanding ceases to reason though it is not, I believe, lost. I mean, it does not function, but rather remains as if amazed at how much it comprehends. For God wills that it understands nothing at all of what his Majesty reveals to it.

During the long hours she spent in prayer following the crisis induced by the contemplation of the wounded Christ and the reading of the *Confessions*, Teresa found herself drawn into regions of strange and ever deepening spiritual experience. 'His Majesty began to give me very frequently the Prayer of Quiet,' she wrote, 'and often too the Prayer of Union, which would last a long time.' In this Prayer of Quiet, the mind would cease from verbal invocation or speculation, emptying itself of all thought before the onrush of an infused sense of marvellous calm and bliss. And sometimes, in this passive but infinitely precious waiting upon God, the spark which filled the soul with its sweet warmth would be fanned by the divine Lover himself into the mystical flame of Union. These were ineffable mysteries, beyond the skill even of Teresa's gifted pen to describe, which she could only adumbrate through the striking images and metaphors of her later writings.

Teresa was now seldom to be seen in the parlour of the Incarnation. Her new-found dedication to mental prayer, and the peculiar states it seemed sometimes to induce in her, became a favourite topic amongst her gossip-loving sisters. Some regarded her with a respect verging on veneration; others spitefully declared that Doña Teresa de Ahumada was setting herself up for a saint and trying to introduce pernicious novelties into the life of the convent. Teresa was greatly distressed – not on account of her reputation, by which she had now learned to set little store, nor yet of the manifest injustice of the nuns' charges, but precisely because she feared there really might be some truth in them. She had been so worldly, so perverse, and the last person in the world with any claim to sanctity – in this they were perfectly right. Although she knew her desires and intentions to be pure, she was also painfully aware of how much of the old Adam still lived on in her. Why indeed should she, Teresa the sinner, be favoured with the spiritual consolations lavished upon her as she trod the hazardous but rewarding path of mental prayer?

It was at this moment of doubt and distress that the path took an alarming new turn. Teresa experienced her first 'locution'. The words which suddenly crystallized in her consciousness as she knelt in prayer imprinted themselves with such vivid clarity and power that she could not possibly mistake them for the familiar voice of conscience. She was given to understand that it was Christ himself telling her: 'Do not fret yourself about this, but serve me.' They were words of comfort and reassurance, but the mode in which they had been conveyed to her filled her with awe.

This was the first of the many locutions which were to guide the course of Teresa's spiritual life and practical activities. Just as visions (which she had yet to experience) were something perceived by the mind's eye, so the locutions communicated themselves as silently uttered 'inner voices', directing her in things great and small, instructing her to do this or refrain from doing that, warning, encouraging, occasionally rebuking. She was sure they could be no mere projection of her own unexpressed desires and hopes, as they often surprised and ran counter to her rational intentions. That they might emanate not from God, but from the Devil, she was anxiously aware, and she learned later to discern and formulate the guidelines by which to test their authenticity: the sway they at once exercised over the soul, the humble gratitude and tranquillity they brought in their train, and their power to remain indelibly engraved on the mind. She learned too to distinguish between the different categories of locutions, similar to those of visions – corporeal, imaginary and intellectual, the latter being the most frequent and the most authoritative. Sometimes her voices told her one thing and her confessors another. When this happened, Teresa, who put obedience above all other virtues, would steel herself to carry out her confessor's commands; God would then reward her, she disarmingly declares, by causing the confessor to change his mind so that the conflict of loyalties was happily resolved.

There was another reason why Teresa should be alarmed at the supernatural experiences she was beginning to receive. 'I was very much afraid,' she writes in her *Life*, 'since there have lately been cases of women who have been grossly deceived and subject to great illusions through the wiles of the Devil.' The occurrences to which Teresa alludes form a curious footnote to the history of her times. They first come to our notice in the period of religious exaltation attending the completion of the Reconquest at the close of the preceding century. We hear of one ecstatic prophesying the fall of Granada and the imminent conversion of all Moors and Jews; another, racked with supernatural wounds and aghast at sacred images weeping blood, laments the corruption of the Church. In Piedrahita, a town not far from Avila, through which Teresa had passed on her way to the *curandera* of Becedas, stood a Dominican monastery where the friars still venerated the memory of a holy woman who claimed to have been favoured with such a plethora of locutions that she could sustain long conversations aloud, and in the presence of others, with her heavenly visitants. 'Oh Virgin,' the *beata* would exclaim, courteously stepping aside on entering or leaving a room, 'if you had not given birth to Christ, it could never have been granted me to become his Bride! It was more fitting then that the Mother of my Spouse should take precedence.' She too prophesied the mass conversion of Moslems and believed that she had a mission to reform the great Dominican Order. King Ferdinand, Cardinal Cisneros and the Duke of Alba were amongst those who took her for an inspired and angelic soul; others dismissed her as a deluded fanatic.

Another puzzling case had been that of Juana de la Cruz. The nun had embraced her vocation in the teeth of violent family opposition, escaping disguised as a man to the Franciscan convent near Toledo where she was eventually to become Abbess. Many and wonderful were the mystic graces claimed for her there: the granting of the stigmata, the mystic espousals with Christ in the presence of the Blessed Virgin and the angels, innumerable and prodigious ecstasies, during which she could be heard discoursing in Latin, Arabic, Basque and other tongues of which she was normally quite ignorant. Some of the nuns venerated her as a saint and recorded her prophetic utterances in a huge tome. But others denounced her, the phenomenon of glossolalia at length ceased, and Juana ended her life in obscurity shortly before Teresa entered the Incarnation. Some years later, an attempt was made to revive her cult. 'Santa Juana' was made the heroine of a trilogy by the dramatist who created Don Juan. But it was the daemonic rake, and not the sainted nun, who lived on in the public imagination.

A more recent and deeply disturbing case was that of another Franciscan nun, Magdalena de la Cruz of Córdoba. For as long as Teresa could remember, Sor Magdalena had been renowned for her extraordinary virtues and for the mystical graces of which, at her confessor's behest, she had written a full account. The Inquisitor General himself had begged for her prayers and the Queen for her blessing. The convent in Córdoba had been rebuilt thanks to the alms lavished upon it by her grateful devotees. Then, towards the end of her life, the revered Abbess had fallen ill and to the general consternation had called for confession and even for exorcism. Her holy life, the old woman declared, had been nothing but humbug, and whatever supernatural powers she possessed were conferred upon her by the Devil, with whom she had made a pact at the age of five. The Inquisition treated these sensational disclosures with remarkable leniency, perhaps out of consideration for the eminence of some of Sor Magdalena's devotees, and let her off with a public recantation and a sentence of lifelong reclusion. This had happened in 1546, some eight years before Teresa's 'second conversion', and the memory of the scandal was to haunt her and furnish arms to her critics for many years to come.

At about the same time there died, in the obscurity of a monastery at Torrelaguna, a friar who was once the protagonist of a hardly less bizarre and notorious episode. Fray Francisco Ortiz had been, in his youth, a rising star of the Franciscan Order and chaplain to the Emperor. But he fell under the spell of a young *beata* whose dubious relations with her devotees led her into trouble with the Inquisition. Such was the friar's infatuation that he even mounted the pulpit to denounce that dread institution for persecuting one who was manifestly a saint, and it was long before he could be reduced to silence and contrition. Fray Francisco's aberration was but one expression of the religious ferment which was stirring Castile in the 1520s. Another was the emergence of informal groups of men and women, dubbed *alumbrados* or 'illumined ones' on account of their addiction to mental prayer and their belief that God speaks direct to the human conscience. Pious laymen, women, and Franciscan friars – many of *converso* stock – were specially attracted to what the Inquisition saw as a sect suspiciously akin to those spawned by Luther in northern Europe. Edicts were issued against them and severe punishments meted out. Anyone with an interest in mental prayer and an urge to consort with others of like mind ran the risk – however impeccably orthodox he might be – of being tarred with the same brush.

Dangers loomed on every side and Teresa did not know which way to turn. Malicious tongues whispered 'Magdalena de la Cruz'. Osuna, author of the *Third Spiritual Alphabet* which had helped to guide her in the practice of mental prayer, had himself once frequented the circle round the dubious *beata* who had brought Ortiz to ruin. *Alumbrados* and false mystics were poisoning the very air round the peaks which the true contemplative aspired to scale.

Where could she find a trustworthy guide? The Dominican friar who had been her father's confessor had encouraged her to persevere, but he was not at hand to map out the way. Who indeed could guide her, unless his footsteps too were set on the same course? In her perplexity, Teresa turned to an old friend, connected by marriage to her family, called Don Francisco de Salcedo. He was a layman, but so noted for his piety and charitable works that he was familiarly known as the *Caballero santo*. He was, moreover, of impeccable orthodoxy, and for the last twenty years had assiduously attended the theology lectures at the Dominican monastery of Santo Tomás which served as Avila's university.

But the *Caballero santo* was scarcely the man to help Teresa out of her difficulties. Meticulous and rigid in the ordering of his own devotional life, and sincerely attached to her by family affection and a fervent desire to help another soul in distress, he was incapable of grasping the nature of spiritual experiences so vastly different from his own. The more he listened to the nun, the less he liked what he heard. It smacked unmistakably of delusion or diabolical possession. The most he could do was to suggest that Teresa should consult someone more qualified and spiritual than himself. This proved to be a priest called Gaspar Daza, noted for the fervour of his sermons, his works of charity and his missionary labours amongst the rural poor. Daza was a man of the same stern mould as Salcedo – dedicated, upright, deeply orthodox – and as totally incapable of understanding her. For a time he acted as her confessor and thought that everything could be settled by pouncing on her slightest imperfections with rigorous severity. But he had no wish to assume responsibility for such an unusual penitent and soon excused himself on the grounds that he was already too busy.

Looking back over those difficult years, Teresa writes of her reluctant confessor with more charity than the good man appears to have shown her. His methods, she declares, were well suited to one more advanced in perfection than herself, but had she remained under his direction, 'I do not think that my soul would have prospered'. Though she also gives much credit to Salcedo for his patience and kindness, it seems that on this occasion, as on many others, it was largely her own humility, courage and good sense which saw her through the crisis.

> I thought to myself that the best thing I could do was to keep a clear conscience and avoid occasions even for venial sin [she concluded]. For if the spirit of God was behind it all, then the gain was clear; if it was the Devil, so long as I tried to please the Lord and keep from offending him, he could do me little harm and would rather be the loser.

Francisco de Salcedo at least made one helpful suggestion. The Jesuits had recently opened the college of San Gil in Avila and quickly gained a reputation for piety and spiritual discernment. The Society was still in the first flush of its apostolic fervour and did not yet view mysticism with the suspicion it later came to harbour. The fervent young Jesuit who studied the general confession which, on Salcedo's advice, Teresa had written out and submitted to the fathers at San Gil, was impressed. He visited the Incarnation, raising a fresh flutter of gossip and speculation amongst the convent busybodies, and after a meeting with the nun declared that 'without doubt, it was the spirit of God'. The verdict was confirmed by a still more authoritative voice. St Francisco Borja, once known to the world as the Duke of Gandia and a former friend of the Emperor, was passing through Avila, and Teresa was given an opportunity to meet him. From these Jesuit fathers she heard the words of encouragement for which she had been longing. Though the young confessor was a man of only mediocre parts and his stay in Avila a brief one, the encounter proved providential. He exhorted Teresa on no account to desist from prayer, and it seems probable that he gave her some parts of St Ignatius Loyola's famous *Spiritual Exercises* as an aid to meditation.

The departure of the young Jesuit left Teresa again to the mercies of Salcedo and Daza. Well-meaning and pious though they were, these men were as far as ever from understanding her, and she found no way of explaining her spiritual state in terms they could grasp. At length she hit upon the idea of marking certain passages in a book called *The Ascent of Mount Sion*, particularly the process of emptying the mind of normal thought in preparation for the infusion of divine enlightenment, which seemed to correspond most closely to her own experiences. The *Caballero santo* had expressed relief on learning the favourable opinions entertained by the Jesuits, but he still stuck to his conviction that it was probably all the work of the Devil. Dejected and frightened, Teresa could not keep back her tears. She even offered to give up mental prayer altogether if they were positive she was being deceived, though she could hardly conceive of life without the practice which alone gave it meaning. Salcedo and Daza continued their grave conclave and even consulted other respectable persons, so that all Avila was soon talking about the strange case of Teresa de Ahumada. It was mortifying to her in the extreme that folk should think that she herself had been divulging these divine intimacies to all and sundry.

Under the stress caused by her friends' scepticism and the absence of her Jesuit confessor, Teresa's health broke down. The easy-going customs of the Incarnation allowed her to leave the convent and stay first with relatives and then with a sister of one of the nuns whose friendship was to become of great importance in her life. Doña Guiomar de Ulloa had married very young and been widowed a few years before. She was celebrated for her beauty and – at one time at least – for her love of extravagant display and her impulsive, capricious, but warm-hearted temperament. She had been left well-off, though her fortune was depleted first by her extravagances and later by her charities. Teresa spent most of the next three years in this lady's household and found that she could practise her prolonged prayers and contemplation as freely there as in the often theoretical seclusion of a convent cell. In Doña Guiomar's house she also met others who were to prove helpful to her own spiritual development. One of these was an old peasant woman called Mari Díaz, well known in Avila for her strict and sometimes eccentric austerities, who now led the life of an anchoress under the rich widow's roof and became Teresa's close friend. But most important of all were the relations which Teresa was able to renew with San Gil, whose Vice-Rector, Father Juan de Prádanos, became her new confessor.

Father Prádanos treated his penitent with a judicious blend of severity and tact which, according to Teresa's own account, began to lead her towards greater perfection through a painful exercise in self-denial. This proved the occasion for a startling new mystical experience. The self-denial was in the sphere of personal relations. There was nothing shameful or wrong in a certain relationship itself – she does not inform us further of its nature – but it distracted Teresa from her goal of total dedication. At first, she saw in the sacrifice demanded of her nothing but a gratuitous and ungrateful rejection of harmlessly proffered friendship and she questioned its necessity. Father Prádanos did not insist or explain, but he counselled her to lay the matter before God in prayer. It was then, whilst she was on her knees reciting the hymn *Veni, Creator* and imploring the divine guidance, that she received her answer in the unmistakable tones of a locution: 'I wish you now to converse not with men, but with angels.' At the same time, she experienced something frightening and unexpected. 'There came upon me a rapture so sudden that it almost carried me away – something so sure that there could be no mistaking it. This was the first time that the Lord granted me the grace of ecstasy.' It was a phenomenon which, as we shall see, Teresa was often to experience and learned to describe with searching and subtle analysis.

Teresa was not long to enjoy the guidance of an understanding confessor. Father Prádanos fell ill, and after being tenderly nursed back to health by Doña Guiomar and Teresa he was transferred from Avila. His successor was Father Baltasar Alvarez, at that time a young and irresolute priest, with no experience of contemplative prayer or of directing souls, but possessing deep spiritual potentialities which time and the influence of his exceptional penitent were to bring to fruition. The inexperience of the youthful Jesuit was the signal for the Salcedo-Daza camarilla to renew their well-meant attempts to convince the nun of the diabolic origin of her experiences. The old sneers and the allusions to Sor Magdalena were revived, and since her new confessor seemed to be siding with the prosecution, Teresa's anguished self-questioning revived with them. She left Doña Guiomar's house and returned to the Incarnation. There she prayed long and earnestly that God would lead her by another and less perilous path. But the mystical graces continued to multiply rather than diminish. 'The Lord would make me recollected during conversation. He said whatever he pleased, and there was no avoiding it; much as it distressed me, I had to listen.' When she was alone, Teresa could neither pray nor read, but remained as if stunned by her wretchedness and by the fear that the Devil was deceiving her after all. Then, in these moments of bitter desolation, her voices would comfort her: 'Have no fear, daughter, it is I, and I shall not forsake you. Have no fear.' Immediately she was filled with peace and unshakeable confidence. These things *were* of God; what cause had she then to fear the Devil? Later, she could comment with robust assurance: 'I am more afraid, indeed, of those who stand in such fear of the Devil than I am of the Devil himself!'

Father Alvarez, unsure of himself and playing for safety, saw things in a very different light. The gentle cheerfulness with which the nun bore her tribulations he took for levity, her unaffected frankness for frivolity. She could only be cured, he concluded, by the bitter medicine of mortification. Teresa was deprived of the consolation of frequent Communion. When she wrote to him about her troubles and implored his speedy guidance, he ordered her to wait a month before reading his answer. He urged her to avoid too much solitude and to seek distractions. Even the books in which she had found the spiritual guidance her confessors so often failed to provide were taken away from her. This was in 1559, when many men and women suspected of Protestant and *alumbrista* heresies were sent to the stake in Valladolid, and the Grand Inquisitor issued a lengthy Index of forbidden books. Teresa felt more frightened and abandoned than ever. Then again there came the inner voices: 'Do not be distressed, for I will give you a living book.'

The mysterious promise was fulfilled in a way which is best described in Teresa's own words:

> When I was praying one day – it was the feast of the glorious St Peter – I saw Christ beside me, or more exactly, I felt him to be at my side, for I saw nothing with the eyes of the body, neither with those of the soul. But Christ seemed to be close beside me, and I saw that it was he who seemed to be speaking to me. As I was utterly ignorant that such visions were possible, I was very frightened and at first could do nothing but weep. But as soon as he spoke to me I regained my usual composure and became calm, happy and quite free from fear. There at my side, so it seemed to me, Jesus Christ stayed, but as this was not an imaginary vision I was unable to see in what form; but that he was all the time at my right hand and witnessed everything I was doing I most clearly felt.

In great consternation, Teresa hastened to her confessor to confide this new and disturbing experience. Father Alvarez questioned her incredulously: 'In what form did you see him?' he asked. Teresa answered that she had not seen him. 'Then how do you know it was he?'

She did not *know* it in any ordinary sense, Teresa tried to explain. 'But I could not but be aware that he was beside me. This I plainly saw and felt. And when I prayed, my soul was rapt in a far deeper and more lasting way than ever before. And the effects of my prayers were altogether different too. Of this I am absolutely sure.'

She searched for words to describe it further. It was like being in the dark, it seemed to her, and aware that some person was there beside you. But this was not a true comparison. If you are in the dark, you may still perceive the person's presence through the other senses, by hearing him move or speak, or by touching him. But in the experience she had just had, this was not so. There was no question of being in the dark either.

> On the contrary [she went on] he appears to the soul through a knowledge brighter than the sun. I don't mean that the sun or any brightness is actually visible to the eyes, but I felt my soul illuminated, as it were, by an invisible light. Nor is it like the awareness of God's presence, which often comes with the Prayer of Quiet or the Prayer of Union. It is not a vision, either. In a vision, the soul distinctly sees Jesus Christ and so knows he is present. But here one just knows God is there by the effects which he produces in the soul. That is how he wishes to make his presence felt. It is not simply the divine influence acting on the soul, though it does this too. But here we find that Christ, the human Christ, has become our companion.

Father Alvarez, still unable to grasp the meaning of Teresa's words, could only repeat: 'Who said it was Jesus Christ?'

'He often tells me so himself', Teresa continued. 'But even before he said so, it was impressed on my understanding that it was he. He would tell me this even when I could not see him.'

Teresa struggled to make her meaning clearer. If someone she had never seen or heard about were to come and speak to her when she was in the dark or had lost her sight, and were to say who he was, she would believe him. But she would not be able to assert it as positively as if she had actually seen him. But here the case was different. For, though unseen, God imparted so clear a certainty to the soul that doubt was impossible. In fact, one would sooner doubt the evidence of one's own eyes. On normal occasions, one might sometimes wonder whether something seen had not really been just imagination. Not so here. If such a suspicion crossed the mind, it at once gave way to an overwhelming and unquestioning certainty. She could only compare the phenomenon to that of locutions, when God is pleased to impress his message direct on the soul, without the use of audible words. A homely metaphor occurred to her which may have startled the serious-minded young Jesuit. It was as if food had been put into the stomach without one's eating it or knowing how it had got there.

Teresa does not tell us how this remarkable interview ended. According to a nun who claimed to have heard it from the lips of the saint herself, the confessor brusquely dismissed her and her story, more than ever convinced that he had to do with an obdurate case of diabolical possession. The same witness relates a remarkable sequel. Shortly afterwards, when Father Alvarez was meditating in his cell, he was himself favoured with a vision of Christ. The next day, their roles now reversed, he confided his secret to Teresa, who replied: 'Do not believe it, Father! Christ appeared to Your Reverence? It could not have been Christ! Just think again!'

The Jesuit assured her that he was not mistaken, and gave many good reasons for his belief. 'Now you see, Father', Teresa concluded. 'This is how it appears to you. But to others it may appear to be whatever they say it is.'

Was it as a consequence of this experience that Teresa found her confessor's incredulity beginning to weaken? She first describes him as 'a very discreet man of great humility', although 'this deep humility brought me great tribulation since, albeit a man of much prayer and learning, he did not trust himself since the Lord was not leading him along this path.' But she then refers to him as now very different in every respect . . . and on the many occasions when the Lord permitted me to be harshly judged – often undeservedly – everything was laid at his door and he was blamed on my account, although he was entirely blameless. . . . He had to answer people who did not believe him and who thought I was on the road to perdition.

Father Baltasar Alvarez remained Teresa's confessor for more than three difficult years, during which time his spiritual direction seems to have been interrupted by absence or sickness. Teresa, charitably mentioning no names, alludes to a substitute confessor, at whose hands she suffered her harshest persecution. When she answered this confessor and her other critics with the frankness and shrewdness natural to her, they accused her of lacking humility and trying to teach *them*. Some declared that she ought to be exorcised, since she was so clearly possessed by the Devil. The confessor ordered that, whenever she saw one of her visions, she was to show her scorn by snapping her fingers at it. Others advised her to spit.

Teresa was thrown into fresh agonies by this new onslaught. It was powerless, however, to shake her belief in the divine origin of what she was experiencing. All doubts had now fled. 'I would gladly have let myself be torn to pieces,' she writes, 'rather than believe it was of the Devil.' What did cause her intolerable distress was to be required to respond to God's favours with scorn and insults, and she fancied herself no better than those who had stood mocking the crucified Christ. She cried out for forgiveness as she forced herself to do as she had been told, pleading that she was only acting under obedience to those whom the Church set in authority over her. Her voices soothed her, bidding her not to fret but to go on obeying, and promising that her persecutors would be shown the truth. When they forbade her to pray, Christ seemed to be wrathful and to bid her tell them that this was tyranny. Once he took from her the rosary she was carrying, and when he gave it back she saw four precious stones set in the cross, exquisitely incised with the Five Wounds and sparkling like diamonds, only incomparably more beautiful, and she was given to understand that from then on that cross would always appear to her so. And though no other eyes beheld the wonder, Teresa adds, 'I have never since been able to see the wood of which this cross is made, but only those stones.'

The tide of mystical graces was now flowing at full flood. The more the sceptics scoffed and threatened, the more copiously were they bestowed, vested with a 'majesty and beauty which remained so deeply imprinted on the soul that they are unforgettable', and leaving such spiritual effects that 'everyone who knew me saw my soul had changed'. They came unsought and often surprising by their strangeness. Not long after the imageless perception of Christ at her side, Teresa received her first 'imaginary' vision and again hastened to her confessor to give an account of it.

One day when I was at prayer, the Lord was pleased to show me no more than his hands. Their beauty was quite beyond description. I was filled with a great fear, as usually happens when the Lord begins to grant me the experience of some new supernatural favour. A few days later I also saw that divine face, and the sight seemed to transport me quite beyond myself. I could not understand why the Lord was revealing himself to me gradually in this way, for later he was to grant me the favour of seeing him whole. Later I learned that his Majesty was making allowances for the weakness of my nature. May he be for ever blessed, for so vile and base a creature as myself would not have been able to bear it, and it was because he knew this that he acted in this way.

These strange, fragmented revelations occurred during the second half of 1559, when Teresa was forty-four years of age. The following January she was granted a vision of the resurrected Christ: 'There stood before me the most sacred Humanity in the full beauty and majesty of His resurrected body, as it appears in painting.' She wrote a description of the vision, at her confessor's urgent behest, stressing that it was wholly 'imaginary' and seen not with the eyes of the body but with those of the soul. Indeed, she wished that she *had* seen it with her corporeal eyes, so that her confessor could not tell her that it had all been a product of her fancy. For a moment, just after the vision had faded, the thought flashed through her mind that perhaps she really had been fancying it. She went to him and told him frankly of her fears.

'Have you described the vision as it really was, or have you made it up in order to deceive me?' Father Alvarez sternly asked. 'Father, I have told you the truth. I would not deceive you knowingly or tell a lie for anything in the world.'

Father Alvarez believed her. But why, then, was she distressing herself with these scruples? Why, indeed? Teresa grew calm, the certainty once more welling up within her that it could only be God's doing, and making her wonder how she could torment herself with doubts which only the Devil was putting into her head. When she later came to write her *Life*, she could indeed recall three or four occasions when the Devil had tried to lure her with some counterfeit likeness of God, but she had seen through his tricks almost at once, for the apparitions left her restless, troubled and nauseated. He must have tried them on in order to destroy her faith in the truly divine visions. But the latter could not possibly be confused with the false. For one thing, the human imagination was utterly powerless to conceive anything resembling them. She had compared them to a beautiful painting, but the comparison was utterly inadequate. They were more real than the most realistic picture, as a man is more real than the most lifelike portrait. When granted a vision, it was no mere likeness of Christ which she beheld, but the living Christ himself.

It seemed to Teresa that if she were to spend many years trying to imagine it, she could never have conjured up anything so beautiful as what she saw in her visions. The whiteness and radiance alone exceeded anything the mind could conceive.

It is not [she declared] a dazzling splendour, but a soft whiteness and infused radiance which brings great delight to the eyes and never tires them with the sight, nor does its brightness prevent us from gazing upon this divine beauty. It is a light so different from what we know here below that the sun's brightness seems dim by comparison with that brightness and light which is revealed to our gaze and makes us quite loath ever to open our eyes again. It is like looking upon very clear water running over a bed of crystal and reflecting the sun, compared with a very muddy stream running over the earth beneath a cloudy sky. It seems rather to be natural light, whereas the other is artificial.

Try as she might – for the sceptics kept urging her to resist – Teresa found no way of preventing the onset of her visions. She sought to still her mind in prayer, but this only increased the overwhelming sense of Christ's presence. The longing to see him, to be with him, swept over her in mighty gusts which left her incapable of action and as if beside herself. She seemed to be dying of love – an irresistible, supernaturally infused love in which pain was mysteriously conjoined with delight. It was in one of these transports that Teresa was granted the vision known as the Transverberation of the Heart. By her side she saw an angel. He was small, very beautiful, his face radiant. In his hand he held a long golden spear tipped with flame. This he seemed to plunge several times into her heart, and when he drew it out, it left her all aflame with a great love of God. So sharp was the pain that she groaned aloud, yet so sweet that she wished it could last for ever, for she knew that now her soul would never rest content with anything but God. The effects of this vision lasted several days and left her in a sort of stupor. 'I had no wish to look or to speak,' she tells us, 'but only to hug my pain, which was a greater bliss than all created things could give me.' Though she has left us only the one celebrated description, it seems that the vision was granted to her more than once – during mass, in her convent cell, in Doña Guiomar's house, and perhaps on other occasions. It was, as it were, the orgasm of the mystic nuptials.

6

The Experience of Ecstasy

Teresa's visions and locutions were secrets between her soul and God – intimacies only divulged, obediently but reluctantly, to those who claimed to be her spiritual guides. Others knew of them merely through hearsay and convent gossip. But what many could vouch for, and had seen with their own eyes and commented upon as they chose, were the ecstatic seizures which left the nun seemingly dead to the world, her spirit transported to realms celestial or diabolical. Such ecstasies were by no means unknown in the convents and monasteries of those times, but they could nevertheless take remarkable and sometimes startling forms. They imparted an agreeable frisson of the supernatural to the uneventful tenor of religious life.

There was sound biblical and ecclesiastical authority for such experiences. St Paul recalls the moment when he was 'caught up into paradise and heard unspeakable words, which it is not lawful for a man to utter'; he is careful to add, 'whether in the body, or out of the body, I know not – God knoweth'. Since his time, innumerable saints of the Church and men and women of holy life had been granted similar favours. But it was also true that in the case of witches, diabolists and dubious mediums, ecstasies and raptures could be induced by the Devil. Trancelike states resembling religious ecstasy could also arise from purely pathological causes, obsessive mental concentration, or from the emotional and aesthetic impact of music, poetry, art or communing with nature. So ecstasy itself, as Teresa well knew, was no sure indication of sanctity. She had first experienced the phenomenon at the age of forty-one when, as we have noted, she was made aware that henceforth God wished her 'to converse with angels, not men'. Her ecstasies soon occurred more frequently and often in public, arousing a curiosity which caused her acute misery. People flocked to the convent parlour, the sisters waited around the chapel and her cell, hoping for a peep-show. 'Matters reached such a pitch', Teresa recalls, 'that I decided I would rather be buried alive than have these things known.' She thought of transferring to a more remote and strictly enclosed convent, perhaps to a Carmelite house in Valencia, or even in France or Flanders. Her confessor would not hear of it; she must bear her cross where God had called her, here in Avila.

Teresa experienced ecstasy as a form of prayer in which she herself played almost no part, but everything stemmed from the mighty power of God. She describes it as more sublime even than mystical union, and leaving deeper and more lasting spiritual effects. In union, the soul communes with God in a purely interior way; in ecstasy, the body is caught up too as the soul is rapt away to God.

In these raptures [she writes] it seems that the soul no longer animates the body, which thus loses its natural heat and gradually grows cold, though with a feeling of very great sweetness and delight. Here there is no way of resisting, as there is in union, where we are on our own ground and can almost always resist, though it costs pain and effort. But rapture is generally irresistible. Before you can be warned by a thought or do anything to help yourself, it sweeps upon you so swift and strong that you see and feel yourself being caught up in this cloud and borne aloft as on the wings of a mighty eagle. You see and know, I say, that you are being borne aloft, yet you know not whither. For though this brings delight, the weakness of our nature makes us afraid at first and we need courage and strength of mind, more so than in the earlier stages of prayer, to risk everything, come what may, and leave ourselves in God's hands to be borne away despite ourselves wherever he will. In such extremity I have very often wanted to resist and have striven against it with all my might, specially when this happens in public, and very often when I am by myself too, for fear of being deluded. At times, by dint of great effort, I have had some success; but it has been like struggling against a great giant and has left me utterly exhausted. At others, it was quite impossible, and my soul has been carried away, and my head after it too most often, without my being able to hold them back. Even at times my whole body has been lifted from the ground.

Here Teresa is alluding to the phenomenon of levitation. This she experienced only rarely, but she singles out one or two occasions:

Once, when we were together in the choir and I had knelt down to communicate, and this greatly distressed me as it seemed a most extraordinary thing which was bound to attract much public attention, so I ordered the nuns (for it occurred after I had been elected Prioress) to say nothing about it. At other times, when I began to see that the Lord was going to do the same with me (once when some ladies and persons of quality were there and we were listening to a sermon on our patronal feast) I lay down on the ground and they came round to hold me down, but it was noticed all the same.

Years later, when evidence was being taken for Teresa's beatification, a nun recalled seeing her enter the chapel, kneel down, and some time later rise bodily into the air and remain suspended there about a foot and a half above the ground. Terrified, the nun came over and placed her hands under the saint's feet until the ecstasy ended and Teresa sank to the ground. A friend and biographer describes Teresa once clutching desperately at the bars of the grille to resist levitation after receiving communion, and on another occasion grasping the reed mats on the chapel floor, only to rise up into the air still tightly clasping them. She herself refers to the extraordinary sensation of weightlessness which often accompanied her raptures; 'Sometimes I felt so light that I did not know whether my feet were touching the ground or not.'

Whether or not the ecstasy was accompanied by the actual levitation of the body, Teresa was conscious of 'mighty forces, for which I can find no comparison, lifting me up from under my feet'. Her pulse would almost stop beating, her eyes remain closed or open yet unseeing.

> The body seems quite lifeless and unable to do anything of itself, and stays in the attitude it was in when seized by transport – seated, standing, with hands clasped or open. Consciousness is seldom lost, though on occasion, and for a short while, I have lost it entirely. The senses are generally disturbed and, though powerless to perform any outward act, one can still see and hear things, but as though from afar off. I do not say that one can see and hear when the rapture is at its height – by 'height' I mean when the use of the faculties is lost, being so closely united with God – then I believe it neither sees, hears nor feels.

The climax – the 'transformation of the soul into God' – would last no more than the twinkling of an eye. Of short duration at first, her ecstasies grew longer but discontinuous, the senses flitting uncontrollably to and fro, whilst the inmost core of her being remained locked in the divine embrace.

The experience, specially when accompanied by levitation, filled Teresa with terror and humility:

> To feel one's body being lifted from the ground in this way, although the spirit draws it gently in its train with no resistance on our part and without loss of consciousness – at least I was still conscious enough to be aware that I was being lifted up – shows

the majesty of one who is able to do such a thing which makes one's hair quite stand on end, and inspires a mighty dread of offending such a great God. It also kindles afresh a burning love for him whose love for this vile worm is so great that it seems he is not content with bearing away to himself the soul, but would have the body too, mortal though it be and befouled by all the sins we have committed.

Whilst the body remains in this trancelike state, the limbs rigid and impervious to sensation and the pulse scarcely perceptible, the soul seems 'raised above itself and all earthly things'. It detaches itself from a world of which it has become utterly weary and is seized with an overwhelming longing for its God. But God remains infinitely far off. So the soul is 'as if crucified between heaven and earth, receiving no help from either'. It is altogether alone in its solitude, yet 'this abandonment and loneliness seem better than all the company in the world'. God then sometimes reveals to it his grandeur in the strangest of ways: by bringing it not comfort, but an understanding of why it is so weary – 'because it is absent from that good which contains within itself all good things'. The bliss of this awareness of God's being is blended with the agony of finding it so unattainable, so that the soul suffers 'a martyrdom harsh yet sweet', rejecting any consolations that may be offered by the world to which it knows it must soon return:

> Oh what torment it is for the soul in this state [Teresa exclaims] to have to return to the company of men, to see and watch the sorry farce of this life of ours and to waste time in satisfying such bodily needs as eating and sleeping! Everything wearies it; it knows not how to escape, but sees itself caught and tied down. Then it tastes to the full the wretchedness of this life and what it means to be the body's prisoner. It understands why St Paul implored God to deliver him from this state and cries out to God with him for deliverance so vehemently that the soul itself often seems about to burst from the body since it can find no escape. It

goes about like this as one who has been sold into slavery in a strange land.

The soul feels strangely detached from everything around it. The full return to normal consciousness may be slow, the body sometimes being unable to move for some hours and the mental faculties as if dazed by the experience and the attempt to fathom it. But if the body had been ill or in pain before, it would feel marvellously relieved and strengthened, as if the Lord wished it to share in the blessings conferred on the soul.

Teresa was granted her first rapture on reaching the point along the way of perfection described as the Spiritual Betrothal. She continued to experience similar ecstasies for nearly twenty years, culminating in the supreme grace of the Mystical Marriage, symbolized by a vision in which Christ placed a wedding-ring on her finger. From then until her death seven years later – except for a short period when she had some recurrence of raptures, mainly during divine service – Teresa remained almost free from such outward manifestations of the mystical life. Their onset and sudden cessation remain as mysterious as the phenomena themselves. In the *Interior Castle* she writes that when the soul reaches the seventh and ultimate 'mansion', where its journey terminates in the Mystical Marriage, raptures cease or occur but rarely, perhaps because the strength which God imparts to the soul is so dominant over the body, or because he no longer wills that what is wrought in secret should be revealed in public. Other mystics are known to have found similarly sudden release from their proneness to ecstasy. Teresa's Italian contemporary St Catherine de' Ricci was famous for her long raptures in which she relived Christ's passion. They recurred regularly, on the same day of every week over a period of twelve years, and then abruptly ceased.

Spiritual blessings, Teresa believed, were the touchstone by which ecstatic experience should be tested. Where these were lacking the 'ecstasy' was sure to be no more than a delusion, the product of weak health or a disordered imagination. Teresa constantly impressed on her nuns that they must never regard raptures, or any physical phenomena, as in themselves evidence of sanctity. Such things indicated at best that the soul had made a certain amount of progress; but it was because the flesh remained weak and the senses insufficiently subdued that the body was liable to be as it were thrown out of joint at the touch of divine grace. She advised her nuns to pay little attention to such things, but to cultivate humility and the other virtues. They must not seek these experiences, or value them for their own sake, or they would fall victims to 'spiritual gluttony'. Nor must they talk about them except to their confessors.

Women were naturally prone to such frailties. Some nuns, she writes, with an ironic play on words impossible to translate, get it into their heads that they are being carried away by ecstasy (*arrobamiento*) when in fact it is only a silly stupor (*abobamiento*), for they are doing nothing but wasting their time and ruining their health. They should be kept from remaining too long in prayer and given a good diet and occupations which would take their minds off themselves. Teresa and the nuns she trained had constantly to be on their guard against exhibitionism and imposture. 'Sister, we don't need you here for your raptures, but for washing the dishes', one of her prioresses tartly observed to a lay sister whose claims to be always experiencing ecstasies and seeing visions ended by getting her into trouble with the Inquisition.

In true rapture, the body might be inert and useless and the mental powers as if atrophied, but the will remained absorbed in God, and through it, as along a wire recharging a battery, flowed supernatural energy. The sense of detachment from worldly concerns, far from inducing passivity, would tend rather to release this energy and galvanize the ecstatic into intense activity. Teresa writes of her overwhelming desire to suffer great penances, to do great things for God, to proclaim his truths from the house-tops.

She describes Pedro de Alcántara, a Franciscan friar famous for his ecstasies, going through the fields singing aloud, so that many accounted him mad, and she adds approvingly: 'What blessed madness, my sisters! – God grant it likewise to all of us!' The legend later grew up that her own books had been composed, by a sort of automatic writing, whilst she was in a state of trance. It seems rather that much of them was written, with a speed which to her contemporaries might well appear miraculous, soon after emerging from ecstasy.

'I know from experience', she declares, 'that the soul in rapture is mistress of all things, and gains such freedom in an hour or even less that it cannot recognize itself.' The discovery was awesome and humbling, for Teresa saw it was God's handiwork alone; her own defects were shown up with painful clarity, like specks of dust caught in a brilliant sunbeam. 'There have been women who have done heroic deeds for love of you, Oh Lord!' she lamented. 'I am myself fit only for talk, and so you have not been willing to put me to the test by deeds.' But the call to deeds was soon to come, and the two paths of contemplation and action to merge into one.

7

The Battle for St Joseph's:
the Opening Round

Life in the Convent of the Incarnation pursued its customary calm course, despite the strange things that seemed to be happening to Teresa de Ahumada. The circle of her friends and devotees, despite the malicious gossip aroused by her case, continued to grow. They would meet together in the evenings in the spacious cell which Teresa shared with two young nieces, Beatriz and María Cepeda y Ocampo, who had taken the place of her sister Juana, now married and the mother of a fine son. There was laughter and youthful spirits as well as a fervent but relaxed piety in these gatherings. The women, bending over their embroidery and seated on cushions and mats of cork, esparto or reeds after the fashion which the Spaniards had adopted from the Moors, would chat quietly amongst themselves or listen, fascinated, whilst Teresa talked. She passed from the sublimest subjects to familiar, everyday topics with such graceful vivacity, such warmth and wit, such an overflowing love for God and all his creation that she seemed to illumine and dominate the conversation, even when she said but few words, by sheer greatness of soul.

One evening in September 1560 the talk turned on the nuns' venerable spiritual forebears, the hermits of Mt Carmel. How splendid to return to their simple and austere way of life, now in our own age, and here in Avila! exclaimed María, a high-spirited and elegant girl in her teens, and seemingly a most unlikely person to wish to emulate the harsh lot of the desert fathers. Others took up the idea enthusiastically.

A return to the primitive simplicities and virtues was no new aspiration in Spain. Various efforts had indeed been made in that direction for more than half a century, and most of the Orders now possessed, or would come to have, their reformed – Barefoot or 'Discalced' – brethren, who sought to practise their Rule in all its ancient rigour, zeal and poverty. But the reform movement had hitherto been restricted almost entirely to the friars. If nuns needed reform, the men whom the Church placed in authority over them would see to it. Devout women, such as that eccentric visionary the Beata de Piedrahita, who believed they had a reforming mission, might gain a small following of fanatics, but were generally regarded askance. After all, any nun who wished to practise exceptional devotions and austerities was free to do so in her own cell. But convents also housed many who felt no such call and saw no need to be reformed, provided they remained respectable in conduct and orthodox in belief.

Back to the primitive austerities of Mt Carmel – or at least to the strict observance of the Carmelite Rule as it existed before the 1432 Bill of Mitigation! Could the niece really be in earnest? She herself later wrote that she had spoken half in jest. Doña Guiomar happened to join the gathering at this point and Teresa explained to her with some amusement that the young enthusiasts were discussing nothing less than a proposal to start a small convent like the simple monasteries of Discalced Franciscans which Fray Pedro de Alcántara had been busy founding. Doña Guiomar was at once won over and impulsively offered to help endow it. María, now quite carried away, volunteered to contribute 1,000 ducats out of her dowry, the share which she expected to receive of the family fortune. Teresa smiled and listened to the others' eager talk. The idea of starting a convent for Discalced Carmelites where she and other like-minded nuns could live quietly according to the primitive Rule had been at the back of her mind for some time. But she had not given the matter much serious thought. For one thing, she disarmingly admits, 'I was very happy in the house where I was. The place was much to my taste, and so was my cell, which suited me excellently.' The discussion ended with general agreement that they would commend the matter fervently to God in their prayers.

Here the matter might have ended. But one day soon afterwards, when Teresa had received Communion, there came to her an unmistakable command. The Lord ordered her to take up the project with all her might. He made her great promises; the convent would assuredly be founded, and he would be greatly served in it. It should be called St Joseph's. That saint would stand guard over them at one of its doors, Our Lady at the other. Christ would be with them, and their new house would shine with all the radiance of a star. Teresa was to tell her confessor what the Lord wanted of her, and that he was not to oppose or hinder it.

It is not clear from her account whether Teresa received her commission as foundress by means of a locution or a vision. At all events, she was made aware of the divine will with such certainty that it was impossible to doubt it. Nevertheless she hesitated, turning over in her mind all the arguments against it which human prudence could raise. The Lord had to repeat his instructions, adding so many divine counter-arguments that it at length became impossible for her to find excuses. Her mind now made up, Teresa took her pen and composed an account of the whole matter for her confessor.

The reaction of the timid but conscientious Father Alvarez was what might be expected. He was already spending much time poring over treatises on Mystical Theology in the hope that they would help him to understand his perplexing penitent. Now he was faced with the intractable practical problems arising from her determination to become a foundress. Father Alvarez foresaw the opposition which would inevitably be aroused. His immediate superior, the Rector of the Jesuit College, was already prejudiced against Teresa. There was bound to be an outcry in the city against the proposed innovation, and the Jesuits would be blamed. Father Alvarez temporized. He replied to Teresa that he would speak to the Father Provincial of the Carmelites about the proposal, and she should do as her Superior saw fit. Teresa was dissatisfied with this answer. She had not divulged the intimacies of her spiritual life to the Provincial, and whether she should go ahead with her practical reforms depended on the priest who had the guidance of her soul and could confirm the authenticity of the commands she believed she was receiving through her visions and locutions. That was why she had laid the matter before Father Alvarez; he should not try to evade his responsibilities and so hold up the plans she believed God wished her to carry into effect. She had already passed on to him what she had been given to understand was the message intended for her confessor.

If Teresa's confessor had declared that her voices and visions were an illusion and had categorically forbidden her to proceed with the St Joseph's project, Teresa would have obeyed. But he would take no stand in the matter and declined to pronounce her revelations either true or false. Teresa determined to consult others reputed to be even more learned and holy and to abide by their counsel. We know that they included three men later canonized by the Church: St Francis Borja, with whom she had spoken when the renowned Jesuit visited Avila, St Luis Beltrán, famed for his missionary labours amongst the Indians of South America and for the penitential life he was then leading in Valencia, and St Pedro de Alcántara. St Luis Beltrán's reply has been preserved. After apologizing for his delay in answering Teresa's inquiry, which was due to his wishing to give her case much thought and prayer, he roundly assures her: 'Now I tell you in the Lord's name to set about your great design with courage, for he will assist and favour you. And I assure you on his behalf that fifty years will not pass before your Order will be one of the most illustrious in God's Church.' It was to prove an astonishingly accurate prophecy.

Teresa has left us an unforgettable pen-portrait of Fray Pedro de Alcántara, founder of the Reformed or Discalced Franciscans. She tells us that he always went barefoot, clad only in a hoodless habit of sackcloth, and ate no more than once in every three days. His cell was so small that he had to take his scanty sleep in a sitting position, his head propped against a piece of wood fixed to the wall. He had lived for three years in a priory without knowing any of his brother friars except from their voices, for he never raised his eyes from the ground. For many years he had not looked upon a woman; but now, he declared, it was all one to him whether he looked or not. Fray Pedro seemed very old when Teresa first met him (though in fact he was little more than sixty) and so emaciated that his body looked as if it had been twisted together out of the roots of trees. He was apt to be swept off into tremendous raptures, as Teresa once witnessed herself. He was also popularly credited with spectacular feats of levitation, though she makes no mention of these. But for all his holiness and fearsome asceticism, Teresa found this latter-day St Francis very courteous and affable and a delight to talk to, for he possessed a quick intelligence and subtle powers of discernment. He recognized her at once as a kindred spirit and assured her that the strange experiences she related to him were undoubtedly inspired by God. He also confided to her many of his own, and encouraged her in her vocation as a foundress. Before they parted, the nun and the old friar agreed to remain in close touch by letter and through their prayers.

Fray Pedro offered not only spiritual encouragement but invaluable practical advice. His work had familiarized him with the formalities needed for obtaining official authorization for new religious foundations, and had given him exceptional psychological insight into the best means of gaining friends and supporters and of disarming opponents. The tactics followed in the campaign for St Joseph's were largely the fruit of the friar's sagacity. Teresa, he urged, should keep as far as possible in the background and leave the initiative to Doña Guiomar, whose rank would ensure her at least a respectful hearing. A request for papal sanction was sent off to Rome in that lady's name. It seems that Fray Pedro also endorsed, and may possibly have himself devised, the piece of holy duplicity by which the house selected for the new convent was to be bought by Teresa's sister Juana and her husband Juan de Ovalle, ostensibly for their own use. If St Joseph's was to be a dovecot for the Lord, its occupants might be as innocent as doves, but their sponsors had to be as guileful as serpents.

The conspirators next moved cautiously to secure two important positions: the acquiescence of Teresa's own superiors and backing from the influential Dominican Order. Following the advice of Father Alvarez, Doña Guiomar approached the Carmelite Provincial, Angel de Salazar, and obtained his consent in principle for her proposed foundation. With Teresa, as companion to one of her own daughters who had taken the veil at the Incarnation and was given permission to visit her mother, Doña Guiomar then approached that bulwark of Catholic orthodoxy, the monastery of St Thomas. Father Pedro Ibáñez, to whom they went for confession and advice, already knew of the project through hearsay. He listened attentively to what the two women had to say and declared that he would let them know his opinion after he had turned it over in his mind for a week. The scheme struck him at first as ill-advised. There was already strong local feeling against it, as he knew from a letter which a gentleman of his acquaintance sent him warning the Dominican not to give it any encouragement. Teresa had not yet confided to him the secrets of her spiritual life nor her real reason for acting in the matter – the divine command which she believed she had been given. 'I merely set out the natural reasons that prompted me,' she tells us, 'for I did not want him to base his opinion on any ground but these.' This approach was soon justified:

When he began to consider what reply he should give us, and to think about the matter and about our aims and how we wished to carry them out, and our concern for our Order, he came to the conclusion that it would be very much in God's service and that the scheme should not be abandoned. So he replied that we should make haste to carry it into effect, and he suggested ways and means of doing so.

Father Ibáñez not only approved but offered his active support, and he undertook to speak personally to anyone who had doubts about it. Thanks to his stout advocacy, and to that of Fray Pedro, important allies were won over to the cause of St Joseph. They included the *Caballero santo* and the stern Gaspar Daza, who had both so long insisted that Teresa's revelations were the work of the Devil.

But in the convent of the Incarnation feeling amongst the nuns ran high against the would-be foundress and her plans for a more strictly enclosed community.

> They said that it was an insult to themselves; that I could serve God just as well where I was, for there were others there better than myself; and that I had no love for my own house and that I should do better to raise funds for it rather than for another foundation. Some said that I ought to be sent to the prison-cell; others – but only a handful – took my side.

Teresa kept silent, sympathizing with much that they said but loath to disclose the supernatural nature of her authority. What particularly distressed her was the attitude of Father Alvarez, who wrote reproaching her for all the scandal she was causing and urged her to drop the matter once and for all. As she pondered her confessor's harsh letter, Teresa's tormenting doubts returned. Could she be deceiving herself, and were her voices and visions then nothing but dangerous illusions? But when others came to her in great alarm and tried to frighten her by warning that 'these were difficult times, and that charges might be laid against me and I might be denounced to the Inquisitors', all her marvellous courage and confidence returned.

This merely struck me as funny and made me laugh [she comments]. On that score I never had any fear. In matters of faith I was quite sure I would rather die a thousand deaths than fail to observe the smallest ceremony of the Church, or in order to defend the Church or any truth in Holy Scripture. So I told them not to be afraid on that account, for my soul would be in a sorry state if there were any reason to fear the Inquisition. I said that if they thought there was, I would go to report to it myself, and should charges be laid against me, the Lord would deliver me and I should only stand to gain.

Nevertheless, Teresa was still hungry for reassurance at the deepest spiritual level. Since her own confessor could not provide it, she turned once more to Father Ibáñez. She had won that learned and fair-minded man's approval for the St Joseph project by convincing him of her sincerity and practical good sense; now she would lay bare to him those supernatural experiences which were shaping the course of her whole life. She described, as best she could, the phenomenon of rapture: how it would sweep her spirit irresistibly away, leaving her consumed with such an ardent love and craving for God that she could scarcely contain her desires to do great things for him, to suffer, to die, if only she might thereby be the more speedily united with him. She wrote of the sense of detachment from all worldly affairs that it left in its train, of the wish for solitude and the pain of having to consort with others, of the marvellous serenity and peace of mind. She described too the periods of aridity, renewed doubt, and the 'dark night of the soul' which God in his mercy would finally dispel, so that when she could again commune with him in prayer 'not all the learned and saintly men in the world, or any tortures to which I might be put, could convince me that these things were of the Devil – for that I simply cannot believe'. This 'Account of Conscience' or 'Spiritual Relation', one of many similar statements prepared at different times for the information of Teresa's spiritual directors, she sent to Father Ibáñez. In due course it elicited an *Opinion* which that conscientious Dominican prepared for the enlightenment of his fellow theologians – an unqualified and closely argued endorsement of Teresa's conviction that her visions, voices and ecstasies were of divine, not diabolic, origin.

Shortly afterwards, Father Ibáñez was transferred from Avila. He had struck a stout blow for St Joseph and helped Teresa through a difficult crisis. Like many of those privileged with the guidance of a great soul, his own life had also thereby been immeasurably enriched.

> He greatly reassured me, and I think this proved of benefit to him too [Teresa artlessly observes]. For good man though he already was, he devoted himself from that time much more to his prayers, and retired to a monastery of his Order where he could find great solitude and give himself more wholly to them.

She missed him greatly. But her voices consoled her with the assurance that he was in good hands. The Dominican had judged wisely thanks to his great learning; to this God now added the spiritual insight born of personal experience.

But the tide of opposition in Avila had not yet turned. Much of it was directed against Doña Guiomar, to whom her confessor refused absolution unless she abandoned the St Joseph project altogether. The good lady was also heavily in debt and unable to raise the money she had promised for the foundation. The Carmelite Provincial, mindful of these things, began to have second thoughts, and he withdrew his authorization when the contract for the purchase of a small but suitable house was on the point of being signed. Juana lost heart and tried to persuade her sister to give up her plans. She and Teresa had been in church when a friar preached a pointed sermon against meddlesome nuns who left their convent on the pretext of wanting to found one of their own. Teresa listened unmoved, smiling serenely to herself. Her voices told her to have faith and to wait. For the time being she was to do just as her confessor said and take no further action.

Why all this uproar in the martial City of Knights and Liegemen over a handful of women who wanted nothing more than to live in peace in their own house? This was no mere squabble amongst priests and nuns; the citizenry, and especially the grave city fathers, were also deeply involved. In many parts of Spain there was a proliferation of religious houses and growing concern at the economic consequences for the municipalities which often had to support them. By the end of the sixteenth century the number of monks alone was estimated at 400,000 out of a population of less than eight millions. Nuns were less numerous, but in those days their role – now so prominent – as teachers, nurses, and in other forms of social work was almost nonexistent, whilst the falling value of money resulting from the influx of American gold meant that their endowments rapidly became insufficient and needed to be supplemented by alms or subsidies. Yet the number of convents continued to grow. The Carmelites of the Incarnation had moved into their large new home the year Teresa was born. When her father had settled in Avila a few years before, the city had had only four convents: the aristocratic Benedictine foundation of Santa Ana, the Dominicans of Santa Catalina, and the miserably poor houses of Santa Escolástica and San Millán. The two latter had then been absorbed, much against their will and despite protracted law suits and scandalous acts of defiance, into Santa Ana. But new foundations quickly took their place; the Poor Clares in 1502, Our Lady of Grace in 1509, the Conceptionists in 1539. Now there was talk of yet another Carmelite house, which would mean fresh demands on local charity. But despite local civic opposition and royal prohibitions, the proliferation continued, religious fervour often prevailing over economic sense as Spain sank into decline. Some years after Teresa's death Madrid was to be agitated over a proposal to establish a convent of Discalced Carmelites. The scheme was vetoed by the Cardinal Archbishop of Toledo, until that dignitary fell mortally ill but recovered thanks to the miraculous effects of a relic – nothing less than a finger of the saintly foundress herself – which at once converted him into an enthusiastic sponsor of the new house. So even from beyond the grave Teresa was able to continue the work to which she felt called. But such triumphs lay in the future. At the time with which we are here concerned the prospects for the first of her foundations were far from bright.

By the end of 1560 it looked as if the battle for St Joseph's had been lost. But Teresa had learned not to fret. The Lord was rewarding her labours with an abundance of mystical graces and a mighty growth of love for him which 'left me so consoled and happy that all the persecution I was suffering seemed nothing at all'. After five or six months, signs appeared that that situation was beginning to change. In April a new Rector was appointed to the Jesuit College of San Gil. With Father Gaspar de Salazar Teresa felt an immediate spiritual affinity. Her confessor, taking his cue from the new superior, started to treat her with less rigour and even exhorted her to resume activity. Encouragement and guidance still came to her through her visions and locutions. St Joseph appeared to her and bade her not worry about money, for that would be provided. The house she had in mind was so small that she was filled with misgivings. 'Move in as best you can', the Lord commanded. 'Oh human greed – to imagine that there will not be room enough for you! How often did I sleep out in the open, having nowhere else to lay my head!'

The Provincial continued to withhold his authorization. Fortunately, he was away from Avila; and what need was there, after all, for him to give approval for a deal between lay folk? Negotiations for the purchase of the house were in the hands of Juan de Ovalle and his wife Juana. It is true that they had no money. Nor could Doña Guiomar provide much beyond the proceeds from pawning one or two of her possessions. Two young nuns, both relatives of Teresa and future inmates of St Joseph's, offered their modest dowries. Alterations were needed to adapt the building to its new purpose, and Teresa was still eighty ducats short of the sum demanded by the masons. They were nevertheless persuaded to put the work in hand, and the following day Teresa received a package from her brother Lorenzo in Quito enclosing more than two hundred ducats. 'I believe it was an inspiration from God that moved you to send me so much', she wrote to him in gratitude; and again, 'I really think that all the trouble you have taken is not just the result of your own goodness – it was put into your heart by God.' As for the little house, which was to accommodate a maximum of fifteen nuns, 'poor and simple though it is, it has lovely views and grounds'. The beauty of nature was for Teresa always a means of nourishing the life of prayer.

On the feast of St Clare, that saint appeared to Teresa in a vision, bidding her take courage and promising help. The convent of Poor Clares was hard by St Joseph's, and far from resenting the competition of a new foundation pledged, like the humble followers of St Francis, to subsist on the alms of the charitable, the nuns were later to assist their Carmelite sisters in times of need. Soon after the vision, during mass in the church of St Dominic, Teresa was favoured with a still more glorious revelation. She saw herself clothed by the Virgin and St Joseph in a robe of translucent whiteness, and was given to understand that she was now fully cleansed of her sins. The Virgin took her by the hand, promising that her plans for the convent would be brought to fruition, and that St Joseph would be greatly served in it. In token of this she placed round Teresa's neck a golden necklace from which hung a jewelled cross of incomparable beauty. Teresa felt herself transported with bliss of such unutterable sweetness that she wished it might last for ever. Even after the celestial visitants had ascended into heaven amidst a great host of angels, she was so rapt in grateful wonder that she remained for a long time unable to speak and consumed with a fervent longing for God.

During this vision something of great practical significance was revealed to Teresa. The application for permission to found a convent originally dispatched to Rome in Doña Guiomar's name had envisaged a house under obedience to the Carmelite Order.

> The Lord told me that this would be unwise [St Teresa writes in a passage of her *Life* which is not altogether clear]. He gave me the reasons why this would not be at all fitting, and he also told me to send to Rome, in a certain way which he also explained, and promised that he would surely arrange matters there. And so it proved to be. We sent to Rome, as the Lord desired me – for the business would otherwise have continued to drag on – and all turned out well.

What appears to have happened is that the papal Brief, which eventually arrived in reply to Doña Guiomar's petition, was found to be unserviceable, as an essential clause had been omitted. So a fresh application was made, this time with the request that the new foundation should be placed under obedience not to the Carmelites, but to the Bishop of Avila. This was to prove no mere formality, but rather – for reasons which we shall see – a matter of the greatest importance and a stroke of remarkable statesmanship.

Family troubles and anxieties threatened to interrupt the pious work. One day in August Juana's small son Gonzalito was found by his father lying senseless on the ground. Some accounts say that he had been injured by the collapse of a wall; others, that he had had a bad fall or a seizure. Teresa hurriedly took charge of the situation to avoid alarming his mother, who was in an advanced stage of pregnancy. Gathering the child up in her arms, she carried him to her room and shut the door. Less than an hour later, they came out together hand in hand. Doña Guiomar's account suggests that Teresa had given her nephew the kiss of life; others frankly proclaimed a miracle. Teresa, when asked, would only smile and change the subject. God had indeed restored the child to life, but it grieved her to think that anyone should take her for a wonder-worker. A few months later something happened which seemed to make it clear enough that she had been endowed with no such powers. The child to whom Juana gave birth lived only a short time. Cradling the ailing infant in her arms, Teresa uttered a strange supplication to her patron, St Joseph: 'God grant the child may either grow up to become a saint, or else be taken, little angel that he now is, straight to heaven!' Juana bore her loss with Christian resignation, consoled by her sister's vision of the celestial hosts bearing away the innocent soul in great glory. 'Doña Juana – God be praised! – has become such an upright and courageous woman!' Teresa wrote to her brother Lorenzo. 'She really has the soul of an angel!'

So the year 1561 drew towards its close. The alterations to the house were now well advanced. Despite all the secrecy, rumours of their real purpose had leaked out and Teresa feared that sooner or later they must come to the ears of the Provincial, who would then command her to desist, 'which would have been the end of everything'. Two days before Christmas she wrote to Lorenzo that she was still Doña Guiomar's guest, which gave her more freedom to expedite the matter she had so much at heart, and would stay with her until ordered elsewhere. She had scarcely sealed the letter when an urgent message was brought her from the Provincial. It left her astonished and at first very perturbed. Father Angel de Salazar said nothing about St Joseph's. Instead, he instructed her to leave with all possible speed for Toledo, where her presence was urgently required.

8

Interlude in Toledo

Doña Luisa de la Cerda was one of the greatest ladies in the land. Scion of the royal houses of Spain and France and daughter of the second Duke of Medinaceli, she had married a nephew of the Cardinal Archbishop, a Toledan nobleman whose death the year before had plunged her into a melancholy from which neither her children, the ladies of her household, nor priests or pious friends could rouse her. So intense and obsessive was the widow's mourning that it was even feared for her reason. Doña Luisa was a devout woman and punctilious in the observance of her religious duties. But she lacked the companionship of one who could treat her with the respect due to her rank whilst offering a woman's understanding and the comfort of a spirit uncrushed by worldly griefs. Such a one, she had been told, was the nun of Avila, a certain Teresa de Ahumada. The Carmelite Provincial, whom Doña Luisa knew well, could scarcely refuse to let the nun stay with her awhile. So Father Salazar was prevailed upon to grant the rich widow's request and orders were sent to Avila.

Teresa received them with surprise and vexation. She feared her absence might endanger the completion of her cherished project. And how could anyone possibly imagine that she, despicable sinner that she was, could presume to be of help to such a great lady, who was no doubt far better than herself? Some of her friends urged her to ask the Provincial to reconsider his instructions. She prayed earnestly for guidance. Whilst attending Matins on Christmas Day she was transported with a profound rapture in which 'the Lord told me that I must assuredly go, and not to heed the opinions of others, for few would give me sound advice, and that although I should have trials, God would be greatly served'. As for the business of the convent, it would be all to the good for her to be away from Avila until the receipt of the papal Brief, since 'the Devil was preparing a great plot' for the moment the Provincial arrived. She was to have no fear, however, for the Lord would help her. Teresa felt comforted and heartened by this revelation. One man who commended her decision to go was the Rector of San Gil, and she was relieved to learn that there was also a Jesuit college in Toledo under whose spiritual direction she could safely place herself. She had already made a resolution which her biographers describe as a 'vow of greater perfection'. In whatever circumstances she might find herself, and whatever decisions she would have to make, whether in matters great or small, she would always – with God's grace – choose that which seemed to answer most closely to Christ's uncompromising call to self-denial, to his command – 'Be ye perfect!'

Despite the decline in prosperity and political importance which followed the failure of the Comuneros rising of forty years before, Toledo still retained its air of imperial grandeur. Though Philip II had just proclaimed the upstart Madrid to be Spain's new capital, many great families preferred to go on living behind the imposing, heavily escutcheoned façades of their mansions in the city on the Tagus. There, like the widowed Doña Luisa, each held court at the head of the hierarchy of relatives, dependants, duennas, major-domos and servants which made up their huge households. It was a world of stiff Castilian protocol where all competed for the favour of master or mistress, vigilantly guarding their place in the order of precedence and quick to resent the instrusion of any new favourite. Even Teresa, for all her affability and tact, her threadbare habit and her distaste for the distinctions shown her, could not altogether escape the shafts of envy. For Doña Luisa at once fell beneath her spell.

It pleased the Lord that this lady should be so greatly comforted that she at once began to show a marked improvement [Teresa writes]. She was a very God-fearing woman and so good that her many Christian virtues made up for the lack of them in myself. She took a great liking to me, as I did to her, when I saw how good she was.

Teresa nevertheless found life in the grand lady's entourage a heavy cross. 'The luxury of the place was a great torment to me,' she wrote, 'and the fuss they made over me filled me with fear.' Pitfalls and temptations surrounded her, so that she dared not relax her guard for a moment. Whenever she could, Teresa escaped to the solace of the discipline and her prayers, oblivious of the inquisitive eyes peeping through the keyhole of her chamber door to spy whether the nun would be carried off into one of her ecstasies, for God continued to shower his graces upon her. How different this artificial and worldly existence from the austerity of convent life which was all she desired! Yet she found she could move through it with surprising ease, 'for I treated those grand ladies, whom it would have been a great honour to serve, with all the freedom of an equal'. She learned, from living at Doña Luisa's side, that 'she was a woman, subject to like passions and weakness as myself', and was filled with compassion at her lot. How terrible to have to live in such state, surrounded by touchy attendants and untrustworthy servants, her whole life governed by protocol, down to the sort of food served and when she should eat it! Great folk like Doña Luisa were not really masters but slaves to their rank and social obligations, yet 'I do not think there are many women humbler and simpler than she is'.

There were other grand ladies whom she met too under Doña Luisa's roof: the Duchess of Medinaceli, the great Duke of Alba's consort who was to become a close friend, and Doña Luisa's wayward niece Ana, the Princess of Eboli, from whose whims and malice Teresa was later to suffer greatly. The nun's fame spread through Toledo, attracting some by the grace and charm of her conversation and others by the example of her holiness. The servants, with whom Teresa liked to chat with the same unaffected warmth as with their mistresses, adored her. One of Doña Luisa's attendants, María de Salazar, then a fourteen-year girl a trifle too aware of her good looks and quick wit, was fascinated by the unusual guest, to whom she slipped cleverly turned verses and confided her desire to take the veil. She was to become one of Teresa's most remarkable prioresses.

Sometimes Teresa would attend Mass in the Dominicans' church of St Peter the Martyr. Did she ever call to mind their predecessors who, seventy-seven years before, had brought the Inquisition to Toledo and thereby the good name and prosperity of Juan Sánchez to a dramatic end? And was the *sambenito* recording his shame still hanging on the walls of some Toledan church? When Teresa was twenty-three years old, commissioners had been sent to Toledo to inspect the *sambenitos* displayed in the Cathedral cloisters and to see that those which were torn and faded were replaced and transferred to their owners' parish church and thus would keep the memory of their infamy green. Was her grandfather's amongst them, or had his money and influence wiped the slate clean for his descendants?

Providence now seemed to have brought the *reconciliado*'s granddaughter back to Toledo almost as mentor to the Dominicans. One morning at Mass Teresa recognized an old acquaintance from Avila – Father García de Toledo, whom she had known whilst he was Vice-Rector at Santo Tomás. Seized by a sudden desire 'to know the state of his soul, since I wished him to be a great servant of God', she rose to speak to him. She checked herself immediately, and sat down again; what business had she to set herself up as some sort of spiritual guide? Three times she felt the same strong impulse, and in the end, she relates, 'my good angel prevailed over my bad', and she went to talk with him in a confessional. 'I began to question him about his life,' she continues, 'and he also questioned me about mine, for we had not seen each other for many years.' The upshot of this strange interchange, in which the nun clearly took the initiative, was twofold. For Father García de Toledo it led, as Teresa fervently prayed it might, to a radical change of heart: 'The Lord transformed him virtually to such an extent that he scarcely recognized himself.' For Teresa it resulted in the obligation to record the odyssey of her inner life. She had already, as we have noted, composed a number of 'Spiritual Relations' for the information of her confessors. Now, at Father García's behest, she was to embark on a full-length account. She set about it at once. Before she left Doña Luisa's house in June 1562, Teresa had completed the first draft of what was to become a classic of spiritual autobiography.

Toledo, as the nodal point of many roads, brought other visitors. Fray Pedro de Alcántara stopped briefly in the great mansion, his coarse sackcloth contrasting still more strangely than Teresa's patched habit with the silks and velvets of Doña Luisa's entourage. Juan de Ovalle, who had escorted Teresa from Avila, returned with the distressing news of her half-sister María's death. She had died suddenly and alone, as had her husband some time previously. Teresa, granted foreknowledge of her approaching end, had previously visited her and earnestly inquired into her spiritual state. Less than a week after María's death, Teresa was assured in a vision that her soul had passed through purgatory and was now at rest.

The visit which left the deepest impression was one from a stranger, whom the Provincial had sent expressly to see Teresa. María Yepes was a widow from Granada, then about forty years of age. After the death of her husband she had entered a Carmelite convent, but instead of taking the veil she had exchanged her status of novice for that of *beata*, which left her with greater freedom to pursue the vocation to which she felt called. Some two years previously, at about the same time as Teresa was made aware of her own mission, Our Lady had appeared to her in a vision with the command to found a reformed Carmelite community. After selling her possessions and sewing the money needed for her journey into her quilted bodice, María de Jesús – as she now called herself – set off, with some Franciscan *beatas* as companions, for Rome. She went barefoot, fell ill on the way, but finally secured an audience with the Pope, who was impressed by her courage and fervour. When she had spent some time with the Carmelite sisters in Mantua, where the Rule was still observed with much of its original strictness, she obtained papal authority to found a reformed community of her own. But back in Spain neither the nuns nor the citizens of Granada would so much as hear of any Reform, and the pilgrim was threatened with a public whipping. Undismayed, she presented herself at Court and secured the support of the pious infanta Juana and the promise of a house in Alcalá de Henares for her projected convent.

Teresa was amazed and moved by the Carmelite *beata*'s courage and by her dedication to an ideal which seemed so providentially akin to her own. 'She had done so much more than myself in the Lord's service that I felt ashamed to come into her presence', was Teresa's typically generous comment. María de Jesús could neither read nor write, but she knew the ancient Carmelite Rule by heart. From her Teresa learned for the first time that it enjoined a poverty so absolute that not even communal possessions or endowments were permitted. 'Until then,' she writes, 'it had never occurred to me to found a convent without any revenue, since I thought we ought not to worry about bare necessities.' But she at once recognized that the *beata* was right. They should live in utter poverty, without financial security of any kind, looking only to the Lord to support them through their own labour and the charity of the faithful. Only thus could they learn true detachment from earthly things and full dependence upon God. For herself, she had no doubts on this score, for it seemed the only life consonant with true discipleship and her vow of greater perfection. But she still hesitated to commit others to such an uncompromising course; not knowing where their next meal was coming from, would not her nuns grow anxious and restless, and their extreme poverty lead not to detachment but to distraction from spiritual things? As always when she was in doubt, Teresa resolved to consult learned and saintly men – Fray Pedro de Alcántara, Father Pedro Ibáñez and others whom she does not name.

Fray Pedro replied with a masterly blend of courteous irony, moral fervour and uncompromising rigour. He addresses his letter, with stately Castilian formality, to 'the most magnificent and reverend lady, Doña Teresa de Ahumada, whom Our Lord make holy', and signs himself 'your worship's humble chaplain, Fray Pedro de Alcántara'. He begins by expressing surprise that she should seek advice from *letrados* on something clearly outside the province of the merely learned. Spiritual guidance should be sought only from those striving to lead a truly spiritual life, in accordance with Christ's precepts. It is not for us to examine whether it is prudent or not to follow them. If Teresa seeks the way of greater perfection, which is open to women no less than to men, then let her obey the call to poverty and all will be well. But if she wishes to be ruled by men of much learning but little spirituality, then let her seek rich endowments for her convents. The counsel given by such persons may be good; but Christ's is better. If there are some houses where the nuns suffer real want, that is because they are poor against their will and cannot help themselves, and not because they are following Christ's precepts. 'It is not poverty itself that I am praising,' the old friar declared, 'but poverty suffered patiently for love of Christ Our Lord, and still more, poverty desired, sought and embraced for his love.'

Teresa needed no further persuasion. Others whom she consulted

> answered me with so many arguments that I did not know what to do. Now that I knew the Rule prescribed poverty, and that this was the more perfect way, I could not bring myself to accept

endowments. They might convince me for the moment, but when I betook myself again to prayer and saw Christ so poor and naked on the Cross, I could not bear to be rich, and I implored him with tears to dispose matters so that I should find myself as poor as he.

Even Father Ibáñez answered her with 'two pages of refutation and theology' in an attempt to dissuade her. She replied tartly that she saw no cause to thank him for all his learning and theology if they would have her abandon her vocation and break her vow of poverty and the precept given her by Christ. Fray Pedro himself could not have put things more bluntly; her reward was to learn that the Lord had enlightened the Dominican's mind and that he now fully supported her stand. Further revelations of divine approval confirmed her in the resolve to found her convent *sin renta* (without revenue).

At about the same time Teresa heard from the Provincial that he had revoked his order to her to be with Doña Luisa and that she was now free to choose for herself whether to stay on or return to Avila. She also received a message from Father García de Toledo urging her to send him as soon as possible the account of her life which she had been writing on his instructions. Teresa did so, with a covering letter apologizing for not having had time to revise the draft and begging him to amend or delete anything in it as he saw fit. The weather had turned very hot, and her confessor advised her to wait some days before returning to Avila. The climate of Toledo was milder than that of her birthplace; her health had been better there and she had been less plagued by the nausea and other ailments from which she constantly suffered. The *mal de corazón* still however sometimes troubled her, and then Doña Luisa would anxiously tend the guest to whom she had become deeply attached. On one occasion the great lady sought to distract her by displaying the contents of her jewel box. Teresa fingered the glittering diamonds and emeralds with polite indifference. Had she not only to glance at her rosary to see with the eyes of the spirit the gems of incomparable splendour which Christ himself had placed there?

Teresa had another reason too for staying on awhile in Toledo. The nuns of the Incarnation would shortly be choosing their new Prioress, and her partisans were confident of securing her election. The news vexed her. Teresa had never had any wish to hold office, and she quailed at the prospect of administrative responsibilities which would dash her hopes of leading a more secluded life at St Joseph's. She wrote to her friends in Avila begging them not to vote for her, and she decided that her election would be less likely if she were to stay away. But just as she was congratulating herself on escaping this tiresome involvement, Teresa was called to face a new challenge. The Lord clearly gave her to understand that she must go to Avila at once. She had asked for a cross, he reminded her, and he had a fine one waiting for her there.

Teresa could not hold back her tears, although she received too the assurance that he would help her to bear it. She took the cross to mean her election as prioress. She was seized with a sudden restlessness which robbed her of all solace in prayer and left her only after she had obtained Doña Luisa's reluctant consent to her departure. Then Teresa's agitation at once gave place to serenity and to a joy which she found hard to explain, for at the same time she grieved to be leaving so many friends. In face of the approaching ordeal Teresa felt weak and defenceless; yet, like St Paul, utterly confident that God's grace would suffice and her strength be made perfect in weakness. She was happy in the knowledge that she was going to suffer for her Lord. He had told her himself that the cross awaiting her would be heavy. 'But I never thought', she admitted, looking back on that hurried return to Avila, 'that it would be quite so heavy as it proved to be!'

9

Victory for St Joseph

The journey to Avila was nevertheless good, and the news which greeted Teresa excellent. The very evening of her arrival, the papers from Rome authorizing the foundation of her cherished convent were received. They took the form of a Rescript dated 7 February 1562, signed by Cardinal Rainucio on behalf of Pope Paul IV and addressed to 'the illustrious widows resident in Avila', Doña Guiomar and her mother Doña Aldonza de Ulloa, granting them leave to make suitable endowment for a Carmelite convent under obedience to the Bishop of Avila, and nominating trustworthy persons charged with seeing the papal wishes carried into effect. The Rescript furthermore sternly commanded that no authorities, either ecclesiastical or lay, should attempt to hinder the foundation, or even to lodge an appeal against it. Rome could not have spoken in clearer or more favourable terms.

Teresa's delight was increased by the discovery that all the key figures necessary for the foundation had providentially been brought together in Avila. Fray Pedro de Alcántara was there, unwavering in his support albeit stricken with a grave illness. Juan de Ovalle, in whose name the house had been bought, had also been detained in Avila by a sudden fever, and since his wife was away in the country Teresa was allowed to leave the Incarnation to look after him. The Bishop, whose active co-operation was now essential, was there too. So was the Provincial, Father Angel de Salazar, who had at first given the project his approval and then withdrawn it in the face of public hostility. Teresa made a final attempt to win him over, though without mentioning that she held the trump card in the shape of the papal blessing which would enable the foundation to be made whether he liked it or not; he persisted in his disapproval and was highly displeased to find himself outflanked and the foundation made.

The Bishop, Don Alvaro de Mendoza, was himself at first far from enthusiastic when he learned that it was intended to found St Joseph's *sin renta*. Pious though he might be, the Bishop was of noble birth and lived in a style suited to his rank. He was no more ready than the Provincial to incur the odium of sponsoring a new community which the charitable public would have to support. Spurning an eloquent appeal addressed to him from Fray Pedro's sick-bed, Don Alvaro prudently turned his back on the problem and made for his country house. The old friar went after him. 'I have made a pact with my body,' he used to say, 'to allow it no respite in this world so that it may enjoy rest eternal in the next.' Calling for an ass to be saddled and himself to be lifted on to it, the sick man set off in pursuit, armed with the papal brief and accompanied by two friends, one of them the *Caballero santo*, Francisco de Salcedo. Shamed by their entreaties, Don Alvaro agreed to return to Avila and at least to speak with the foundress. His conversion was instantaneous and wholehearted. Never was Teresa's 'gift of pleasing' put to better use; Don Alvaro de Mendoza was henceforth to be the foremost friend and protector of the reformers. His support was the more timely in that they were soon to lose the friar's. Within a few weeks, Pedro de Alcántara was dead. 'His Majesty seems to have preserved him expressly until this affair was concluded', Teresa observed. She saw that every minute was now precious. The Bishop's licence was issued in the middle of August. On the twenty-fourth of that month, in the year 1562, the first convent of the reformed or Discalced Carmelites began its humble existence.

Fray Pedro had highly approved of the little convent. He said it was a true house of St Joseph – small and poor, just as he imagined the stable at Bethlehem. One of the rooms had been turned into a chapel. Small statues of St Joseph and Our Lady had been acquired and one was placed at each entrance, in fulfilment of the promise given to Teresa in her vision that they would stand guard over her home. Gaspar Daza, the priest who had once so sternly told Teresa that her visions were inspired by the Devil, celebrated the first mass. The bell was small and cracked, for they had bought it second-hand. It summoned the neighbours to witness a ceremony that was novel but moving in its simplicity. Teresa and two other nuns from the Incarnation (who were also her cousins) were there and also four novices, whom she describes as 'poor orphans, who were accepted without dowry and were great servants of God'. They were given the rough, unfamiliar habit of the Discalced Carmelites and professed obedience to the primitive Rule. Their names have been preserved: the 27-year-old Antonia de Henao, María de Paz, a girl of humble birth whom Teresa had come to know and respect in Doña Guiomar's household, Ursula de los Santos, a woman already in her early forties, and the slightly younger María Dávila, whose brother was to become the chaplain, friend and biographer of the foundress. Such was the nucleus of the band of sisters, never more than thirteen in number, who were to inspire similar communities throughout the world. For Teresa it was an hour of deep joy and gratitude. Not for a moment did she claim any credit for herself.

> I have always known that it was the Lord's doing. My part in the business was so full of imperfections that I clearly deserved blame rather than thanks. But it was a great joy to me to see how the Lord had made me, sinful though I was, his instrument in this grand design. I was therefore filled with such happiness that I felt quite carried away by the ardour of my prayer.

The euphoria gave place almost at once to a mood of doubt and self-reproach. Had she not broken her vow of obedience, gone behind her superiors' back, and given them every reason to be angry? Would not her nuns be wretched leading such a poverty-stricken, hand-to-mouth existence, and quickly run short of food? And what about herself? How could she bear so strict and secluded a regime, with her poor health and her happy memories of the friends and pleasant house which she wished to leave behind? Perhaps she would find it hard to get on with the nuns who were to be her companions. Perhaps she had been altogether too ambitious in launching the new venture, when she was already a professed nun herself and ought to have been content with the common lot. The Devil, in short, might have put the whole idea into her head and beguiled her into believing it was inspired from on high. 'Everything God had commanded me, all the advice I had sought and the prayers I had been offering almost incessantly for more than two years were quite blotted out from my memory as if they had never been.' The gloom and anguish which enveloped her took away even the power to pray, and Teresa could only kneel in utter dejection before the Blessed Sacrament humbly invoking the divine mercy. Then suddenly the clouds cleared. A ray of light penetrated her soul, and she began to recognize her fears as put there by the Devil and to recall God's promises and her resolve to serve him, come what may. Had not the Lord plainly told her he would send her a cross, and a heavy one at that? Fixing her eyes on the Blessed Sacrament, Teresa vowed that she would do everything in her power to obtain the consent of her superiors for a transfer to the new house and there live a life of penance and strict enclosure.

'The moment I did this,' she tells us, 'the Devil turned tail and left me calm and happy; and thus I remained, as I have done ever since.'

The turmoil within her was stilled, but outside the storm was only beginning. News that a community of penniless nuns had surreptitiously sprung up under their very noses spread quickly and filled great and small with indignation. The Corregidor and notables saw it as a slight to their authority and a probable drain on their purse. Tradesmen closed their shops to join the demonstrators protesting that the nuns would take the bread out of their children's mouths. The Inspector of Fountains declared that the convent buildings would interfere with the city's water supply. The friars feared for their alms.

The Town Council met in emergency session and announced that an Assembly would be held the following day, 26 August, at which representatives of all local interests and institutions, the parishes, and the Orders could voice their objections and decide on the action to be taken, which few doubted would be the instant dissolution of the upstart foundation. A deputation waited on the Bishop to voice their objections. But Don Alvaro, now firmly committed to the Reform, had already visited St Joseph's and assured the nuns of his continued support. Whilst he was there a messenger arrived from the Incarnation with a peremptory order from the Prioress summoning Teresa to appear before her. Leaving the eldest of the novices in charge and commending them all to the spiritual care of Gaspar Daza and the protection of the Bishop, she set out at once.

The Town Council, eager to take advantage of Teresa's absence without provoking a head-on clash with the Bishop, attempted to frighten St Joseph's tiny garrison into surrender. An angry group gathered outside the convent shouting abuse. Then the Corregidor appeared in person and called on the nuns to leave. Otherwise, he threatened, he would order the doors to be forced. The nuns replied that they were under not his authority but the Bishop's; the Corregidor might violate their enclosure if he chose, but let him think well before doing so. Both sides prepared for battle. Some of the Council's men hammered on the doors, but the nuns reinforced them with wooden beams and the locks held. A crowd of onlookers collected, some of them more curious than hostile. Four defenceless orphans pitted against the City of Knights! The commotion could not have been greater, sarcastically observed Julián de Avila, brother of one of the beleaguered women, if the whole town were on fire or under attack by the Moors! Coercion having failed, the Assembly considered what next to do. Amongst those present we find the name of Father Baltasar Alvarez, but there is no mention of that timid and irresolute man speaking up for his penitent. The name of Father Pedro Ibáñez also appears in the records, but he, it seems, was absent from Avila and his place was taken by a learned young colleague, Father Domingo Báñez, who did not know Teresa personally but defended her with great courage and eloquence. The Bishop sent a respresentative who made an impression by producing and reading the papal bull authorizing the new foundation. In the face of this evidence the Assembly, though still bent on the destruction of the convent, felt obliged to refer the case to the Bishop. And so for the next six months the battle continued to rage, Gaspar Daza, on behalf of the Bishop, performing prodigies of valour for St Joseph's and suffering bitter persecution, Teresa tells us, for his pains.

Teresa, confined to her cell at the Incarnation, was obliged to watch the conflict from the wings. On returning to her old convent she had immediately prostrated herself at the feet of the Prioress. Doña María Cimbrón, an elderly nun who was distantly related to her and had only recently been elected to the office for which Teresa feared she herself might be chosen, was mollified by the culprit's serenity and submissiveness. But many of the nuns made no attempt to contain their indignation. The Provincial arrived and administered a sharp rebuke. Teresa quite expected to be sent to the prison cell; at least she would have found there the quiet and solitude which she craved after the strain of the last days. Now that the Lord had permitted the storm to unleash its full fury she felt strangely elated and 'most happy to have some suffering to offer up and some way in which to serve Him'. María, the young niece who had been the first to suggest, half in jest, that a convent of the primitive Rule should be founded and was herself to take the veil the following year, noticed that her aunt was so brimming over with joy that she had difficulty in restraining her laughter. Teresa herself writes that she had to make a show of contrition for fear her accusers would think she was not taking their rebukes seriously. But how could they say that she had offended the Order, when her one wish was to serve its Rule and traditions more perfectly? She knew she had not acted, as they claimed, out of ambition or an itch for notoriety. But when they taxed her with having led a life, even under the Mitigated Rule, far more 'wicked' than that of many others, she admitted that they were right. Teresa hung her head in shame, made no attempt to excuse herself, and begged them to forgive her.

The Provincial then ordered Teresa to speak up and put her case. 'As I was inwardly quite calm,' she writes, 'and the Lord helped me, I defended myself in such a way that neither the Provincial nor the nuns who were present found any cause to condemn me.' Afterwards, when she was alone with the Provincial, she even managed to win him round to the extent of promising that, as soon as all the fuss had died down, he would allow her to return to St Joseph's.

But the militants on the Town Council still kept up their pressure. Unable to dissolve the convent on the spot, they decided to refer their case to no less an authority than the Royal Council. Delegates were nominated and funds raised, for it was clear that the lawsuit would be long and expensive. Teresa was at first forbidden to take any part in the proceedings, but the following day the Provincial lifted the ban. He had now moved at least from hostility to neutrality. 'Although he did not help us,' she comments, 'he would not stand in our way.' Teresa had no money and at first found no one willing to represent her cause. Finally a well-disposed priest, Gonzalo de Aranda, offered to speak up for her before the Royal Council. In Avila, the *Caballero santo*, Daza, Julián de Avila and other faithful friends stoutly resisted the pretensions of the Corregidor. Teresa was much upset by the unpopularity they incurred whilst she herself was forced to remain inactive. 'I was amazed at all the efforts the Devil was making against a few poor women,' she wrote, 'and how convinced everyone was that a dozen sisters and their prioress would bring great harm to the town.' The same people who objected to a handful of women whose only wish was to be left in peace to serve God, Julián de Avila added pungently, cared nothing for the hundreds of men and women in the town who never did a stroke of work and whose loose living showed that they preferred to serve the Devil.

In November an official of the Royal Council arrived in Avila and began to take statements from the contending parties. There were signs that the Town Councillors, realizing that they were not going to have things all their own way, might consider a compromise. They finished by suggesting that, provided the convent were to be adequately endowed and so less likely to become a burden on local resources, they would tolerate its existence. Teresa began to waver. She was anxious to see an end to the tiresome wrangle and to the persecutions suffered by her valiant helpers. It seemed to her that it might be prudent to yield for the time being on the question of endowments and revert to the idea of absolute poverty once the storm had died down. A compromise was accordingly worked out and only awaited signature. But the foundress was not a free agent. She had always believed that she was acting under higher authority which might transcend the dictates of human reason. 'When I was at prayer,' she writes, 'the Lord told me that I was not to do any such thing, for once we agreed to live on the income from endowments, they would never let us do otherwise.'

Nor was this all. Fray Pedro de Alcántara, who had followed the fortunes of the foundation with undiminished interest as his life ebbed and had sent her a final letter of encouragement and exhortation not to compromise on the issue of holy poverty, appeared to her one night in a vision. Teresa felt no alarm. Twice already since his death she had seen him in his glorified body, radiant with a celestial splendour which filled her soul with something of the bliss the saintly friar was enjoying in recompense for his earthly sufferings. But now 'he looked on me sternly, repeating that I must on no account accept an endowment, and asking why I was not following his advice. Then he immediately vanished.'

Shaken by this startling experience, Teresa at once instructed the *Caballero santo*, who was handling the negotiations, not to sign the proposed agreement. They must stick to their principles, she declared, and the lawsuit would go on. Salcedo, who had never liked the compromise, did as Teresa said. To silence their opponents once and for all, a petition was sent to Rome asking that the convent should be allowed to continue *sin renta*. At the beginning of December a papal Rescript to this effect was issued. The prioress and nuns of St Joseph were granted an unusual privilege: 'to possess no goods, either individually or collectively, but to maintain themselves freely from the alms and charitable assistance which pious Christians may offer and bestow'. The little band of the Discalced were beside themselves with joy; they thought themselves the most fortunate creatures in God's world.

The horizon was beginning to clear, though menacing stormclouds still blew up from time to time over the battlements of the City of the Knights. Someone suggested that the contending parties should refer their differences to a panel of learned men. Teresa, mindful of Fray Pedro's admonition not to seek the advice of *letrados* on spiritual matters outside their competence, scented danger and refused. Then, providentially, Father Ibáñez arrived. Though the respected Dominican had himself first opposed the project of a convent *sin renta*, Teresa's remonstrances had converted him into an ardent supporter, and he now threw the weight of his authority into the scales, encouraging the Bishop to stand firm and finally persuading the Provincial to allow Teresa to return to St Joseph's. By the end of 1562 or the following spring, the foundress and four nuns from the Incarnation were permitted to join their sisters in the new house. They remained under the jurisdiction of the Carmelite Order, being merely seconded to instruct the novices of the new institution whose status remained somewhat ambivalent. Teresa took with her a straw pallet, a discipline and an old patched habit, which she received on loan against a signed receipt and a promise to return them.

The suit in the Royal Council still remained to be settled; an entry in the Avila records for June 1563 mentions it as still dragging on. But passions had cooled, and much money been spent to no avail. Avila had gradually come to accept the little house where a handful of nuns lived out their secluded and inoffensive lives. But they were not forgotten; enough food and money continued to come in from well-wishers to satisfy their modest needs. Teresa's heart was brimming with gratitude. As soon as she entered the tiny chapel to pray, an irresistible rapture swept her into celestial realms where Christ seemed lovingly to place a crown on her head and to give her thanks for what she had accomplished for his mother. Soon afterwards, when the nuns were on their knees in the choir after Compline, Our Lady appeared to Teresa in glory and spread her radiant robe around them in token of her protection. The battle had been won and Teresa's vow to St Joseph fulfilled.

10

The Way of Perfection

For the next four and a half years Teresa led the simple, spartan existence which she believed to be the Carmelites' true calling. 'Those were the most restful years of my life,' she later wrote, 'the peace and quiet of which my soul often sorely misses.' She saw the importance of keeping the community small. The maximum number of nuns had been fixed first at fifteen – in token of Christ, the twelve Apostles, the Blessed Virgin and St Joseph – and then reduced to thirteen. The nuns took the names of those saints to whom they professed a special devotion, distinctions of rank or ties of kinship having no place amongst those who renounced the world. Doña Teresa de Ahumada was henceforth simply Teresa de Jesús. Her niece María Cepeda y Ocampo became María Bautista. After almost casually suggesting the idea of a return to the primitive Rule and pledging 1,000 ducats of her dowry – for which she was rewarded by a vision of Christ who thanked her and promised great things for the new convent – María had for a time been beguiled by the world and had contemplated marriage, until a true change of heart led her to take the veil. Teresa refused all but 300 ducats of the proffered dowry – just enough to settle some outstanding debts and pay for the little chapels or 'hermitages' she wanted built in the convent grounds. The community indeed at first seemed almost a family affair. María's two sisters Beatrix and Isabel followed her, to join another elegant and well-connected cousin, María Dávila (María de Santo Jerónimo). Others, like Isabel Ortega – now Isabel de Santo

Domingo – were spiritual daughters of Fray Pedro de Alcántara. These young and ardent spirits were to form the nucleus of the wider Reform and to rank amongst its leading figures. Teresa loved them as tenderly as a mother. Though she would test and correct them sternly, she wrote of them as angels, innocent and holy souls amongst whom it was a blessing to live, for they were far better than herself; 'for what his Majesty has not achieved in me in all these years since I began to pray and he to grant me favours, he has wrought in them in three months, and sometimes even in three days'.

Like the disciples of Pedro de Alcántara and the Reformed of other Orders, the Carmelites of St Joseph's became known as the 'Discalced'. The Constitutions which the Foundress at once began drawing up for her little community laid down that its members should go barefoot, except in *tierras frías*. Avila, high on the bleak Castilian plateau, might well have qualified for this exemption, but it seems that, for the first years of the convent's existence at least, this rule was observed with full rigour. On 13 July 1563, possibly to mark the coming into force of the Constitutions, there is a reference in the records to a ceremony at which 'our holy Mother was discalced'. But prudence must quickly have prevailed. Four years later we find Julián de Avila, who had assumed his duties as Chaplain to the nuns, referring to them being shod in the Spanish hempen sandals known as *alpargatas*. The habit which they wore under the white Carmelite mantle, like the blankets on their straw pallets, was of rough brown frieze, the coif, closely framing the face so as to cover any stray wisp of cropped hair, of coarse linen. Whilst insisting on the utmost austerity and simplicity of dress, Teresa liked her nuns to maintain the standards of fastidious neatness and personal cleanliness which came naturally to her.

In the primitive conditions prevailing at St Joseph's this was not easy. One of the witnesses at Teresa's beatification recalls that their habits and bedclothes became so infested with lice that the nuns complained to their Prioress. They were distracted by this plague, they told her, from their prayers; could their Mother please do something about it? Such incidents Teresa took not only as a test of faith but as an opportunity for some innocent fun. One night after Matins, a little procession formed up and went from the nuns' dormitory to the chapel. One nun carried a cross, and all sang psalms and some little verses composed specially for the occasion. They implored the Lord who had clothed them with their habit to deliver them from the *mala gente* – the tiresome creatures now infesting it. Teresa knelt in prayer before the Holy Sacrament. Then, chanting the Litany and taking with her a bowl of consecrated water, she went with them to each cell in turn sprinkling and blessing the pallets. From that time on, the witnesses declared, the plague ceased. Some controversy later arose as to whether this immunity extended to other communities of Discalced Carmelites as well. At all events St Joseph's was freed for all time from the pest. The cross carried in the procession became known as the Christ of the Lice.

At the heart of this life of poverty and penance throbbed a joy which found vent in outbursts of spontaneous song, poetic composition and even dance. The childlike spirit of St Francis seemed to have been reborn amongst the Discalced. To celebrate the feasts of the Church, or some event such as the taking of the veil, Teresa loved to improvise verses, and she encouraged and even ordered her daughters to do the same. Though her later friend and collaborator in the Reform, St John of the Cross, was to dwarf all others by the magnitude of his genius, many lesser talents flourished on Mount Carmel. They ranged from the 'literary nun' and competent prioress María de San José, whom we have already met as the bright-eyed María de Salazar in Doña Luisa's household at Toledo, to Ana de San Bartolomé, Teresa's devoted nurse, whose rustic verses bespoke her simple peasant origin. But not all of Teresa's nuns found such things to their taste. 'What – we are being asked to sing?' one of them once complained. 'It would be better to contemplate!' The Prioress overheard the remark and was displeased. The kill-joy was sent to her cell to reflect that there is a time for innocent pastimes as well as for prayer. Another nun was once made to copy out some verses which she thought beneath the dignity of the Foundress. 'Don't take this amiss', Teresa gently chided her. 'We need everything that helps to make life bearable.' *Villancicos*, ballads, and other poems in popular verse-forms – often anonymous or collective compositions – passed from mouth to mouth and later from convent to convent. We find Teresa sending them to her brother Lorenzo and frequently referring to them in her correspondence.

Some of Teresa's verses seem to have come to her whilst she was in a state of ecstasy. 'I know a person', she writes, referring to herself, 'who, albeit no poet, yet suddenly and without the help of her intellect composed some stanzas which most feelingly expressed her pain.' A movingly sung verse might, literally, send her into rapture. One Easter, the beautiful voice of a young novice carried her off into such a deep ecstasy that the nuns had to take her to her cell as if dead. On regaining her senses. Teresa is said to have composed her well-known verses beginning, 'I live; yet 'tis not I that live'. On another occasion it is recorded that 'during the nuns' hour of recreation the holy Mother came from her cell rapt in a marvellous ecstasy and fervour of spirit, singing and dancing, and made the whole convent join in, which they did most merrily'. The drum which the saint is said to have played is still treasured by the Carmelites of Avila.

This irrepressible inner joy seemed to be nourished, rather than quenched, by privation. The fasts observed at St Joseph's were frequent and strict. The longest lasted from the Feast of the Exaltation of the Cross in September until Easter. Even when the nuns were not officially fasting they often went short of food and other necessities, despite the generosity of their well-wishers, especially the Bishop. The principal meal of the day was frequently no more than a little bread, cheese or fruit. Eggs and fish were a treat. A single frying-pan was the chief piece of kitchen equipment. One day when the Prioress was on duty at the stove, a nun found her deep in ecstasy, the pan still clasped firmly in her hand. The sisters gathered round in consternation. Not that they were alarmed to find her in this state, even in such a place, for they had grown used to such things; but the oil in the frying pan was in danger of being spilt, and it was all they had. Teresa liked taking her turn in the kitchen. She was an excellent cook, and her daughters found she could do wonders with their meagre provisions. She seemed to be both Martha and Mary. 'The Lord walks amongst the pots and pans', she was fond of telling them. At one time she wanted to renounce her status as a choir-nun and devote herself wholly to the menial tasks of a lay sister. She only desisted on being told by her confessor that this was impossible for one who had already taken the veil.

The nuns' day was apportioned between work and prayer, as prescribed by the Constitutions. They rose at dawn and after private prayers, the saying of the Little Hours of Prime, Terce, Sext and None, and a pause for examination of conscience they attended Mass at nine before dispersing to their respective tasks. Dinner, when there was anything to eat, was at ten or eleven. Then followed an hour's recreation, when they might chat to one another whilst they sewed, spun, or weaved, avoiding any elaborate work on which they would need to concentrate a mind which should have thoughts only for God. They might sell their handiwork for the common good, but not haggle over it: if they thought the price offered by the purchaser insufficient, they would know that this form of labour was unproductive and turn to something else. Teresa was a great enemy of all idleness, firmly believing that those who were able yet unwilling to work should have no right to eat, and she was seldom to be seen without a distaff or spinning wheel. These she plied even whilst speaking with visitors in the *locutorio*, and desisted only out of respect when the Bishop came or to please the *Caballero santo*, who found the whir distracting and gave her alms in return for the privilege of silence.

Vespers was at two, followed by an hour's reading from the lives of the saints, the *Imitation of Christ*, and edifying books by Pedro de Alcántara, his much-read Dominican contemporary Luis de Granada and other spiritual writers. Any odd moments when the sisters were not in chapel or busied with their duties they were expected to spend in prayer and meditation in their cells. At eight, after Compline, the bell rang for silence, which had to be observed until Prime the following morning. After Matins, which was preceded by an hour's prayer and said a little after nine in the evening, the nuns remained for a time in chapel absorbed in self-examination or listening to the reading of the mystery which was to form the subject of their meditations on the morrow. When the bell rang at eleven, each returned to her cell, whitewashed and bare except for the straw pallet, an earthenware pitcher, a plain crucifix on the wall, perhaps a mat of cork or esparto grass and a book or two, and they might not leave it to visit another sister without permission. Such was their daily life, and such their home – 'a heaven upon earth', it seemed to their Mother, 'if ever there is one!'

Once a week the nuns held a disciplinary Chapter. The enumeration of the offences and the penalties prescribed for them, comprising more than one-third of Teresa's Constitutions (which were read aloud in these conclaves), bespeak the severity of the primitive Rule. The categories ranged from minor transgressions to matters of *gravísima culpa* (very serious guilt). The first included such misdemeanours as being late for meals or services, walking either too fast or too slow, mislaying a book or making mistakes when reading or singing, unseemly chatter, giggling or making others giggle, breaking things, making a noise in the dormitory, eating or drinking without leave, and treating others with discourtesy. *Gravísima culpa* included the crimes of breaking out of the convent, laying violent hands on the Prioress, refusing to do penance, acquiring personal possessions, revealing confidential matters and indulging in malicious gossip with outsiders, ambitiously scheming to acquire office, and falling into the sin of sensuality. Irreverence in chapel, ill-intentioned fault-finding, loose, insulting or threatening language, idle chatter, answering back, slandering or striking another sister or taking her to court, forming cliques, committing acts of insubordination and generally disrupting the life of the convent formed a gamut of intermediate offences, each with appropriate penalties ranging from reprimands and light penances to ostracism by the community, imprisonment, excommunication and expulsion.

This arsenal of disciplinary weapons was sparingly used, though Teresa would wield them unflinchingly when it seemed to her necessary. Baseless or maliciously motivated denunciations, such as those which often brought the victim into the clutches of the Inquisition, were discouraged by application to the informer of the punishments appropriate to the alleged offences. The Constitutions also gave the Prioress discretion to mitigate the penalties prescribed, and such were Teresa's tact and gentleness in dealing with transgressors that punishments received at her hands often seemed more like favours. Nor did the Foundress spare herself, and she was constantly urging her nuns to criticize her own faults as readily as they would those of others. She would submit too to humiliating mortifications with all the meekness she expected of her daughters. One witness at her Beatification describes a scene which, given Teresa's known aversion to anything smacking of eccentricity or sensationalism, it is hard to believe: the Prioress, in penance for some self-confessed misdemeanour, saddled and laden like a mule and crawling on all fours before the startled nuns as they sat at dinner in the refectory. Other accounts speak of the Prioress, brought up with her father's taste for fine things, eating off broken crockery and drinking from a human skull.

Such gestures seem meaningless and even repugnant unless we grasp the superlative value attached by Teresa to the practice of humility, the chief of all virtues in her eyes. In a Spain dominated by the cult of 'honour' – pride of lineage, disdain for plebeian occupations and manual work, and a touchiness which led to ferocious revenge for every imagined injury – the practice of self-abasement stood in dramatic contrast. Even her pious father and brothers had not been immune from the poisonous obsession with 'honour', and Teresa feared the contagion might spread to the Discalced. The latter, however exalted their birth, were required to drop the honourable style of '*Doña*', and those of her correspondents who persisted in addressing the Foundress as '*Señora*' were severely taken to task. The surest antidotes to the current obsession with honour were searching self-examination, criticism, and the practice of humility. Closely allied to these virtues was that of obedience – another concept which, as interpreted in her convents, the modern mind finds difficult to grasp and approve. Teresa practised unquestioning obedience herself – obedience to her Rule, her superiors and confessors, and (once she was convinced of their divine origin) to her revelations. She expected the same obedience from her nuns, testing them out and requiring utter submission to her orders in ways which may strike us sometimes as comic, sometimes as wrong-headed.

Ursula de los Santos, being somewhat older than the others, was singled out for a particularly severe test. 'How ill you look!' Teresa remarked to her one day. Then, feeling her pulse, she added: 'Just as I thought! Off to bed with you at once; you really must be in a bad way!' The nun went to her cell without a word and lay down as she had been ordered. The others were sent to visit her and inquired how she felt. 'Poorly, my sisters, very poorly!'

'Where does it hurt, then? What's the matter with you?' they asked anxiously. 'I can't tell. Our Mother says I'm very ill!' The nun had passed the test with flying colours. Her spiritual health was clearly as sound as her physical.

Another incident is recorded which recalls St Francis of Assisi's testing of two postulants by telling them to plant a row of young cabbages upside down and then rejecting the one who put reason before obedience. María Bautista was one day handed a rotten cucumber and told to plant it in the garden. She obeyed immediately, pausing only to ask: 'Upright or lengthwise, Mother?'

'Lengthwise!' Teresa watched her depart on her errand with satisfaction. 'It never occurred to her that what she was going to do was absurd', she explained approvingly. 'Obedience had blinded her common sense.'

The episode of the cucumber shows how easily the nuns might find themselves at the mercy of a capricious or autocratic Prioress. The latter, Teresa warns, must never put their obedience to the test in such a way as to lead them into even venial sin. Nor must they forget that the Lord gives his children different spiritual graces and leads each along her individual path to perfection. A Superior should not try to force them all into her own mould. Teresa mentions the case of a Prioress much addicted to penance who would keep her community scourging themselves and reciting penitential psalms far into the night, when they ought to be in bed. Superiors must also bear in mind that their slightest word may be taken literally. She knew of one who told a nun to get some fresh air by going out for a stroll and then forgot all about her until some hours later when her absence was noted and the exhausted nun was found still trudging round the garden. Of another she tells the following story:

A nun once brought a very large worm for her Prioress to look at and admire. 'Go and eat it, then!' said the Prioress jokingly. The nun went off and promptly started frying the worm. The cook asked her what she was doing. She answered that she was going to eat it, as she really intended to do. So a thoughtless remark made by the Prioress might have done her a great deal of harm.

Though she realized that, like all good things, it might be liable to abuse, obedience remained for Teresa the touchstone of her spiritual life, the motive force behind her actions, and the lifeline protecting her from error or delusion. It was under obedience that she wrote her books, founded or desisted from founding her convents. For this granddaughter of a *converso* penanced by the Inquisition there could be no higher good than to be recognized as a loyal daughter of the Church. Submission to those set in authority by the Church and acceptance of all its dogmas, customs and ceremonies were axiomatic. She wanted her nuns to be formed in the same mould. This accounts for some attitudes which may appear paradoxical. The future Doctor of the Church distrusted and discouraged book-learning amongst her daughters, though she esteemed it highly in men. It seemed to her incompatible with the simplicity and lowliness of their vocation and liable to lead to intellectual pride and perhaps even into heresy. 'God forbid that any of my daughters should make a show of their Latin', she wrote to one of her prioresses. 'I would much rather that they showed themselves to be simple, as is very fitting for saints.' She was extremely wary of accepting any postulant who seemed to have the makings of a blue-stocking; one she rejected out of hand for saying she would bring a Bible with her.

Teresa firmly believed, as did others of her day, in the inequality of the sexes. Her writings are full of allusions to 'us frail women', and to their natural timidity, inconstancy and limited intelligence. Most were docile and could be handled with gentle kindness, but troublemakers needed to be dealt with firmly. 'If a few of the nuns are punished the rest will keep quiet; women are like that – timorous creatures, for the most part. . . . I know by experience what it is like when a lot of women get together', she wrote to one of her male correspondents. 'God deliver us from them!' Yet she stoutly defended two basic rights – that the nuns should elect their own prioresses and choose their own confessors – which her successors had to fight hard to preserve against the dominating pretensions of the friars. The relationship between the latter and their penitents, even in genuinely reformed communities, remained fraught with potential danger, and Teresa insisted that, however much the friars' counsel was needed in the confessional, they should see as little of the nuns as possible.

Teresa knew too what poisonous weeds might flourish in the hothouse atmosphere of a strictly enclosed female community. The Foundress discouraged the use of sentimental terms of endearment, favouritism, and close intimacies; her ideal was that of a family of sisters in which each should be bound in equal love to all. They were to behave like 'strong men', not 'weak women'. The Constitutions laid down that no nun was to embrace another or caress her hands or face. Nor, on the other hand, were they to 'mortify' one another by a sudden slap or pinch – an unpleasant practice apparently in vogue at the Incarnation which seems to have lingered on in some of the reformed convents, for we find Teresa later writing to her prioress at Seville: 'It looks as if the Devil is teaching them to do these things under the guise of perfection. You must on no account ever order, or permit, any nun to strike another – and that applies to pinching too!'

It was this low view of woman's natural abilities and status which paradoxically led to Teresa's high view of the nuns' calling. She summoned them to nothing less than the pursuit of spiritual perfection. Women might not, like their menfolk and crusading forebears, take up arms for the Cross; they might not evangelize the heathen, preach or teach; society had not yet even conceded them a public role in tending the sick or working amongst the poor. The religious life meant for them enclosure in a convent and dedication to prayer and contemplation. But were not prayer and contemplation, if practised with perfection, the highest form of human activity? Moreover, Teresa saw it linked organically to the great issues of the day: the struggle waged by the Most Catholic King against the Lutherans, against the Moslems of Barbary and Turkey, against the obdurate pagans of the New World. Convents and monasteries should be so many spiritual power-houses, where the ceaseless intercession of monks and nuns provided logistical support for these great enterprises. In the global battle between good and evil the humblest nun could play her part by living the Christian life in its full perfection.

At the outset of *The Way of Perfection*, the little book which Teresa wrote at St Joseph's, at their urgent entreaty, for the guidance of her twelve nuns, she describes how she came to see this truth for herself. It was not, she tells us, her intention at first to live a life of absolute poverty, but

> at this time it came to my ears what mischief and ravages those Lutherans had wrought in France, and how that unhappy sect was fast increasing. I was deeply distressed and implored the Lord with tears, as if I were somebody and could do something, to remedy so great an evil. Had I a thousand lives, it seemed to me I would give them all to save a single one of the many souls which were going to perdition. But since I was only a woman, and a base one at that, powerless to help as I should have liked in the service of the Lord, and as my desire was – and still is – that since he has so many enemies and so few friends, the latter should be trusty ones, I resolved to do the little that was in me: namely, follow the evangelical precepts as fully as I could, and endeavour that those few nuns who were with me should do likewise . . . dedicating ourselves to prayer for the preachers and learned men who are defending the Church, and do all we could to help this our Lord who is now so sorely beset.

Though they had renounced the world for a life of humble obscurity, Teresa explained to her nuns, they were still, in a sense, in the thick of the fray. They were like standard-bearers, unable themselves to wield the sword, but charged with rallying others by holding high the banner of Christ, despite the blows rained upon them by the enemy. And in this battle, as in any other, there were casualties. Some simply found things too hard and gave up. Ana Dávila, an older nun who had come to St Joseph's with the Foundress and was chosen prioress, on Teresa's insistence, instead of herself, could not stand the severities and returned to the Incarnation on the plea of ill health. Nor could her successor, one of Teresa's Cepeda relations and sincerely devoted to the same ideals, who likewise had to go back to the Incarnation where she remained bed-ridden for twenty years. There were others who found the life difficult but having nowhere else to go stayed on, victims of 'melancholy' – that scourge of monastic life known in medieval time as *accidie*, and comprising a gamut of disorders ranging from listlessness and chronic depression to nervous breakdown and even madness. Teresa, who well knew and feared its ravages, declares that 'it is far better not to found any convents at all than to admit melancholics who will soon be the ruin of them'. Her letters contain many allusions to the baneful effects of melancholy and she devotes a whole chapter of her *Foundations* to analysing its various manifestations and prescribing ways of dealing with them.

She begins by distinguishing between the different degrees of the malady and the spiritual states of those whom it afflicts. If they remain humble and obedient, they do no great harm to others and simply arouse compassion. Teresa may have had in mind the case of her own niece Leonor de Cepeda, who accompanied her to St Joseph's, where her ardent mortifications caused her to lose her health and finally her reason. The girl returned to the Incarnation and died there, in all holiness but quite mad. Teresa had no doubt that she went straight to heaven. But with many victims of melancholy it was not so much their health and reason that came in peril as their very soul. Experience convinced Teresa that they became despondent and restless because of their failure to conquer self-will. They made their melancholy humour an excuse for refusing to obey their Superior, for speaking ill of others and for all sorts of indulgences. The Prioress must therefore treat them severely; 'if words are not enough, they must be punished'. It was fatal to give way to them out of misguided kindness, for their bad example would quickly infect others and a whole convent might be ruined. The trouble generally stemmed from lack of discipline or humility, and stern measures were called for; 'I have often seen them become docile when brought before someone of whom they are afraid.' In one of her letters she gives advice on how to deal with a case of melancholia which appears to be verging on madness. Two strong nuns must remain in constant attendance and look after the sufferer as they would anyone else who was ill, and 'perhaps if you were to whip her too she would stop crying out as she does now'. Here Teresa may be writing with her tongue in her cheek. But though she never loses her humanity or good sense (for she also recommends that melancholics should not spend too much time in prayer and fasting but should be kept usefully occupied) we see the Foundress here at her sternest – the offspring of crusaders, the sister of *conquistadores*, and a true daughter of Avila of the Knights.

Teresa, indeed, regarded her nuns as auxiliaries in the great counter-offensive which the Church, reinvigorated by the decisions taken at the Council of Trent, was preparing against the heretics. In the Netherlands, the Duke of Alba (later to become, with his Duchess, a great devotee of the Foundress) was soon to strike against them with fire and sword. Malta, the bulwark of Christendom in the Eastern Mediterranean, was holding out against the besieging Moslems. From the New World, those of Teresa's brothers who had not fallen fighting for the faith sent her news of the consolidation of Spanish power and the spread of the gospel amongst the Indians. One day, nearly four years after the founding of St Joseph's, a Franciscan friar called Alonso de Maldonado visited the convent and painted such a vivid picture of the need for a still greater missionary effort to save these pagan souls that Teresa was deeply moved. 'I went in tears to a hermitage,' she writes, 'imploring our Lord to devise some way whereby I might be of help in gaining some soul for his service, since the Devil was carrying off so many; and that if I could do nothing else, at least my prayers might be of some avail.' Teresa's petition was not granted at once; but when it came, the answer was to set her life on a new course.

One outlet for Teresa's yearnings, which seemed to increase rather than diminish with the long hours spent in contemplation, she found in writing. During the years spent at St Joseph's she put the finishing touches to her *Life*, adding at her confessor's bidding an account of the founding of the convent. There, too, she composed her second work, *The Way of Perfection*, which she completely rewrote several years later, giving a more formal tone to the intimate, conversational style, so revealing of Teresa's warm and vivid personality, in which she addressed her daughters; both versions of the book have fortunately come down to us. She also began a third book to which she gave no title, but which is generally known as *Conceptions of the Love of God* or *Meditations on the Song of Songs*. The work is a discursive commentary on certain passages in the Song of Solomon, whose evocative lyricism has so fascinated the many mystics who have seen in its erotic oriental imagery an edifying allegory of God's love for the human soul. To treat of it was a daring undertaking – specially for a woman. Though she obtained the written approval of Father Báñez, the devout and learned Dominican who had championed her cause before a hostile Town Council, the manuscript later aroused the misgivings of a confessor, who ordered her to burn it. Teresa's superiors had cause for alarm. It was about this time that the poet-scholar Luis de León was delated to the Inquisition for translating and circulating a translation of the dangerous poem, and though he was finally acquitted he prudently refrained from including the *Meditations* in Teresa's collected works, which he edited after her death.

The *Meditations* and the concluding chapters of the *Life* reflect the intensity, variety and frequency of the mystical graces which Teresa experienced during the years at St Joseph's. Many flowed from her loving concern for the salvation and spiritual progress of those around her. Their physical suffering too was often the object of her ardent intercession. We read of a relative cured through her prayers from an agonizing kidney complaint, of sight restored to one going blind, after Christ had appeared to Teresa in a vision and pulled a nail from his bleeding flesh to show her that he spared himself no pain to succour those who turned to him. Deliverance from sin and spiritual distress demanded long and ardent intercession. It took more than a month before a devout man who had fallen into Satan's clutches could be restored to virtue; Teresa could only be sure of victory when she saw the Devil furiously tearing up the infernal contract. Sometimes it was revealed to her that a grave sin was in danger of being committed. She was once praying with great fervour for one she knew to be exposed to such temptation when 'I heard a very soft voice addressing me in a whisper. It made my hair quite stand on end with fear. I tried to hear what it was saying, but could not; then it soon ceased.' Fear quickly gave place to a feeling of serenity and inner bliss, which left her convinced that the petition had been granted. But it was an uncanny experience all the same, for, unlike her customary locutions, Teresa tells us that she heard the voice with her bodily ears, though she could not distinguish what it said.

Nor did Teresa's concern for souls cease with their departure from this earthly life. It then became indeed more intense, her prayers on their behalf more fervent. At death she knew the soul passed into Purgatory, whence it emerged after due purification; her visions often revealed its final ascent into glory. Only the saintly Pedro de Alcántara, Pedro Ibáñez and an unnamed Carmelite friar did she ever see ascend into heaven without a spell in Purgatory. But the soul's sojourn there might be short, as she earnestly prayed it might be, though sometimes, when it had already attained a high degree of perfection in this mortal life, to offer such prayers seemed 'like giving alms to the rich'. Such, she believed, must have been the case with a devout Carmelite Provincial who died at a great age but appeared, when caught up into heaven in her vision, with the radiant face of a young man. So, too, it must have been with a very young nun, whose soul she saw ascend into heaven after a brief life of spotless purity. In short, she could write that 'the Lord very often delivered souls from grave sins and brought others to greater perfection in answer to my prayers. As for delivering souls from purgatory and other notable things, the Lord has granted me so many favours of this kind that it would only weary my readers and myself to relate them all.' This she could affirm with wonder and totally without pride, knowing it to be solely the Lord's doing. In fact, experience had taught her that the Lord put into her heart the desire to intercede only when he was already disposed to grant the petition. If it was inexpedient to do so, she remained as if tongue-tied and scarcely able to find the words or thoughts in which to frame it.

With so many blessed spirits passing into the celestial realms, Teresa lost all fear of death. Sometimes she longed for it passionately, as the gateway into a far fuller life and a release from the weaknesses and restraints of the flesh. One night, she tells us, when suffering from the nausea to which she was prone, whilst her spirit craved the liberty and bliss of contemplation, she was overcome with deep dejection and burst into tears. Then Christ appeared to comfort her, exhorting her to endure all earthly trials for love of him. Her courage immediately returned. 'Once I made up my mind to serve our Lord with all my might,' she affirmed, 'I don't think I ever felt depressed again.' What cause, indeed, was there for sadness when she knew that those she had loved and honoured in this life were now in a state of glory which, through God's mercy, she hoped soon to share? 'The first persons I saw there', she writes in describing one vision of heaven, 'were my father and mother.' Pedro de Alcántara, who had helped her so much whilst alive, continued to strengthen her with his ghostly counsel. Such visitations inspired no fear in her. 'I sometimes feel', she wrote, 'that my real companions, and the friends who give me the greatest comfort, are amongst those I know to be living in the hereafter; whilst those who remain below seem quite dead and unable to keep me company.'

Which was the real world, and which the imaginary? 'Everything around me here below seems like a dream,' she wrote, 'everything I see with my bodily eyes a mockery. The soul longs for that which it has seen with the eyes of the spirit.' Calderón was to give dramatic expression to the same thought in the sublimest of his plays, *Life is a Dream*. Whether the stage was set in this world or in the next, Teresa saw the same characters going about their creator's business. For the Jesuits, still in the first flush of their apostolic ardour, she cherished a special veneration. She saw them at Communion beneath a celestial canopy or moving through her visions bearing white banners. The Dominicans, paladins in the battle against heresy, appeared to her with swords in their hands, striking out valiantly, their faces afire with holy zeal, many falling martyrs for the faith. Father Ibáñez stood transfigured before her, his head illuminated by the rays shed from a hovering dove or clad by the Virgin in a robe of dazzling brightness. Unnamed saints addressed her, prophesying a glorious future for their Order. These exalted accounts are sometimes tempered by discretion. 'I do not say which Orders I am speaking of', she explains. 'If the Lord wishes their names to be known he will declare it, so that none will take offence.' Jesuit, Dominican and Carmelite champions have voiced competing claims to the celestial inheritance.

On the Feast of the Assumption it was Our Lady whom Teresa was privileged to see ascending into heaven. At Whitsun, when she was in a hermitage meditating on the coming of the Holy Spirit, she fell into a deep rapture and seemed to hear the rustling of wings above her head. She looked up and saw a dove, 'very different from the doves of this world, not feathered but covered with what appeared to be tiny, scintillating shells'. She was filled at first with fear, and then with a joy which left her 'bewildered and foolish'. Another vision, vouchsafed to her four times and the most sublime, she tells us, ever granted her, kindled in her soul a flame which seemed to consume all its imperfections and annihilate every earthly desire. 'I beheld the Most Sacred Humanity in greater glory than ever before', she wrote. 'I seemed to see him in the most clear and marvellous way in the bosom of the Father.' This she apprehended, without seeing, in a sense impossible to describe, as if transported into the presence of the Supreme Being. In another grandiose vision the heavens were drawn aside like a curtain to reveal a host of angels in the midst of whom she knew to stand the throne of the Godhead. It was a mystery utterly beyond human comprehension – 'all I knew was that I could know nothing, and that everything else was nothing in comparison' – and from it there emanated the same supernatural fire of God's love in which she felt her old nature purged away and her soul reborn, phoenix-like, from the ashes.

The revelations showered upon Teresa in such abundance came by means of locutions or by wordless communications which, she says, conveyed their meaning more clearly than any form of speech. Her visions were both 'imaginary' and 'intellectual'. Of the latter she records many instances. Once, whilst reciting the Athanasian Creed, it was given her to comprehend the nature of the Trinity, and the mystery enshrined in the words 'Three Persons and one God'. At other times she perceived with complete clarity 'how all things are seen in God, and how he contains all things within himself'. She was granted an awareness that God is Truth as well as Love – the Truth which is the fulfilment of all lesser truths. 'Ah, daughter,' she heard in her mystic colloquy, 'how few there are who truly love me, else would I not hide my secrets from them! Do you know what it is to love me truly? It is to know that everything which is not pleasing to me is a lie.' This revelation left Teresa with an overwhelming sense of the vanity of all earthly things; she now understood that 'all other truths depend on this Truth, and all love on this Love'.

It was at Mass, particularly when approaching to receive the Sacrament, that Teresa was most liable to be rapt in ecstasy. 'The

Lord has often graciously appeared to me in the Host', she tells us. 'Then my hair stands on end and my whole being seems to shrink into nothingness.' But once, when she was about to take Communion, Teresa had a very different and terrifying experience. 'I saw with the eyes of my soul, more clearly than ever I could with those of my body,' she writes, 'two most hideous of Devils.' Their horns seemed to be around the throat of the celebrant, and she knew that the hands which held the Host were stained with mortal sin. Teresa could hardly say how she was able to take the Sacrament. But she did so for the vision, she came to believe, had been granted in part to teach her that God is present in the Host by virtue of the prayer of consecration, and not through any merit on the part of the priest. She was also given to understand that she should pray for the soul of the sinner, which she did most fervently.

Teresa was no stranger to devils. In the person of the Father of Lies himself or of his minions, they had constantly assaulted and pestered her ever since she set out on the Way of Perfection. They had striven to distract her from her devotions, and one had once actually alighted on her prayer-book and stayed there until being driven off by holy water. They tempted her to doubt the truth of her revelations, to drop her plans for reform, and in a thousand other ways. She had been attacked by them physically as well as spiritually. Teresa had learned to foil all their tricks and see through their disguises, for they might assume the form of a loathsome toad or a horribly grinning little negro. Sometimes their presence would be betrayed by an unmistakable whiff of brimstone. Teresa had watched in impotent horror as they gleefully tugged at the shroud of a dead man about to be laid in his grave. But generally she had found that they could easily be routed at the mere sight of a cross or by a good sprinkling of holy water. Though they still pestered her from time to time, she came to lose all fear of devils and could say that 'in fact it is they who have grown afraid of me. The Lord of all things has given me such power over them that I take no more notice of them than of flies.'

If Teresa's horned and fire-breathing demons seem to step straight out of the illuminated pages of some medieval book of hours, her vision of hell might have been taken from a psychiatrist's case-book. By contrast to her glimpses of heaven, which brought a sense of exhilarating release and expansion into an infinitely greater reality, her hell was to feel imprisoned in an isolated and painfully contracting self:

> I seemed to be on the threshold of a long, narrow passage, like a very low, dark and cramped oven, the bottom of which seemed to be covered with slimy, foul-smelling water full of vile reptiles. At the far end was a cavity scooped out of the wall like a cupboard where I found myself closely confined.

She had the sensation of being crushed to pieces, stifled in a fiery agony more excruciating than any bodily pain she had ever known. Depair overwhelmed her, for the torment promised to be without respite or end:

> I had been cast into what seemed a hole in the wall, and the very walls, which were hideous to behold, kept pressing in and suffocating me. There was no light but only the blackest darkness. And yet whatever could affright the eyes could somehow clearly be seen.

This terrifying experience had come to Teresa whilst she was still at the Incarnation, in order to give her a more vivid awareness, she believed, of God's mercy in saving her from the deserts of her sins. It still made her blood run cold when she remembered it.

At St Joseph's Teresa was spared any repetition of this infernal ordeal, although she suffered the recurrent phases of aridity and tormenting self-doubt which are the mystic's portion. She suffered too, despite the strict enclosure and the silence she imposed on her nuns, from the curiosity and sensation-mongering of pious well-wishers. The Bishop, despite his sincere veneration for the

Prioress, was not entirely blameless in the matter. He brought his sister with him, and Doña María de Mendoza brought her friends. These high-born ladies, and other prelates who frequented the nuns' humble chapel, were eager to see the ecstasies which so frequently came upon the Prioress during divine office. Try as she might, by grasping the grille, getting the nuns to tug at her habit, and sometimes even by throwing herself on the ground, she could not prevent them from witnessing the disconcerting phenomenon of levitation. Her raptures, which sometimes lasted for more than two hours, were the talk of Avila. Teresa's anguished supplications that she might be spared at least these public exhibitions seemed to go unheeded. Her locutions gave her rather to understand that, for a while, such things were necessary.

Teresa resigned herself humbly to the divine will.

Though some with the best of intentions speak ill of me, and others are afraid to have anything to do with me or even to hear my confessions, and others tax me with all sorts of things, I care very little, since I believe the Lord has chosen this means of benefiting many souls [she concludes her autobiography]. He has given me a life which is a sort of sleep, and everything I see appears for the most part like a dream. I find neither great happiness nor unhappiness in myself, and when I do feel something of either it passes so swiftly that I am amazed, and it leaves behind the feeling that I have been dreaming it.

Teresa could not know when she penned those lines that it would soon be the Lord's pleasure to rouse her from that dream. The period of acute psychic sensitivity – the plethora of raptures, levitations, and visions of every sort – was soon to draw to an end, though they would never leave her entirely and the inner voices would still continue to guide her.

One day – it was after the visit of the missionary from Mexico, whose harrowing description of the benighted Indians inspired her with a burning desire to spend herself in the Lord's service – a clear locution came to her: 'Wait yet awhile, my daughter, and you will see great things!'

The weeks passed, and the calm tenor of convent life remained unchanged. Then at length an important piece of news reached St Joseph's. The General of the Carmelite Order had come from Italy on a tour of inspection and would shortly be in Avila. Rumour had it that he was resolved to carry through a thorough reform of the whole Order.

11

God's Gadabout

Giovanni Battista Rossi, known in Spain under the hispanicized name of Rubeo, was an Italian aristocrat in his early fifties. Cultured, upright and energetic, he resolved on his election as Father General to apply the reforms laid down by the Council of Trent to all houses of the Carmelite Order, even in the distant Spanish provinces which none of his predecessors had visited. He was a man after the heart of the Pope, the former Dominican Inquisitor-General and fervent reformer who, at the beginning of 1566, ascended the throne of St Peter under the name of Pius V. The General's personal sobriety and his desire to see the practice of holy poverty strictly observed in Carmel did not rule out a strong sense of the respect due to his office. He travelled in style with a retinue which included two assistants, a secretary, a steward, two valets, two grooms, a messenger, a laundryman, a cook and a barber, whom he would call upon to shave off the beards of unkempt friars. The General had been known to seize the scissors himself to snip off unauthorized adornments from their habits, and even apply the rod to an offender's bare shoulders with his own hands.

Philip II had backed the election of Pius V and was no less anxious to promote the reform of the Franciscan, Augustinian, Trinitarian, Mercedarian, Carmelite and other relaxed Orders in his own domains. But he would have preferred to see it entrusted to Spanish bishops rather than to Generals from Rome. Ever suspicious of papal encroachments on the royal prerogatives, he wished to keep ecclesiastical reform, like all matters great and small, under his personal control. Nor was there much love lost between Spaniards and Italians. Though the King received him with prudent courtesy, Father Rossi was not to find his mission an easy one. In Andalusia, where laxity was at its worst, he faced open rebellion. It centred round the three Nieto brothers: Melchor, former Prior of Ecija, who had scandalously assaulted the Procurator previously sent to look into the abuses, Baltasar, who had rescued his brother from punishment by force of arms, and Gaspar, who had misused his office of Provincial to protect the miscreants. Partisans of the Nietos held key positions in the Order throughout the Province and enjoyed the backing of influential nobles. The General stripped Gaspar and other offenders of their offices, whipped Baltasar in front of his brethren in Seville, excommunicated the fugitive Melchor and condemned him to the galleys *in absentia*. Leaving his own nominees in power and discipline outwardly restored, he then moved on to Portugal and Castile.

By the middle of April 1567 Father Rossi had reached Avila, begun his visitation, and attended a Chapter of the Castilian Carmelites. Here the situation was much more encouraging. Angel de Salazar, who now ended his term as Provincial and became Prior of Avila, seemed no enemy to reform, if not a man to risk much in its cause. His successor, the elderly Alonso González, was virtuous and amenable. The Incarnation, though hardly a model establishment, was not as black as Teresa's biographers have sometimes painted it. As for St Joseph's, the General soon had an opportunity to see things for himself. The Foundress, with some trepidation, pressed an invitation on him to visit it. She was apprehensive on two counts. He might well resent her having placed the house under the jurisdiction of the Bishop, and she feared he might order her back to the Incarnation. Her own position remained somewhat anomalous. The Provincial had given his permission, first verbally and then in writing, for her secondment, and this had been confirmed and extended by the nuncio, subject to the Provincial's continuing approval, and endorsed by a papal brief. But Teresa was still a nun from the Incarnation, and St Joseph's was a Carmelite convent. Complete frankness seemed to her not only the wisest course, but since, as she believed, the head of her Order stood in the place of God, it was also her duty and her ardent desire. She opened her heart to the General, relating with eloquent sincerity how she had been led to make the foundation, showing him the Constitutions drawn up for her nuns, and confiding to him every detail of their life and devotions.

Father Rossi was deeply impressed. He had come to Spain to promote reform and here, in microcosm, he saw reform already in action – 'a picture, albeit imperfect, of our Order in its early days, with the primitive Rule being kept in all its rigour'. Of all the persons of rank and influence who came under the spell of Teresa's charm and goodness, none was to prove a more important conquest than the Carmelite General. Without his blessing and support her work could never have transcended its humble local origins. Seeing the General so well-disposed, she would have liked to transfer the formal obedience of her community to him there and then, but felt unable to do so without the risk of offending the Bishop who had been such a staunch friend in difficult days. Father Rossi enthusiastically commended everything he saw at St Joseph's and gave Teresa and her nuns permission to remain there. A further mark of his confidence was to issue a patent authorizing her 'to receive houses, churches, sites, and places anywhere in Castile in the name of our Order so as to found convents of Carmelite nuns under our direct obedience', and forbidding provincials, priors, or any other superiors to prevent her doing so. Then, with many assurances of his continuing concern and support, the General left for a final audience with the King before returning to Italy.

Whilst waiting in Madrid to be received by the King, Father Rossi sent Teresa a further patent reiterating and elaborating her powers to found convents. The authorization was valid for all

Castile, but not (probably on account of its still-simmering discontent) Andalusia. The approval of the respective Bishop or Archbishop was required, but once it was obtained the Foundress might take two nuns from the Incarnation to form the nucleus for each new foundation. From Valencia, in reply to a request from Teresa, an even more important document was dispatched by the General on the eve of his departure from Spain – a patent authorizing the foundation in Castile of two priories for friars, subject to the consent of the Provincial and his predecessor in office. Teresa was beginning to see that the existence of her Discalced nuns would never be secure until a parallel reform was carried out amongst the friars. Pedro de Alcántara, the Bishop of Avila, and other supporters of the reform had favoured such a development and the General himself took soundings but let the matter drop on discovering the marked lack of enthusiasm amongst those who would be affected by the proposal. That Teresa, a mere woman without rank or resources, should be entrusted with the enterprise was a mark of extraordinary confidence. It would also have been presumptuous even to contemplate and totally beyond her powers without the promise of the 'great things' foretold by her voices. So ardent was her desire to see its fulfilment and so powerful her conviction that God meant to bring it about through her that – as she tells us – 'I seemed to see the foundations already made.'

The next four years were to prove a time of extraordinary activity. The contemplative became a 'gadabout' – as a hostile nuncio later dubbed her – but a gadabout for God, with a dedicated energy and capacity for practical affairs. The devotee of poverty was to show a shrewd head for business, and the humble nun a courteous and easy grace which won her the friendship of some of the greatest in the land. In that short space of time Teresa founded seven convents and reorganized another, launched the reform of the friars, wrote innumerable letters, the first nine chapters of her *Book of the Foundations* and other miscellaneous works, and all this at no cost to her inner spiritual life, but rather to its enrichment. The odds seemed heavily against success. There she was, she recalled, 'a poor Discalced nun with no one to help her except the Lord, well supplied with patents and good intentions but with no means of carrying them into effect'. Yet she was not in the least daunted. The humanly impossible seemed to her not only possible but, since it was God's will, certain. She would go forth in the strength of the Lord – the Lord who was pleased to 'show his power by putting heart into an ant'.

Teresa decided to make her next foundation at Medina del Campo, the flourishing commercial and international market centre to the north of Avila. It was apparently a decision reached after mature reflection rather than the result of any specific guidance revealed to her through locutions or visions. In her account of the foundation Teresa adduces several reasons for the choice. Fray Antonio de Heredia, whom she had known when he was Prior of the Carmelites in Avila, had recently been transferred to Medina; she believed she could count on his help, and in this she was not mistaken, for he was to become a leading figure in the Reform. Father Baltasar Alvarez, the confessor who had once treated her with harsh scepticism but later came to enjoy many mystical experiences himself, was now also there. Teresa could be sure too of his support and through him of the support of the many respected and well-to-do merchants who held the Jesuit in high esteem. Was it her acute intuition, or some revelation which she did not think it prudent to record in the pages of the *Foundations*, which persuaded Teresa of the help she might expect from such well-disposed laymen? Typical of these shrewd, influential and often deeply religious members of the Medina bourgeoisie – many of them of *converso* stock – were the rich merchants Simón Ruiz and Francisco de Dueñas. The great hospital founded by the former and the school which was once the palace of the Dueñas family still bear witness to their wealth and benefactions.

But opposition was only to be expected too. One grave prelate asserted that Teresa de Jesús was no better than an *alumbrado* or an impostor like Magdalena de la Cruz. Some declared she was crazy to think of founding when she had not a ducat of her own, others that a convent *sin renta* would be a burden on the town. The Augustinian friars were particularly dismayed at the prospect of fresh competitors for the alms of the faithful. The Vicar-General, who was administering the see in the absence of the Bishop, was reluctant to give his consent to the new foundation without taking further soundings. It was only after a number of leading citizens, both priests and laymen, had stated their opinions in due legal form and the consensus was found to be favourable that the necessary licence was issued. Amongst those warmly supporting the project were Francisco de Dueñas and Simón Ruiz. The administrator of the latter's hospital offered to rent his own house to the nuns whilst Fray Antonio de Heredia continued his efforts to find them a permanent home.

Cheered by the news from Medina and by a postulant's proffered dowry, which would at least cover the rent of the temporary accommodation she expected to find awaiting her, Teresa decided to set out at once. She was accompanied by the postulant, two nuns from St Joseph's, four from the Incarnation, and her chaplain, the genial Julián de Avila, who was to be her escort and negotiator on many such occasions. The road led through Gotarrendura, dear to her from childhood days, to Arévalo. There bad news awaited her. The owner of the rented house, under pressure from his Augustinian neighbours whom he did not wish to offend, had changed his mind and was unwilling to let the nuns move in. Fray Antonio was negotiating the purchase of another house, but its dilapidated condition rendered it at present uninhabitable.

The Foundress was at a loss, 'not knowing what to do with so many nuns'. If they turned back, the Discalced would become the laughing-stock of Avila. She sought the answer to her dilemma in

130

prayer. Someone brought word that Father Báñez, the Dominican whose support and advice had already proved so valuable in other crises, was in Arévalo. He assured her that the Augustinians would soon be placated and the new convent established. Fray Antonio arrived with further details. The tumbledown house had a large porch or entrance hall which was in fair condition and could serve as a chapel, and the lady who owned the house, he added, was staying not far from Arévalo. Teresa went to see her at once and told her of their difficulties. The lady proved sympathetic and gave her a letter to the caretaker instructing him to move out and do everything possible to help the nuns settle in. Teresa sent off all but her two nuns from St Joseph's to a cousin who happened to be the priest of a nearby parish, and dispatched Father Julián post-haste to Medina to prepare her arrival. Then, with their few belongings and the ornaments collected for their chapel, Teresa and her remaining companions climbed into a cart which rumbled on through the night towards Medina.

It was after midnight when they arrived; Teresa had thought it worth making a further detour in order to visit the Bishop of Avila who was staying with his sister and brother in their country house nearby. The Bishop, who had not been pleased at the prospect of Teresa's leaving Avila, was still the nuns' chief friend and protector, and his support could be valuable to them even though they were going outside his jurisdiction. They were about to enter unknown, and perhaps hostile, territory. Medina was not yet asleep, even at that late hour, for the morrow was *fiesta* and an added hazard would be the fierce bulls shortly be be loosed through the streets as a prelude to the day's sport. The driver took them by a roundabout route to the Carmelite monastery where Fray Antonio and Father Julián were awaiting the travellers. They unloaded the cart together in haste, and set off furtively carrying the vestments and sacred vessels needed for celebrating mass. 'We looked like gipsies who had been robbing churches', Julián recalled, and they thought themselves lucky to escape an encounter with some night patrol which would assuredly have clapped them all in jail.

Nuns, friars and caretaker bustled about clearing the house, or at least the entrance hall which was to do duty as a chapel, in time for the dawn mass. The place was in a far worse state than the optimistic Fray Antonio had led them to believe. 'It seems that the Lord was pleased to blind the eyes of the good Father so that he failed to see it was no fit place for putting the Holy Sacrament', Teresa observed ironically. There were gaps in the roof and piles of rubbish on the floor, and in places the walls had fallen in. They worked as if their lives depended on it, removing rubble, sweeping away the dirt and covering the crumbling walls with hangings which the caretaker produced from his mistress's store-cupboard. They had brought no nails with them, but Teresa found some old ones and extracted them from the walls. By dawn the makeshift chapel was beginning to look presentable.

Teresa saw the need for quick action. Once a chapel had entered into service, it could not easily be dismantled or the religious house attached to it dissolved. The celebration of the first Mass was therefore of the utmost importance. It denoted the official 'taking possession' of the new establishment, as the raising of the royal standard and the reading of a proclamation marked the 'taking possession' of territory discovered and claimed for Spain by the *conquistadores*. But one more formality was required in that legalistic age before the 'taking possession' could be regarded as complete and the nuns feel secure. The proceedings must be recorded in a sworn affidavit. So a notary was found and roused from his bed by the resourceful Fray Antonio. A document was drawn up declaring that a new convent had been founded with the blessing and permission of the relevant authorities. At dawn, on the feast of the Assumption of the Blessed Virgin, the small bell which the nuns had brought with them rang out to announce the glad tidings to the people of Medina del Campo.

Teresa was filled with joy and gratitude. 'It is always the greatest consolation to me to see one more church where the Holy Sacrament is', she wrote. But euphoria quickly gave way almost to panic. When daylight came she could see just how flimsy were the chapel walls behind the camouflage of hangings, and what danger the Sacrament might run from desecration at the hands of sacrilegious breakers-in, specially 'in the dangerous times we now live in on account of those Lutherans'. The quarterly fairs brought many foreigners to Medina, and who could tell whether there might not be Frenchmen or Flemings amongst them infected with heresy? Teresa arranged for armed men to stand guard over the Holy Sacrament, but her fears kept her awake at night, and she would rise from her bed to peep into the chapel and make sure that all was well.

The Devil too was busy counter-attacking, just as he had done after Teresa had moved into St Joseph's at Avila, with other fears and doubts. She saw how much still remained to be done before the new foundation could be consolidated, and she could dwell only on her own sins and inadequacies instead of on the Lord's mercies. Again the thought returned to torment her: how could she be sure that God had really entrusted her with this mission and that she was not the victim of some diabolical illusion? A Jesuit father sent to her by Father Baltasar Alvarez somewhat allayed her fears, and she kept them from the daughters who were sharing her trials lest their innocent faith might be shaken too. The physical conditions under which they were all living in the half-ruined house were deplorable, yet they never complained. After a week, a charitable citizen offered them the use of the upper storey of his own home. Teresa sent for the four nuns she had left in the care of her cousin near Arévalo, and together they converted their new quarters into a temporary convent, using the largest room as a chapel, whilst work went on to make the dilapidated house habitable. Two months later they were able to move into their new home.

The foundation at Medina del Campo had turned out well after all. The convent quickly found friends and benefactors and was soon attracting vocations. Teresa's eyes were already fixed on the next goal – the promotion of reform amongst the friars. Fray Antonio surprised her by offering to be the first recruit. At first she thought he was joking; the prior was a good man, of dignified appearance and settled and scholarly habits, and used to wielding authority. Could he stand the privations, and perhaps the persecutions, of a stricter calling? She advised him to wait awhile and test himself in secret for such an exacting vocation. Teresa was also told of another friar who had just entered the Order but was already thinking of leaving it for the more solitary life of the Carthusians. She persuaded him that he could find what he was looking for with the reformed Carmelites who were to be the counterpart of her Discalced nuns. The ardent young friar agreed – on condition that he was not made to wait too long. Teresa intuitively recognized his exceptional qualities. Beneath the reserve and austerity she sensed a keen intellect and an intense and exquisite sensitivity – the earliest records refer to him as an 'art student' or 'artist-friar' – and the passionate, unyielding dedication of a soul already committed to the quest for sanctity. He was of delicate and diminutive build; 'although he is small in stature, I hold him to be great in the sight of God', she wrote to a friend. To her nuns she exclaimed in an outburst of elation: 'God be praised, my daughters; I have already a friar and a half for a foundation!' The 'half' was to become known as St John of the Cross.

The news that Teresa de Jesús had successfully founded another St Joseph's spread quickly and fired the enthusiasm of would-be benefactors and benefactresses. At Medina, the pious merchants had given her their support; now the nobility was to extend its gracious patronage. The Bishop of Avila's brother, Don Bernardino de Mendoza, whose gay bachelor life had left him little time for such thoughts until he met Teresa, offered her his country house outside Valladolid. Doña Luisa de la Cerda, anxious to make a propitiatory offering on behalf of her late husband, urged her to found a convent at Malagón, a small town to the south of Madrid over which he had acquired seignorial rights. But first Teresa was requested to undertake a task of some delicacy. María de Yepes, the courageous and dedicated woman who had walked barefoot to Rome to obtain the Pope's permission to found a house of strict observance, had finally, in the teeth of much bitter opposition, started one at Alcalá de Henares. Though loosely under the aegis of the Carmelite Order it was in fact following an idiosyncratic and fanatically austere mode of life of its own. Teresa was to use her tact and experience to persuade the saintly but eccentric foundress, who was now also its Prioress, to moderate the penitential excesses of the community and adapt it to the more sober and humane interpretation of the Primitive Rule set out in her Constitutions. The Prioress had imbued her twenty young nuns with her own uncompromising spirit. Even after the new Constitutions had been officially adopted, some of them continued to emulate her austerities and to spurn the use of stockings and *alpargatas*. Teresa makes no mention in her extant writings of her mission to Alcalá, and one is left with the impression that it can have been neither pleasant nor very successful. She must have been relieved when the ubiquitous Father Báñez appeared and gave her the sensible advice to resume founding convents of her own and not to concern herself further with those of others. After some three months in Alcalá we find her back again with Doña Luisa in Toledo.

Doña Luisa's project raised a serious scruple in Teresa's mind. Malagón was little more than a village where nuns could not possibly subsist on public charity. Their convent would need to be endowed. Teresa had hitherto resolutely set her face against any such arrangement and had insisted that the Discalced must live *sin renta*. Would she not be betraying the spirit of the Reform if she were now to accept the generous offers made to her by Doña

Luisa? Once again she had recourse to Father Báñez and accepted his ruling with surprising equanimity. Since she had been permitted, and indeed encouraged, to make foundations, the Dominican argued, it would be wrong to neglect this opportunity; her nuns could still live in virtue and poverty, even though their basic necessities were provided for. So Malagón became Teresa's third foundation. One of the novices who took the veil there was María de San José, the lively, quick-witted maid of honour María de Salazar who had listened spellbound to Teresa's talk six years before and peeped into Doña Luisa's guest-room to watch the saint in ecstasy.

Of the course of Teresa's mystical life in this year of intense practical activity we know but little. The autobiography in which she had so vividly described its early phases stops short before this date, and her *Book of the Foundations* is mainly concerned with the matters indicated by its title. In answer to her prayer, the raptures which she had found so embarrassing when they came upon her in public seem to have become less frequent. The aura of the supernatural nevertheless still hovered around the busy Foundress, to judge from the depositions made later in her process of beatification. We are told of a mighty levitation sweeping her off her feet during mass at Malagón, and of the Host being miraculously conveyed to the lips of the enraptured saint. Another account describes a vision in the refectory when Christ appeared to her bleeding more profusely from the wounds inflicted by the present sins of the world than from the thorns of his crown. In Alcalá news had reached her of the sudden death of Don Bernardino. It was revealed to her that his salvation was in jeopardy and that he would remain in purgatory until mass had been celebrated at the convent he had wished to found at Valladolid. This she records in her *Foundations* and adds that, though she was anxious after Malagón to found in Toledo itself, she decided for the sake of Don Bernardino to press on to Valladolid. The vision was repeated in Medina when she was revisiting her nuns. Whilst at prayer in her oratory, 'the Lord told me to make haste, for his soul was suffering greatly'. With the patronage of the Bishop of Avila and his sister Doña María the necessary formalities for the Valladolid foundation were quickly completed. During the Mass which marked the 'taking of possession', Teresa had a vision of the departed *caballero*, 'his countenance radiant and joyful' after his release from Purgatory.

Don Bernardino's house was pleasantly situated on low ground between the banks of two rivers. But it was to prove so unhealthy that the community had to be transferred to another in the centre of the city. The nuns went down with fever, and Teresa became so ill that she thought she was dying. It was some months before she was well enough to return to Toledo where Father Pablo Hernández, the Jesuit who had been her confessor there, had persuaded a pious and wealthy merchant to bequeath part of his fortune for the endowment of a Carmelite convent and chapel. From her sick-bed Teresa sent power of attorney to Father Hernández and begged Doña Luisa to use her influence to obtain the necessary permits for the foundation. This was to prove more difficult than she expected. Toledo already possessed twenty-four convents and communities of *beatas*, with a total of some 1,200 nuns. No new foundations were allowed without special permission from the King. Consent had also to be obtained from the City Council and from the Archbishop – or rather, from his Vicar-General, since the Primate of all Spain had been suspended from office to answer charges of heresy brought against him by the all-powerful Inquisition.

By the spring of 1569, when Teresa was back in Toledo, negotiations for the new foundation were at a standstill. Father Hernández had been transferred to other duties and Doña Luisa was showing herself strangely reluctant to further her friend's designs. The situation was one of some delicacy, as we can deduce from the guarded references to it in Teresa's *Foundations*. Neither the nobles nor the wealthy merchants were wholly disinterested in their munificent offers of patronage. In Spain, as in other Catholic lands, the custom had grown up of endowing chantry chapels where masses might be said for the souls of the illustrious dead. The testator Martín Ramírez, and his brother and executor Alonso Alvarez Ramírez, were merchants and in all probability *conversos*, though they may have used their wealth to secure (as Teresa's grandfather had done in his time) a formal certificate attesting their nobility and 'pure blood'. They were no doubt as anxious to raise their social status and demonstrate their piety by some imposing endowment as the aristocratic 'Old Christians' were determined to prevent them. Doña Luisa de la Cerda, despite her charitable disposition and her affection for Teresa, was unwilling to take a stand against the prejudices of her caste. She prudently washed her hands of the affair and only reappeared on the scene when Providence and Teresa's determination had overcome all obstacles and the convent had been established.

For more than two months Teresa tried in vain to obtain a licence, find suitable accommodation, and settle affairs with the executors of Martín Ramírez. Her task was complicated by the insistence of Diego Ortiz, who was acting for his elderly father-in-law Alonso Alvarez Ramírez and was for ever raising pettifogging quibbles and new conditions which Teresa found unacceptable. 'Although he was a theologian and a very good man,' she writes, 'he was more unyielding in his opinions than Alonso Alvarez and less open to reason.' The theologian, in short, seems to have been a thoroughly tiresome character, though we find Teresa later writing to him, or referring to him in her letters, with her usual warmth and courtesy. The Vicar-General, who had persisted in his refusal to grant a licence, capitulated more quickly once Teresa had secured a personal interview with him. After she had spoken her mind 'with a great firmness which the Lord gave me', he agreed to the foundation provided it had no endowment – a condition which was the very reverse of that which the opponents of the first St Joseph's had wished to impose. In Avila, they had feared that a convent *sin renta* would become a financial burden on the town; in Toledo, they were more concerned with preventing *conversos* from gaining prestige. So it began to look as if Teresa would get her convent, and on terms which she had always favoured – without endowment and the obligations due to a patron.

But where then was she to find the house and helpers she still needed? Toledo had other preoccupations. The streets were astir with armed men mustering to suppress the rebellion which had broken out in the mountains round Granada, where the Moriscos had never genuinely accepted the faith and customs forced on them by their Christian conquerors. One day after Mass, a young man called Antonio de Andrada – a student, to judge from his down-at-heel appearance – approached Teresa and offered his services. He had been informed by his Franciscan confessor that the Mother was in trouble and he thought he could help her. Teresa's companions were incredulous when she told them of the unexpected offer. How could an impecunious student be likely to help them? And was it quite proper? The future prioress, Isabel de Santo Domingo, was slightly scandalized at the thought of nuns mixing with such dubious characters. Teresa made light of their misgivings. The youth had struck her as sincere and she sent for him and told him frankly of her difficulties. Andrada replied confidently that, although he had no money to give them, he knew the city inside out and was sure he could find somewhere suitable where they could live. The following day he was back with the keys of a house which Teresa inspected and rented on the spot, a charitable merchant standing guarantor for the rent. As it was small, the house next door was rented too, although the women who lodged there were told nothing in case they raised difficulties. Where the service of God was at stake, Teresa acted decisively, even ruthlessly. She was determined to move in with the minimum of delay and publicity and to face Toledo with a *fait accompli*. Their only belongings were a blanket, a couple of straw pallets, two holy pictures, a hand-bell, and some sacred vessels borrowed for the celebration of the mass. The nuns feared that the student, when he realized they were even poorer than himself, would no longer bother to help them. But Teresa brushed their fears aside.

Andrada and a mason he had brought with him worked through the night helping the nuns adapt their home to its new functions. Access to the chapel had to be through the house next door. When they started to pull down the partition wall, the women woke up in terror and cried out that robbers were breaking in. By some miracle of persuasion, and with the help of 100 *reales* borrowed from Doña Luisa's butler, Teresa managed to appease the indignant tenants; 'the Lord calmed them', she simply tells us. She also had to face the wrath of the lady who had rented her the house without knowing it was to be converted into a convent. More serious still was the anger of the gentlemen of the City Council on discovering that a mere woman had dared to make a foundation under their noses without their consent. They sent a threatening letter demanding the immediate suspension of all further chapel services. Teresa returned a conciliatory reply promising that, although she had official permission for the foundation and was not obliged to obey them, she would do as they wished. With the help of a friendly canon of the Cathedral she then obtained written confirmation of the Vicar-General's consent, and the Council found itself forced to acquiesce.

Negotiations with the Ramírez heirs were also resumed and a complicated legal arrangement worked out to satisfy their wish to endow chaplaincies without infringing the Vicar-General's conditions or the convent's independence. The 12,000 ducats of Don Martín's legacy eventually purchased a new house which remained the nuns' home for many years. It was a triumph of Teresan faith and diplomacy, but one which left her disconsolate rather than jubilant. 'When I saw that our poverty was coming to an end,' she writes, 'my distress was as great as if I had been robbed of many precious jewels and left quite penniless.' Her nuns looked equally crestfallen, and when asked the reason replied: 'How can it be otherwise, Mother, for now it seems that we are no longer in need!'

Their need had indeed been great during those first days at the new St Joseph's, and merrily borne. At night they had only their capes and the one blanket between them, and when the Foundress, who felt the cold keenly, asked her daughters to cover her more warmly, they told her that she already had on everything there was. They forgot their discomfort in laughter. There was no brushwood for a fire – 'not so much as a few sticks of wood on which to grill a sardine' – until someone providentially left a bunch of faggots in the chapel. Doña Luisa, who had so generously welcomed them to her house, seemed to have forgotten their existence. 'Why it was I do not know,' Teresa comments, 'unless God wished us to learn what a great blessing there is in that virtue [poverty]. I did not ask anything from her, as I am loath to cause others trouble, and perhaps it did not occur to her, for however much she gives us I am always needing something more.' Another lesson which her experience with the Toledans taught her was the futility of all their pretensions to honour, rank and privilege. 'I had never – God be praised – bothered much about these things,' she tells us, 'and always set more store by virtue than by lineage.' But now 'the Lord was pleased to give me more light on this, and once he told me how little all this rank and lineage would count before God's judgement-seat, and he rebuked me sternly for lending an ear to those who talked about it.' It was a warning which was to stand her in good stead in the greater trials ahead.

For the next two weeks Teresa worked tirelessly to put her new house in order. The hostile needed to be appeased, the workmen supervised, and nuns summoned from her other convents and settled in. It was Whitsun eve, and the little community had gathered in the refectory. Teresa was relieved and grateful to think that they could now celebrate the festival in peace; she felt so happy, she recalls, that 'I could scarcely eat a mouthful'. A flustered sister approached to say that a messenger from the Princess of Eboli was in the parlour and demanding to speak with her urgently. Princess and Foundress had first met in Doña Luisa's house six years before. Doña Ana de Mendoza y de la Cerda was married to Ruy Gómez, the most affable of husbands and the most powerful man in Spain after the King. She seemed to enjoy every blessing: high birth, the titles of Princess and Duchess, wealth, youth, beauty, children, the intimate favour of the Queen (and of the King too, malicious tongues added). But one thing struck her as still lacking: the patronage of her own convent and of the fashionable 'saint' of the day. And the Princess was accustomed to having her every whim obeyed like a law.

Teresa was nevertheless determined not to comply with her imperious summons, though the coach sent to fetch her was at the door. It seemed essential that she should remain in Toledo to consolidate the still precarious foundation. The messenger insisted, declaring that his mistress and the Prince had returned specially to their palace at Pastrana to receive her. The Foundress was courteous but firm; she sent the worried messenger off to get a meal, telling him that she would give him a letter for the Princess which would explain everything to her satisfaction. But how could she put matters in such a way that would not mortally offend two such important personages? In her perplexity Teresa knelt before the Holy Sacrament in the chapel and implored enlightenment. But the divine guidance which came was as unexpected as it was clear; Teresa was not to refuse, but to go at once. Even more was at stake in Pastrana than the projected foundation of a convent. And she was to be sure to take the Rule and Constitutions with her.

Natural prudence told her to stay in Toledo; the locution ordered her to go. Could she be sure that this inner voice of hers was not an illusion or the work of the Devil? Teresa turned, as she did always in moments of grave doubt, to her confessor. The latter, at this time, happened to be the Dominican friar Vicente Barrón, who had been her father's confessor and also given her good counsel in Avila. He came at once, and after Teresa had explained her troubles and he had paused awhile in thought he gave it as his opinion that she should go. She had said nothing to him of the locution, and now all her doubts were removed. The messenger was informed and travelling companions were selected. On Whit Monday, 30 May 1569, they set off for Pastrana.

The road led south through Madrid, where two other great ladies wished to speak with Teresa — Princess Juana, the King's devout sister, and Doña Leonor de Mascareñas, who had sponsored the foundation at Alcalá and many other works of charity. Through Doña Leonor Teresa made the acquaintance of two unusual Italians who were proposing to lead the life of hermits. Teresa persuaded them to become Discalced Carmelite friars, in whose ranks we shall meet them again.

Her brief stay in Madrid was also notable for an episode of which she says nothing herself but which is mentioned by several witnesses in her process of beatification. Teresa is alleged to have received the following laconic and enigmatic locution: 'Tell the King to remember King Saul!' This admonition she is said to have duly transmitted in a letter entrusted to Princess Juana for her royal brother. That the King's subjects, however humble, did not hesitate to approach him with their complaints, petitions and visionary exhortations there is ample evidence. We know that Teresa later wrote him a letter imploring his intervention in favour of the Reform. Did she, whilst in Madrid, obtain an audience, and if so what was the meaning of the strange message she conveyed to him? We read that Saul lost the divine favour and was eventually replaced by David because he disregarded the command to destroy the heathen Amalekites and all their possessions. Philip, at the time of Teresa's alleged communication, had not yet crushed the rebellious Moriscos, and though he had placed the young and energetic Don Juan of Austria in command of his armies the prince's hands were tied by the appointment of a supervisory council. Were the Moriscos then to be treated like the Amalekites, and was Don Juan a potential David? The implications of Teresa's alleged locution seem uncharacteristically melodramatic. At all events, the rebels were destroyed with exemplary thoroughness, and the Morisco remnants expelled altogether from Spain forty years later; the prudent, suspicious King needed no supernatural enlightenment to see the possible threat posed by a half-brother who was idolized by the people. If we are puzzled by the affair it is worth bearing in mind that Teresa did not always herself understand the full meaning of the messages she believed she had to pass on to others. A note found amongst the saint's private papers and apparently written a year after this incident may perhaps refer to the mysterious locution:

> When I was thinking about a warning the Lord had given me to pass on, and how (although I begged that I might) I did not understand what it meant and so feared it could come from the Devil, he told me that it was not so, and that he would explain it to me when the time was right.

In Pastrana Teresa and her companions were given a princely welcome. Without waiting to consult them, Doña Ana had arbitrarily selected and stripped a house intended for the convent, so her guests were given temporary rooms in the palace. Teresa saw at once that the house would be too small; furthermore, the endowment proposed for it would be insufficient, and the nuns would be left continually dependent on their capricious benefactress. The latter insisted that Teresa should take a certain protégée of hers who was already a nun of another Order, and kept pressing other demands on her which the Foundress felt unable to accept. Her stay under Doña Ana's roof grew more and more intolerable, 'so I determined', she writes, 'to leave without founding rather than do what she kept asking'. But her voices told Teresa that there was more at stake in Pastrana than the founding of just another convent. The divine plan was beginning to become clear; it included the establishment of a monastery for Discalced friars. The Carmelite General had given permission for two such foundations. One had already been started by Antonio de Heredia and John of the Cross, whom she had met in Medina. The second would be founded here by the two Italian hermits under the patronage of the Prince. They were shortly to be joined by Baltasar Nieto, one of the rebellious friars previously disciplined by the General in Andalusia – a disquieting hint of the storm-clouds which were soon to gather over Pastrana.

The Princess was twenty-nine and at the height of her charms. Portraits show her as small and delicate in build, with imperious, finely-chiselled features, and always wearing a black patch over one eye to conceal injury received from a fencing accident or – by less romantic accounts – because of a bad squint; rather than appearing as a blemish it seemed to add a touch of piquancy to her haughty beauty. She was a creature of violent moods, impulses of generosity and fervent piety alternating with ungovernable rages and implacable resentment. The Princess had never met anyone like Teresa. Admiration, sincere at first, gave way to incredulous rancour on discovering she could not bend the Foundress to her will. Doña Ana soon found a malicious way both to indulge her curiosity and to vent her spite. She had heard from her aunt Doña Luisa, who had been asked by Teresa to forward the manuscript to the saintly John of Avila, that the nun had written an extraordinary account of her mystical experiences. Both Ruy Gómez and Doña Ana pressed their guest to let them read it, promising the most inviolable secrecy. Teresa, who had stood firm against so many demands, reluctantly consented. Soon the palace servants were cracking sarcastic jokes over the pages intended only for the eyes of learned confessors, and their mistress was enjoying the fun, and the embarrassment of her guest, more than anyone. Teresa had never known a more agonizing shame and humiliation.

Teresa says little in her *Foundations* about this wretched time beyond stating that 'Ruy Gómez, with his good sense – which was very great – smoothed things over and brought his wife to see reason'. She endured the martyrdom for the sake of the two foundations, and by the middle of July, when both had been completed, she took her leave with relief, promising to return in a year's time for the ceremony of clothing the two ex-hermits. The Princess insisted that, in keeping with her hosts' dignity, their guest should travel in the ducal coach. On reaching Toledo one last humiliation awaited Teresa. As she alighted at her convent, a priest thrust himself forward exlaiming: 'So you are the "saint" who has been taking everybody in! And driving around in a coach too!' Her nuns clustered round her, shielding their Foundress from the priest's insults and consoling her by declaring that he must be out of his mind. 'He is the only one with the courage to tell me my faults!' she replied calmly. The coach returned to Pastrana with Isabel de Santo Domingo, chosen to be prioress on account of her sound common sense, tact and firmness of character. But Teresa vowed that she would herself never again travel by coach, if she could possibly avoid it. A cart or the back of a donkey would be more than she deserved.

Two more foundations were to follow in less than a year. The first, arranged with the help of the Rector of the Jesuit College, was in the university city of Salamanca, where houses were hard to come by on account of the many students seeking accommodation. Teresa was fortunate to have one offered her by a well-wisher, though legal wrangles over the purchase dragged on for years. The Foundress had now learned that the 'taking possession' could be valid without the need to keep the Holy Sacrament displayed in the chapel. This was a great relief to her, since the house had been left in a lamentable state by the student tenants who had been hurriedly evicted. The memory of the first night passed in the future convent inspired some of her liveliest pages:

We spent the night of All Saints, my companion and I, quite alone. I tell you, my sisters, that when I recall the terror of my companion María del Sacramento, a nun who was older than myself and a great servant of God, I really want to laugh. The house was very large and rambling, and with a great number of attics. My companion could not get it out of her head that some of the students, who had been very annoyed at being evicted, had hidden themselves away somewhere in it. This they could easily have done, for there were plenty of suitable places. We shut ourselves up in a room where there was some straw, which is the first thing I had provided when making the foundation, for having that we did not lack for beds. We slept on this straw that night, with a couple of blankets that had been lent us. When my companion saw herself shut up in that room, her fears about the students somewhat abated, though she kept looking this way and that, still in some uneasiness. The Devil made matters worse by putting fearsome thoughts into her mind so as to upset me too, for having a weak heart I easily get alarmed. I asked her why she kept looking about her, as no one could possibly get in. 'I am thinking, Mother, what you would do here all by yourself if I should die now!' she said to me. Were that to happen, I should indeed find it very dreadful. I could not help my mind dwelling for a while on the thought and even becoming rather frightened myself. For although I am not scared of dead bodies, I always come over faint at the sight of them, even when I am not alone. And the tolling of the bells made matters worse – for it was All Saints' Eve, as I have said – so that the Devil was in a fair way to distract our minds with childish fears. So I said: 'Sister, if that should happen, it will be time enough then to think what I should do. But now let me go to sleep.' As we had had two restless nights, sleep soon drove away our fear. The next day more nuns arrived, and we lost it altogether.

Alba de Tormes, where Teresa made her next foundation, is

only fifteen miles from Salamanca. But from Pastrana, which she briefly revisited as promised for the clothing of her two Discalced friars, it was separated not only by a distance several times as great but by the gulf which divided the Spanish Court into two factions – the partisans of the Prince of Eboli, who generally stood for moderation and conciliation, and those of the haughty, intolerant and inflexible soldier, the third Duke of Alba. That the Foundress was able to move so impartially between two such irreconcilable camps is a measure of the extraordinary tact and lack of self-interest with which she went about her mission. The Duke himself was in the Netherlands striving to crush the rebellious heretics. Teresa's foundation was made under the aegis of the administrator of his estates, the *contador* Francisco Velázquez, who had rescued Salamanca University from bankruptcy and doubled its revenues before passing into the Duke's service. He was in all probability a *converso* of the same pious, canny breed as those who had helped Teresa in Medina and Toledo. His wife Teresa de Laíz, whom she describes as 'the daughter of well-born parents, of noble stock and "clean" blood', was equally eager for the foundation. The couple, to their grief, were childless. But the lady had been favoured with a dream or vision in which St Andrew told her that they were to nurture a family of a different kind. The apostle had appeared to her standing beside a well in a courtyard, with a glimpse of flowers and green fields beyond. As soon as she saw the house awaiting her in Alba, the *contador*'s wife recognized it as the place revealed in this prophecy. From Teresa's sister Juana and her husband Juan de Ovalle, who lived in Alba, and from others as well, she learned of the convents of Discalced Carmelites which were beginning to spring up all over Castile. The meaning of the revelation was now clear. Her 'family' was to be a community of nuns, and they should live in the house which she and her husband promptly made over to them.

With the blessing of the Duchess, the endowment generously provided by the *contador* and the assistance of John of the Cross, who joined them not only to offer his spiritual ministrations but also to help the masons with his own hands, the nuns took possession of their new home at the beginning of 1571. Preparations would have been completed earlier had not Teresa been called away to cope with troubles which had arisen in her convent at Medina. A niece of the rich philanthropist Simón Ruiz had become a novice there and wished to make over to the convent her huge dowry of 8,000 ducats. Her relatives were indignant at the proposal and demanded at least in return the sort of patronage rights which had caused so much discord in Toledo. Father Salazar, who had adopted an equivocal position over Teresa's first foundation in Avila and had recently been re-elected Provincial, had reasons of his own for siding with the wealthy Ruiz relatives against the nuns of his own Order. But the novice, the Prioress and the whole community stood firm and refused to bow to pressure. The Prioress was Inés de Jesús, a cousin of Teresa, to whom she now turned for help. Her three years' term of office was nearly up, but with Teresa's backing she was re-elected in preference to Teresa de Quesada, a nun from the Incarnation who was favoured by Father Salazar as likely to prove more pliable. Furious at their defiance, the Provincial overruled the nuns, who strongly resented having one of the Calced imposed upon them, and declared his protégée elected. On the Foundress he served an order of excommunication and immediate expulsion from Medina.

It was a high-handed and unjust act, for Teresa had been vested by the General with full powers over her convents and also held papal briefs to the same effect. But she did not attempt to defend herself, or even to plead stay of execution on the grounds of ill health or the winter weather. Obedience had ever been for her the supreme virtue, and the humble submission expected from her daughters she practised unsparingly herself. She left the convent at once with one nun as a companion, hired a donkey from a water-carrier, and took the road to Avila. How different from those journeys in a ducal carriage which she had vowed never to repeat!

They set off in the bitter December night and arrived exhausted but undismayed at St Joseph's. The Foundress had never before been treated with such harshness by a superior but she did not complain or repine. 'Daughter, obedience gives strength!' her voices had assured her, and she found it to be true. The lines she inscribed in her breviary summed up Teresa's simple but heroic creed:

Let nothing perturb you, nothing frighten you.
All things pass;
God does not change.
Patience achieves everything.
Whoever has God lacks nothing.
God alone suffices.

In the confused and difficult months ahead Teresa needed all her God-given fortitude. Even though the Provincial mastered his wrath and dared not keep her long in disgrace, Teresa could now give him only her obedience, not her trust. Her own position was far from clear. Although Prioress of St Joseph's, she was still a nun seconded from the unreformed community at the Incarnation. Her fledgling foundations needed her constant guidance and frequently her presence. She revisited Alba, Salamanca and then Medina. Her return to that scene of her recent disgrace was discreetly triumphant. Teresa de Quesada was a good woman, and indeed a friend from their days together at the Incarnation. She had been a mere tool in the hands of the Provincial and only awaited a suitable opportunity to return to her own convent. It came with the visit to Medina of the Apostolic Delegate, a dignitary vested with papal powers to authorize new foundations, inspect existing ones, and depose or transfer office-holders. Father Pedro Fernández, Apostolic Delegate and Provincial of the Dominicans, was a just and vigorous administrator, if not the equal of his Carmelite colleague in intrigue. Though distrustful of reputedly visionary nuns, he firmly supported Teresa once he had convinced himself of her sincerity and innocence. Her namesake from the Incarnation was only too glad to resign, and the nuns enthusiastically elected the Foundress as their Prioress.

Father Salazar now made an unexpected and subtle move. When the Apostolic Delegate went on to Avila and visited the Incarnation, Salazar persuaded the Dominican that it badly needed reforming. And who, he suggested, could better undertake this task than Teresa de Jesús? Teresa was filled with foreboding and tried desperately to evade this unwelcome responsibility. She feared it was a pretext to lure her back to her old allegiance and allow the Calced to swallow up the Discalced. Far from promoting the Reform, the project could well sound its death-knell. But the Apostolic Delegate, with the best of intentions, was as much in favour of the proposal as the Carmelite Provincial. He did however take one step which, though it might further complicate her personal status, at least protected Teresa from any danger of permanent reabsorption into the Incarnation: he declared her formally transferred to the community at Salamanca. Teresa was also permitted to reaffirm her vow of following the Primitive Rule, no matter whether she was in a convent of the Mitigated Observance, to the end of her days.

Teresa could no longer resist the strange destiny which was to send her back as Prioress to the community she had left nearly nine years before. She was conscious of acting under the orders of one higher than any Provincial or Apostolic Delegate. 'Take courage', her voices told her. 'It is my will for you. It will not be so hard as you think. Gain will come to those houses where you now fear only loss. Do not resist, for my power is great.' But when her daughters at Medina learned that she was leaving them and she saw their dismay, Teresa broke down. She threw herself into the arms of a novice and sobbed. Then she grew still, lost in ecstasy. When she came to herself, she hastened to cover her confusion by exclaiming, 'Oh what trouble my weak heart is giving me! Go and bring me a little water!'

Teresa was not unaware of the irony of her position. The

Provincial, whom she believed to be basically hostile to the Reform, now figured as her chief defender. Her authority was to be imposed on a defiant community in the same way as that of her namesake had been imposed against the wishes of her nuns and herself at Medina. *Fiat voluntas tua!* (Thy will be done!) she cried in anguish, and a strange calm and strength seemed to be given her. The battle was to be joined in October, and after returning to her little stronghold of St Joseph's Teresa fired the opening shot. It took the form of a message to the Incarnation – although she had not yet assumed office – requesting the removal of all lay persons – relatives, friends and hangers-on – who used the place merely as a sort of hostel and constituted a grave distraction and drain on its inadequate resources. Somewhat surprisingly, and despite much grumbling, she was obeyed. In return, the numerous nuns who had gone to live with friends or family began to rejoin their convent. The first step had been taken towards restoring the integrity and purpose of the community. But there remained a serious cleavage between the nuns who were well disposed towards their new prioress and those who opposed her. Even amongst Teresa's partisans there were many who felt indignant over the Provincial's interference and so were only lukewarm in her defence.

The opposition came to a head when the new prioress made her formal entry into the Incarnation. The Corregidor and officers of the law accompanied the procession in the hope of averting trouble by their presence. A crowd of spectators followed, some bragging that they would keep the intruders out by force, others merely curious. The Provincial, flanked by two sturdy friars, headed the procession. Teresa, wearing her white cape and carrying the tutelary statue of St Joseph which she took with her on all her foundations, trod the familiar path from the city walls and sat down on a stone outside the porch to wait quietly whilst the friars forced their way into the church and through the small door which led to the nuns' enclosure. A throng of angry women screaming out insults and protesting that they would have nothing to do with the Provincial or his nominee attempted to bar their way. The hubbub could be heard from far away. The Provincial, disregarding the abuse and interruption, read out the decree installing the new Prioress and raised his voice above the tumult to ask: 'Will you not have Mother Teresa de Jesús, then?' Teresa's supporters took heart and one of them shouted back: 'Yes, we want her and we love her!' They surged forward to receive the Prioress, and in the scuffle the cross was knocked to the ground. The friars began to intone the *Te Deum* and the hostile cries and jeers were drowned. Gradually the storm subsided.

Teresa, as if quite unconcerned at the hurly-burly, made her way towards the Holy Sacrament and fell on her knees before it. She could be heard murmuring something about the Devil being to blame for all the fuss, not the nuns. When she saw that some women had fainted and others appeared to be suffering from palpitations, she got up and leant tenderly over them. They grew calm at her touch. It was a holy relic she had with her, she told them, that had this healing virtue. One novice had been so upset by the scandalous scene that she tried to force her way into the Provincial's presence to renounce her habit there and then. A nun led her to Teresa, who took her by the hand and calmed the girl with her blessing. Only a small clique, dubbed the *valerosas* or 'valiant ones', continued their vociferous remonstrances. Teresa, they declared, was a willing stooge of the Provincial, who wanted to impose a Prioress to 'reform' them against their will and in disregard of the conditions under which they had accepted the Mitigated Rule.

The following afternoon the nuns held a chapter to give formal obedience to their new prioress. Teresa entered the church and went, as if from habit, to her old place in the choir. All eyes were turned towards the prioral stall which the nuns saw to their astonishment was already occupied. There sat a life-sized statue of the Blessed Virgin, holding the keys of the convent in her hands. Teresa moved to the foot of the statue and began to address her nuns. They had a new prioress indeed, she told them, as they could see for themselves. With such a saint at its head, what great things could not the community expect? Teresa had come under obedience, unworthy though she was, merely to act for her. She would work with them, learn with them, strive to make progress with them. Their welfare, both physical and spiritual, was her only concern. They should follow the path which God wished for them; she would not force on them any unfamiliar Rule of her own devising. The nuns were amazed, and some deeply moved, by her words. Even the *valerosas*, who had come prepared to refuse their obedience and make a scene, were abashed. Teresa's candour and humility had transformed what might have been a *coup de théâtre* into the symbolic opening of a new and happier phase in the life of the convent.

The first sign of change was a marked improvement in the lamentable material conditions under which the nuns had been living. Often there was simply not enough food to go round. With great energy and resourcefulness Teresa began raising funds. The Duchess of Alba sent 100 ducats, the brother of one of the nuns offered a monthly subsidy to eighty of the poorest inmates, and other alms flowed in. The neediest and the sick had the first call on Teresa's charity. The poverty from which the Incarnation was suffering was not the apostolic poverty, willingly sought for the love of Christ, which she wanted for her small Discalced communities, but a poverty caused by neglect and thwarted worldliness, and it was bitterly resented. Teresa worked late into the night struggling with the convent's innumerable administrative problems, but replenishing the springs of her spiritual life with prayer. With the nuns she was always approachable, listening patiently to their troubles and complaints, consoling, encouraging, diverting them. Even the *valerosas* found their rancour melting away in the warmth of her love, and some were transformed into devoted supporters. Her chiding was gentle but could sometimes harden into an awe-inspiring severity. The relatives and friends who waited around the parlour had always been tiresome and Teresa found means of discouraging this source of distraction. One gallant, vexed at finding his attentions no longer welcome, summoned the Prioress to the parlour and started berating her. She answered with spirit that if he continued to pester her daughters she would complain to the King, who would have his head cut off. The man slunk off in alarm and never showed himself there again.

After only a few weeks Teresa could write to her friend Doña Luisa at Toledo:

Glory to God, there is peace here – and that is no small blessing! We have gradually been cutting down their distractions and giving them less freedom, which they have been taking in good part – for there is certainly a great deal of virtue in this house – but a change of habits can be death, as the saying goes. They are putting up with it all very well and treat me with much respect. But there are 130 of them, after all, and Your Ladyship will understand what trouble I am having with getting things straight. But even in the midst of this Babylon I still manage to keep my peace of mind, which I take to be a special favour from our Lord.

Four months later she wrote to Doña María de Mendoza, the Bishop's sister:

The Lord be praised for the change he has wrought in them. The most recalcitrant are now more contented and get on better with me. This Lent no visitors have been allowed, either women or men – not even parents – which is something quite new for this house. They put up with everything and are very peaceful. Some of them are really great servants of God, and almost all are better than they were.

There was one difficulty which Teresa prudently refrained from mentioning to her friend: little or no support was forthcoming from her nuns' confessors. The latter were Carmelite friars of the Mitigated Rule who jealously guarded their prerogatives and showed little sympathy for the stricter standards encouraged by the Foundress. Many indeed feared that she would try to reform *them*; had not such a move already been set in train with the foundation of the first communities of Discalced Friars? Teresa saw that no lasting improvement was to be expected at the Incarnation without the co-operation of confessors who shared her own ideals. Her thoughts turned to the young friar whose spirituality and firm character had impressed her when she first met him and who had since helped her at Medina and other foundations. She wrote to Fray John of the Cross inviting him to become chaplain at the Incarnation. His coming was to mark a new stage in the Reform.

12

The Reform of the Friars

The reform of the friars had made a modest start three years before. Teresa had been offered a small farmhouse in the remote hamlet of Duruelo, some thirty miles from Avila. She obtained the consent required from the Provincial and from his predecessor, Father Salazar; the latter was fortunately anxious to remain in the good books of the Bishop's sister and he did not raise the objections she expected. On the way to her new convent at Valladolid, Teresa made an exhausting detour to Duruelo which she found only after great difficulty. The house consisted of a porch, a room with an alcove, a small kitchen and a loft. 'No one, however good, could possibly put up with it here, Mother!' exclaimed the nun who was with her. But Friar Antonio and Friar John of the Cross both declared, when the Foundress described it to them, that they were perfectly willing to live in Duruelo, or even, if necessary 'in a pigsty'.

Teresa had many talks with her two recruits, and it seems likely that they worked out together how the Constitutions drawn up for her nuns should be adapted to the needs of the friars. John also spent some time in Valladolid, acting as confessor to the nuns and learning their way of life, though Teresa adds that 'he was so good that I at least had more to learn from him than he from me'. Then, clad in the rough habit sewn for him by the nuns and accompanied by a mason to help with the alterations needed for their tiny monastery, he set off for Duruelo. Friar Antonio followed later, after resigning his office of prior. He could never entirely forgive the younger man for not having waited for him, and so depriving him of the honour of being the very first Discalced Carmelite friar. When he took leave of Teresa she was amused to notice that 'he was well supplied only with hour-glasses, of which he had five. He told me that this was to help him keep the prescribed Hours strictly. I don't think he had even anything to sleep on.'

A few months later, at the end of February 1569, Teresa visited the new community. She was deeply affected by what she saw, and she tells us that the friends who accompanied her – two of the merchants who had been helping with the Medina foundation – were moved to tears. They found the ex-prior cheerfully sweeping the entrance to the little church. The inside was adorned with a profusion of skulls and crosses:

> I shall never forget [she writes] the little wooden cross above the holy water stoup, with a figure of Christ made out of paper pasted onto it, which inspired more devotion than the most elaborate work of art. The loft served as the choir, for it was high enough in the centre for them to say the Hours, but they had to bend down low before they could enter and say Mass. At the corners on either side of the church were two chapels, where there was only room enough to sit or lie down. They were filled with hay, for the place was very cold, and the roof almost touched their heads. Two small windows looked out onto the altar, and there were two stones which served as pillows, with some crosses and skulls. I was told that after finishing Matins they stayed there so absorbed in prayer that when they went to say Prime their habits were quite covered with snow without their noticing it. . . .

The friars went barefoot, Teresa adds (though they were later ordered to wear *alpargatas*), despite all the snow and ice. They were out all day preaching and hearing confessions and did not return for their frugal supper until well into the night. 'Such was their joy,' Teresa concludes, 'that all this seemed to them of very little account.'

For all her admiration, Teresa was not blind to the dangers inherent in a life of such hardship. 'I begged them not to be so rigorous in the many penances they imposed on themselves', she writes. Friar Antonio was nearly sixty; she was not to know that he had an iron constitution and would live to be over ninety. A donkey was procured for him, and Friar John would tuck the older man's bare feet into saddlebags stuffed with hay and wrap his frieze habit warmly around him before starting out for their day's work. John was sometimes accompanied by his brother Francisco, a good, simple soul, with a song or devout ditty always on his lips. Their arduous, apostolic life began to attract postulants. The little house could soon no longer provide even the simplest shelter, and the growing community moved to the larger neighbouring village of Mancera. Duruelo was abandoned, the hamlet and the first Discalced Carmelite priory crumbling in time into the dust of the Castilian landscape.

Teresa's second foundation lasted longer but posed grave problems for the future. Never so firmly under her personal influence, it suffered from the very dangers she had warned against at Duruelo. The founding fathers of Pastrana were highly eccentric. Teresa tells us that Ambrosio Mariano Assaro was a learned and versatile Italian, a former court chamberlain to the Queen of Poland, who had taken to the life of a hermit after spending two years in prison on a trumped-up charge of murder. He also seems to have been a soldier, inventor and resourceful engineer whom Philip II consulted more than once on problems of irrigation and river navigability. After a time he was joined by a compatriot who was no less unusual. Giovanni Narduch is described by Teresa, with her usual blend of charity and shrewdness, as 'a great servant of God, and simple in the things of this world'. Juan de la Miseria, as he chose to style himself, moved in a world of visionary fantasies. After making his way barefoot to the great shrine of Santiago de Compostela, 'as if borne along by invisible hands', he had stayed on in Spain, first as a pilgrim and then as a hermit, carving wooden images of the Virgin. Moved by a sudden impulse to live under obedience, he sought out and placed himself in the hands of his fellow hermit, the ex-chamberlain. After further adventures together, the two wanderers found a protector in the Prince of Eboli, who allowed them to settle on a hill outside Pastrana. Following their meeting with Teresa, the hermits were transformed into friars and their hermitage into the nucleus of a Carmelite community.

The monastery, which Friar Mariano ingeniously devised out of a series of interconnecting caves, grew rapidly, but its foundations – both human and physical – proved unstable. The untrustworthy Baltasar Nieto wormed his way into the Prince's confidence and was appointed prior. Recruits flowed in from the nearby university of Alcalá de Henares. One, the youthful Angel de San Gabriel, became novice-master and subjected his charges to the most spectacular mortifications. They were sent to sell firewood at inflated prices so as to endure the abuse of the townsfolk. He even made them soak their piles of wood with water and continue scourging themselves whilst praying that God would send down fire from heaven, as he had done in answer to the prayers of Elijah. The novice-master was determined that the friars should emulate, and even surpass, the penances practised by the desert fathers. When these things came to the ears of Teresa, she sent John of the Cross to bring the zealots to reason. Though he succeeded for a time, Friar Angel was soon behaving more fanatically than ever, and he sent Teresa a letter justifying his excesses and denouncing the faint-hearts who objected to them. Teresa showed it to the judicious Father Báñez, who at once scented danger. 'If he is looking for mortifications,' he observed, 'here is one in very truth: to believe that he is mistaken.'

The situation was exacerbated by the appearance of assuredly the strangest of all that strange company. Catalina de Cardona, an illegitimate offspring of the ducal house of that name, had been brought up in Naples and came to Spain in the service of the Princess of Salerno, after whose death she passed to that of the

Princess of Eboli. Always eccentrically pious, she one day disappeared from the Eboli palace to live as a hermit in the wilds of La Roda. For eight years the recluse kept to her cave, subsisting on roots and herbs and the bread occasionally brought her by a shepherd. The fame of her penances and sanctity spread, specially when it was discovered that the hermit was really a woman. Great was their mutual jubilation when the recluse of La Roda and the friars of Pastrana discovered each other. Catalina declared that it had been revealed to her in a vision that she was to sponsor the foundation of a Carmelite monastery, and after she had had herself clothed with the habit of a Carmelite friar she went to the Court to beg alms. The sensation caused there by the arrival of the holy transvestite was enormous. Secure in the veneration of the King (whom she addressed familiarly as 'my son') and of Don John of Austria, whose imminent victory at Lepanto she foresaw in a vision, Catalina collected a considerable treasure and returned with it to found a monastery at La Roda. Baltasar Nieto, Mariano, and Juan de la Miseria were amongst those who left their troglodyte monastery to follow the new star, whilst the youthful Friar Angel, spurred on by her blessing to fresh extravagances, remained in charge of the community at Pastrana. He, and others of the same persuasion, were to look on the hermit-saint rather than the Carmelite Mother as the true foundress of the Discalced. Teresa herself revered Catalina, whom she never met personally, and wrote of her with admiration. She even wondered, until reassured by a locution, whether she was wrong not to emulate her savage penances. Amongst Teresa's papers we find the following note:

> Whilst I was once reflecting on the great penances practised by Doña Catalina de Cardona, and how I might have done more myself, following the desires sometimes given me by the Lord, had I not been kept from doing so by the obedience due to my confessors, and [whilst I was asking myself] whether it might be

better not to obey them any more in this, he said to me: 'No, my daughter. The road which you are following is a good and sure one. I value obedience more than all those penances you see.'

Amongst the novices who came to Pastrana to be initiated into the contemplative life but found there only the harsh absurdities of Fray Angel's arbitrary rule was the exceptionally gifted Jerónimo Gracián. Intelligent, refined, attractive and persuasive, he was to play an outstanding part in Teresa's life and in the troubled fortunes of the Reform. At the age of twenty-eight, only six months after making his profession, he was vested with the Apostolic Delegate's powers 'to visit and reform' all Carmelite houses, whether of the Mitigated or of the Primitive Rule, in Andalusia. To understand the significance of this appointment, and of the conditions which made it necessary, we must briefly review the troubled course of events and the struggles over jurisdiction which had occurred since Father Rossi, the General of the Order, had confronted and – as he thought – subdued his rebellious sons in that Province.

After the General's departure from Spain, the rebels, with the backing of influential nobles in Andalusia, continued to appeal to the King and to exploit his preference for a reform of the Order carried out by Spanish bishops. With the royal support, papal Briefs were quickly obtained to this effect. The bishops were to be assisted by two Dominicans having the authority of Apostolic Delegates, Commissaries or Visitors. We have already noted the activities of the Apostolic Delegate Pedro Fernández in Castile; his counterpart in Andalusia was another Dominican prior, Francisco de Vargas. A system of dual control was thus set up. This had little adverse effect where, as in Castile, the Apostolic Delegate collaborated tactfully with the Carmelite Provincial, but it could lead to serious friction if good will was lacking. The General, on learning of the arrangement made over his head, indignantly pressed the Pope for the revocation of the offending Briefs in so far as they applied to his Order. He succeeded, at the beginning of 1570, in securing a Counter-Brief to the desired effect, but Ormaneto, the papal nuncio in Spain, ruled that the Apostolic Delegates should continue to hold their appointments until the expiry of their three-year terms of office. Rossi then instructed his Provincials to resist any Apostolic Delegate who might seek to change the existing Constitutions or impose new ones. Finally, he appointed a 'Vicar' as his personal representative in Spain and nineteen 'Defenders of the Liberties of the Order' to provide whatever support might be necessary. The scene was thus set for a trial of strength over the control of the new communities of Discalced Friars.

The General had given Teresa a licence to found two houses of Discalced friars. He had at first forbidden her to found either monasteries or convents in Andalusia, though a patent dated 6 April 1571 seems to have extended her authority to found in any part of Spain. In an effort to arrest the friction developing within the Order, Father Rossi wrote in August 1570 to the Carmelites of Castile forbidding any more Calced friars to join the new Discalced houses, and he specifically banned from the latter the leading Andalusian dissidents whom (except, out of consideration for the Prince of Eboli, Friar Baltasar Nieto, now prior in Pastrana) he singled out by name. The General feared, in short, that those who flouted his authority would rally to the Reform and perhaps cause a schism in the Order. Yet he could do little to stop the flood of new foundations. At the Prince's behest, a College for the Discalced was opened in Alcalá, and zealous friars from Pastrana started offshoots at nearby Altomira and close by the venerated hermit's cave at La Roda. Other influential personages, whom the General dared not refuse, also solicited permission for new foundations. The Apostolic Delegate too gave them every encouragement. Three or four further houses seem to have been established without the General's permission or even knowledge. Altogether, more than a dozen communities of Discalced friars sprang up during Teresa's lifetime in the uncertain soil of Andalusia.

This rapid and ill-co-ordinated growth raised problems which the inexperienced Gracián strove manfully to solve. Father Salazar ordered him and Fray Mariano, who had become his companion, back to Pastrana. Vargas, in Andalusia, confirmed his powers as Visitor for that Province and advised him to disregard Salazar's commands, which he did. Finding the rift between the Calced and the Discalced in the Andalusian communities already too great to be healed, Gracián founded a separate priory for the Discalced in Seville, thereby antagonizing his General. The heads of the Portuguese and Spanish Carmelite Provinces met in conclave and, as 'Defenders of the Liberties of the Order', drew up a joint report for Rome. Gracián could count on the powerful backing of the King, the Nuncio, the Apostolic Delegate and the Archbishop of Seville, who had been rescued from insolvency by the financial talents of Fray Mariano's friend Nicolás Doria, of whom we shall hear more in the history of the Reform. On receiving his Provincials' disturbing report, the General obtained from Pope Gregory XIII a Brief annulling the powers of the Apostolic Delegates. But the Nuncio, who favoured the Discalced, countered by appointing 'Reformers' in their place; the well-disposed Pedro Fernández for Castile, Vargas and Gracián jointly for Andalusia – appointments which the Pope, somewhat surprisingly, confirmed. The Nuncio strengthened Gracián's position still further by nominating him also Provincial for Andalusia, with jurisdiction over both the Calced and the Discalced Carmelites.

Teresa followed these growing dissensions with distress and found herself inevitably drawn into the imbroglio. Her three-year term as Prioress of the Incarnation was due to end in the autumn of 1574, and we must now briefly consider the course events had been taking there since she had secured the collaboration of Friar John of the Cross. 'I am bringing you a saint for your confessor!' she had jubilantly announced to her nuns. In spite of their differences in age and temperament, prioress and chaplain worked together perfectly. 'Although we have had a few disagreements over business matters,' she wrote in recommending him to her old friend the *Caballero santo*, 'and I have sometimes been vexed with him, we have never seen the least imperfection in him.' Her respect for his learning and confidence in his spiritual discernment were unbounded; 'everything I have ever been told by other scholars my "little Seneca" can make clear to me in a few words', she declared. The young friar, for his part, venerated the Foundress, though he would nevertheless sometimes exercise a confessor's prerogative to mortify or rebuke her. 'When you make your confession, Mother,' he once gently chided her, 'you have a way of finding the prettiest excuses!' Yet his attachment was deeper than sometimes seemed to him fitting. Years later a friend found Friar John in evident distress burning a bundle of papers. They were letters he had received from her and treasured so dearly that he feared they had become an obstacle to his creed of stern detachment. When he finally left Avila for other duties, Teresa described him as 'a man celestial and divine', whose like she had not found in all Castile.

In a letter to the Prioress at Medina we find Teresa referring to her chaplain having 'just cast out three legions of devils from a certain person in Avila'. The allusion seems to be to a young Augustinian nun, whose knowledge of the Scriptures was so phenomenal that her superiors suspected it could only have been inspired by the Devil. Amongst other reports of diabolical possession we read of one nun being lifted bodily from her feet during divine service and left suspended upside-down in the air until ordered back to her stall by St John of the Cross, and of another glued so firmly to the ground that no one could make her budge until she was released by a mere glance from the friar. A suspected case also occurred amongst the Discalced at Medina.

Friar John, sent to investigate, pronounced that the nun was not possessed but was suffering from the common convent complaint of 'melancholy' of which Teresa has much to say in her writings; the girl seems to have had a nervous breakdown from which the friar helped her to recover. But not all the problems of Teresa's scattered communities could be so easily settled, and many required her personal intervention. The Bishop of Avila sought the Pope's permission for her to leave the Incarnation but was refused. The request was then renewed by one still greater than the Bishop – the Duchess of Alba, who persuaded the King that she stood in great need of the saint's spiritual ministrations. The Pope, pressed by Philip, deemed it politic to yield. The Prioress of the Incarnation was given leave to visit her nuns and the Duchess at Alba de Tormes. She was also permitted to go to Segovia, where a house had already been provided and only her presence was needed for a new convent to be formally inaugurated.

The foundation at Segovia, whose Bishop was absent on account of his duties as President of the Council of Castile but had given his permission verbally, seemed to offer little difficulty. Teresa followed her usual tactics of moving in unobtrusively at night and signalling the *fait accompli* by the celebration of Mass early the following morning. But she had reckoned without the touchy and choleric Vicar-General. Furious on discovering that a new convent had been established without his knowledge, he stormed into the chapel, brushing aside Friar John's quiet explanations and sending a terrified Julián de Avila scurrying for safety under the stairs, and ordered its immediate dismantling. The hangings and ornaments were stripped from the walls, the culprits threatened with imprisonment, and a constable was posted at the door. Teresa and her nuns watched in consternation from the other side of their enclosure. It needed all her diplomacy and the production of witnesses and documentary confirmation of the Bishop's permission before the Vicar-General was pacified and the foundation allowed to proceed.

There was a special reason why Teresa was eager to see a convent opened in Segovia. The situation at Pastrana had now become intolerable, and she had reached the conclusion that the only course left was to dissolve the community and move her nuns elsewhere. So long as the Prince of Eboli had been alive his tact and good sense had placed some restraint upon his wife. But in 1573 he died, and in a paroxysm of grief the widow theatrically declared that she was renouncing the world and taking the veil. 'The Princess a nun! Then this is the end of the house!' exclaimed the prioress of the Discalced, the prudent Isabel de Santo Domingo. The prophecy was all too quickly fulfilled. The gentlest attempts to guide Doña Ana's capricious spirit into the quiet and disciplined rhythm of convent life proved wholly unavailing. 'The news from Pastrana', wrote Friar Antonio to her rival, the Duchess of Alba, 'is that our novice the Princess is five months pregnant, and is ordering everyone about as if she were prioress and insisting that the nuns treat her with great ceremony and address her on bended knee. Tell our Mother this, if she does not already know.'

Teresa knew, and was resolutely laying her plans. Father Julián de Avila and a trusty gentleman called Antonio Gaitán were sent in all secrecy to arrange the evacuation of the nuns. Leaving the five covered carts which were to take them to their new home in Segovia a little outside Pastrana, they made their way under cover of darkness to the convent where the prioress and her nuns were in readiness. Doña Ana had already been ordered by the King to return to her palace and attend to her fatherless children, and she vented her spite by cutting off the nuns' revenues and harassing them in a thousand ways. Teresa had insisted that all gifts made by her to the convent should be carefully recorded, and these were now returned to the Corregidor for safekeeping. The fugitives crept stealthily through the deserted streets to the waiting carts, which then drove off with all speed until they were safely beyond the ducal domains. They had thwarted the woman who was not only one of the most powerful in Spain, but also the most implacably vengeful. Unable to settle scores with the nuns, the Princess took the copy of Teresa's *Life*, which had caused such derisive merriment in her household, and denounced it to the Inquisition.

By the end of September 1574 Teresa was back in Avila after visiting Alba, Salamanca and Segovia. She concluded her term at the Incarnation a few days later, and then moved to her beloved St Joseph's. Throughout the past three years of trials and relative inactivity, when constant ill health had added to her troubles, Teresa's visions and voices never ceased to sustain her. Some of them are recorded in her private notes or 'Accounts of Conscience'. Not long after she had begun to exercise her new office, she saw Our Lady herself descend from heaven, amidst a host of angels, to take the place of the image in the prioral stall, and remain there whilst the Salve was sung. On Palm Sunday she suffered Christ's passion with such intensity that she felt her mouth filled with blood. At Whitsun, as on some other occasions, a white dove alighted on her head and shoulders. On 18 November 1572, she had a vision in which Christ appeared before her and showed her the nail in his hand, promising that she would henceforth be his Bride, never to be separated from his love. The vision left her 'as if crazed' for bliss, which not even the heightened awareness of her own unworthiness could diminish. But the sufferings to come were also revealed to her, and once

> I saw a great storm of tribulations, and how we should be persecuted, as the Children of Israel were by the Egyptians, but that God would lead us through in safety whilst the enemy would be engulfed in the waves.

Perhaps it was the foreboding aroused by this prophetic vision which led Teresa to write to the King. In a letter dated Avila, 11 June 1573, she recalls the prayers which she and her daughters were continually offering on his behalf, 'for Christendom has need of you', and commends to His Majesty the bearer of her letter, Father

Juan de Padilla, who would explain certain matters relating to the Reform and solicit the royal favour and protection. Teresa scented danger, but she was not to know that it would come from the quarter she least expected – from Father Rossi, the Carmelite General who had always given her such fervent support. In October, and again in January of the next year, he wrote to the Foundress asking her to explain what was happening to the reform of the friars which seemed to be getting more and more out of hand. These letters unfortunately did not reach Teresa until the following June. She then hastened to pacify him, but it was too late. Teresa had counselled Gracián to keep the General fully informed of everything he was doing. He had begun by following her advice, but later let his correspondence lapse. Though Teresa leapt to his defence, the General now regarded him as an ambitious young friar in open rebellion against his authority, and suspected that the Foundress was aiding and abetting him. Father Rossi's displeasure struck Teresa with amazement and distress. She was to endure its consequences with humble submission but she never, to her sincere grief, succeeded in regaining her venerated superior's favour.

Her duties at the Incarnation ended, Teresa was free to turn again to the needs of her Discalced nuns. She spent Christmas at Valladolid, where a wealthy young heiress called Casilda de Padilla had caused a stir by running away to become a nun in defiance of her family's wishes. A mere child at the time, she became a great favourite of Teresa's. Proposals for new foundations poured in; Torrijos was considered and rejected, Madrid postponed, and Zamora fell through. Finally Teresa decided in favour of Beas de la Segura, where two sisters wished not only to give a house but to take the veil themselves; the story of their conversion, visionary guidance, and triumph over parental opposition is related with relish in the *Foundations*. Rather to Teresa's surprise, a licence was obtained without much difficulty from the Apostolic Delegate and from the Knights of Santiago, who held jurisdiction over the little town. It was pleasantly situated on the banks of a small river, where the Sierra Morena slopes down to the fertile valleys of Andalusia. Teresa assumed it to lie within the borders of Castile, as indeed it did for administrative and political purposes, though it also belonged to the ecclesiastical province of Andalusia. This ambiguity was to be a source of future trouble.

At the beginning of 1575 Teresa set out from Valladolid with ten nuns, travelling in four covered wagons, and their male escorts. The party included the future prioress of the new community, Ana de Jesús, whose intelligence and graceful bearing had earned her the sobriquet of 'Queen of Women', Doña Luisa's clever maid-of-honour María de San José, and Isabel de San Jerónimo, whom St John of the Cross had cured of 'melancholy'. They travelled slowly, revisiting the convents at Medina, Avila, Toledo and Malagón, and crossing the dreary plain of La Mancha, soon to be immortalized as the scene of Don Quixote's adventures. In the defiles of the Sierra Morena the muleteers lost their way. Through the chinks of her covered wagon Teresa caught glimpses of the precipices which seemed to be opening beneath its wheels. She exhorted her nuns to pray; their patron saint surely would not let them perish. A voice from the ravine shouted back, as if in answer to their prayers, directing the drivers where to go. They could see no one, and it was no use looking, Teresa told them; was it not enough that St Joseph had heard and saved them? Ana de Jesús, describing the episode many years later, adds that even the muleteers were convinced of their miraculous escape, and from that moment their beasts seemed to fly rather than toil along over the stony tracks.

The new convent was founded soon after Teresa's arrival. Catalina, the more forceful of the two sisters, was a visionary of the type we have often met with before. She had once dreamed that she was in a room with a company of nuns wearing black veils and carrying lighted tapers. When asked to which Order they belonged, they had answered only by raising their veils. Now, looking around her at her Discalced sisters, Catalina recognized the radiant, smiling faces she had seen in her dream.

Some sixty miles south of Beas, but separated from it by wild and lofty mountains, lay Caravaca, another township under the patronage of the Order of Santiago. There too Teresa had been invited to establish a convent. But the Foundress was now over sixty and beginning to feel her age. She had started out on the long journey to Beas so racked with fever and other pains that she could never have withstood the hardships of the road unless the Lord had taken pity on her and miraculously renewed her strength. The General, she believed, still wished her to go on making new foundations – 'as many as the hairs in your head' he had told her in a letter. If the road to Caravaca was too hard, she had the faithful Julián de Avila and Antonio Gaitán, who would go in her stead. The report they brought back was favourable, and Ana de San Alberto, an exemplary nun from Malagón, was sent to establish the convent and remain there as its prioress.

The days at Beas passed in an atmosphere of ineffable peace and gratitude. The Lord renewed his assurance that Teresa was indeed his Bride and that he would give her whatever she desired of him, 'in token whereof he bestowed on me a beautiful ring, the stone of which was like an amethyst, only very different in its splendour from our earthly ones, which he placed on my finger'. This favour seems to have been the culmination of the mystery of the Spiritual Marriage granted to Teresa two and a half years before and similar to the sublime and intimate experience of the bestowal of an espousal ring ascribed to a number of other mystics: to St Catherine of Siena in 1376, to St Catherine de' Ricci in 1542, and after Teresa's day to such visionaries as St Mary-Magdalen de' Pazzi and St Veronica Giuliani in Italy, to St Rose of Lima, and to the Spanish ecstatic Marina de Escobar.

Soon after Easter, it seemed to Teresa that the divine promise made to her was being fulfilled in a marvellous way. She had been in correspondence with Father Jerónimo Gracián, whom the Nuncio had appointed 'Reformer' and Carmelite Provincial for Andalusia, and the two had conceived a mutual respect and sympathy for each other. Gracián was now on his way back to Madrid from Seville and he made a detour in order to meet the Foundress personally. There were many things relating to the Reform which had to be discussed. Teresa also felt the need for something more: the quickening touch of another spirituality as pure and deep as her own, the comfort of one who would be at the same time confessor, spiritual director, superior, confidant, and the most innocently intimate of friends. In the young friar half her age but already distinguished by high office, imbued with her own zeal yet gentle and exquisitely courteous, eloquent and learned but at the same time spontaneous, candid and at times even ingenuous, Teresa found all these things and more. Gracián was a man whom she could revere as a spiritual daughter yet cherish and care for as a mother. The attraction was instantaneous and mutual. 'She so captivated me', Gracián later recalled, 'that from that moment I did nothing of importance without first consulting her.'

Gracián stayed on in Beas waiting for Fray Mariano, whom he had asked to join him there. Teresa was delighted with the delay. For her it was a time of rare euphoria, 'without exaggeration, I believe the best days of my life!' she exclaimed in a letter to her prioress at Medina.

> Father Gracián has been here for more than twenty days. I assure you that, much as I have had to do with him, I had not realized his full worth until now. In my eyes he is quite perfect, and more suited to our needs than anyone we could have asked God to send us. What you and your nuns should do now, Mother, is to implore the Almighty to give him to us as our Superior. Then I could get some rest from governing these houses, for I have never met anyone so perfect and yet so gentle.

Teresa went on to tell the prioress that she had now learned that

Beas was, in fact, in Andalusia. So, without knowing it, she had come under Gracián's jurisdiction and would give him her obedience. The plan was for her to go to Seville and found a convent there – a prospect which, in the Andalusian heat, frankly appalled her.

The letters written by Teresa at this time breathe a very human delight at the unexpected meeting of two minds, the comprehension of a superior who would unreservedly further her life's work, and the discovery of a fascinating companion to confide in and cherish. But we glimpse too that other mysterious dimension which the mystic brings to human relationships. The new friendship is ordained of God. This revelation, we learn from one of Teresa's most remarkable Accounts of Conscience, occurred at a disconcerting moment – when she was sitting down to a meal in the refectory! With the blinding speed and clarity of a lightning-flash, Christ stood before her. She saw Father Gracián on his right, and herself on his left. Taking each by the right hand and placing it in the other's, he said that it was his wish that she should take this priest in place of himself as long as she lived, and that they should be at one in all things. The vision came upon her with the authority of a divine mandate, making all doubt impossible. Teresa tried to call to mind all the confessors she had had during her life, and how much she owed them, and the resentment they might feel at this new allegiance. It was to no avail. She *knew* that it was God's will. Never again would she need to turn from one to another trying to weigh up and decide between their contradictory advice. God had at last given her a permanent and infallible guide, whose will she should obey in all things, unless – but that was unthinkable – it was clearly contrary to God's teaching. Twice the same vision was repeated, leaving her with a sense of peace and certainty beyond any words to describe. Whenever she recalled it, the thought filled her with joy. Nothing could now disturb her serenity or shake her resolve.

Fray Mariano reached Beas at last, and he and Gracián set out together for Madrid. The Italian's exuberant imagination painted a glowing picture of the opportunities awaiting the nuns in Seville: the favour of the Archbishop, the enthusiasm of the people, the rich harvest of vocations ready to be garnered, and the great service it would be to the Order to found a convent. Teresa, with her accustomed prudence, reminded the friars of the ban which the General had originally imposed on new foundations in Andalusia and how unwise it would be to risk provoking his displeasure. Gracián, confident in the powers with which he believed the Nuncio had vested him on behalf of the Pope, and full of candid zeal, brushed aside her misgivings. Without more ado, Teresa took leave of Ana de Jesús, the founding sisters and the other nuns, and set out for Seville. The companions she chose to share her venture were 'souls such as I believe I would dare to go with into the land of the Turks'.

Before reaching Seville, the cavalcade stopped at Ecija to hear mass and rest. The Foundress left her companions and withdrew to the solitude of a wayside chapel. It was Whitsun, and her thoughts dwelt with wonder on the promised gift of the Holy Spirit and she was filled with a desire to spend herself more wholly in the Lord's service. The moment had come to renew the vow she had made of absolute submission to the will of the Superior whom God had given her in place of himself. Had she not hitherto always held back, preserving a remnant of innate pride and attachment to the spiritual independence she now felt called to surrender? 'This seemed to me the most difficult decision I have ever made in my life,' she declares in a revealing Account of Conscience, 'save when I left my father's house to become a nun.' She fell on her knees, ardently renewing her pledge. The renunciation brought her a strange joy and contentment.

It was almost exactly at this time that Father Rossi in Italy summoned a Chapter General of the Carmelite Order to consider the situation in Spain. It met at Piacenza on 21 May 1575. As no representatives of the Reform were present their case went by default. The General began by reading the papal Brief revoking the powers of the Apostolic Delegates. A resolution was then passed calling on 'certain disobedient, rebellious and contumacious friars commonly called the Discalced' to leave the houses which they had founded (at La Peñuela, Granada and Seville) without their General's permission, and to return to Castile, where they were to rejoin the Calced. They were to cease going barefoot and should be known in future as Primitives or Contemplatives. No more convents or monasteries whatsoever were to be founded. An even more drastic instruction, apparently drawn up by the Definitors appointed to restore discipline, laid down that no Discalced nun 'under pain of excommunication, was to leave her convent'. The name of Teresa de Jesús was specifically cited in this connection, and she was ordered to return to Castile and to remain confined there in a convent of her choice.

The General was terrible in his wrath. It seemed that he was now bent on destroying the Reform which he had hitherto seen as the salvation of his Order and warmly encouraged. Teresa journeyed on in ignorance towards Seville. Her mind was set on the tasks which awaited her there and on her resolve to give full obedience to the man she had taken as her superior, friend and fellow worker. Nor did she know that there were other storm-clouds too, besides the General's displeasure, about to burst over her head.

13

The Andalusian Expedition

The four covered wagons which carried Teresa and her party to Seville took over a week to complete their fifty-leagues' journey. Although it was only mid-May, the heat was already intolerable. 'I tell you, my daughters,' Teresa wrote, 'that with the sun beating down on the carts with all its might, getting into them was like entering Purgatory.' The nuns were accompanied by Father Julián, Antonio Gaitán and a Discalced friar called Gregorio Nacianceno. They took few provisions with them – Fray Mariano had optimistically assured them that they could easily live off the land – and those they had were quickly spoiled. Their pigskin water-bottle was soon emptied, and in the wretched inns on the way drinking water was dearer than wine. Even the coarsest food was seldom obtainable, for the scarcities which in less favoured parts of Spain reached famine proportions were affecting Andalusia. 'It was something of an event,' one of the nuns recalled, 'when we managed to find an egg for our Mother.' With the heat, the jolting and the discomfort, Teresa found herself developing a high temperature and sinking into a daze. The nuns splashed her face with water, but it was too warm to bring her much relief.

As far as circumstances allowed, the disciplined rhythm of convent life was nevertheless still maintained. Mass was heard each morning before the journey was resumed. Then, at intervals throughout the day, there would come from within the darkened enclosure of the covered wagons the tinkle of Teresa's little bell summoning the nuns to their appointed hours of prayer, meditation and spiritual reading. The muleteers would cease from their shouts, songs, and curses until the bell signalled the all-clear. As the heat rose to its midday peak, a sharp lookout was kept for some shady spot for the siesta. On their first day, they were fortunate enough to come upon a beautiful wood carpeted with flowers. Teresa wandered off by herself for a while in deep delight; her soul was as readily raised to God by the contemplation of nature as by the solemnities of divine office or the stillness of her convent cell. Once the travellers had to put up with the shade of a bridge under which a herd of pigs was resting; they drove them off and were happy to take their place. Later in the afternoon, the little bell would ring for 'recreation'. The sound of laughter and animated voices came from behind the swaying awnings. The Foundress was taking the lead in a favourite pastime – composing *coplas* or rhymes celebrating the misadventures and mercies of the day. And so, recalls María de San José, whom Teresa had chosen to be the prioress of her future convent, 'laughter helped us to put up with everything'.

Teresa's motherly concern extended to the humblest of her travelling companions. When they stopped for the siesta she would walk over to the muleteers and thank them in her winning way for their courtesy in respecting the nuns' times of silence, perhaps rebuke them gently for their profanity, and talk with sympathy of the difficulties and dangers of the road. These were sometimes very real. Once, when a boatman was ferrying the travellers across the Guadalquivir, the guide-rope snapped and two of the wagons with their mules were swept away. The men shouted and swore and the nuns prayed. Help arrived from a nearby castle and the wagons eventually came to rest on a mudbank some way down stream. Teresa's observant and compassionate eye had noticed a detail of this near-tragedy which few might think worth recording – the consternation of the boatman's small son, whose 'distress when he saw his father in such straits made me praise the Lord'.

The sorest trials were the inns. As evening drew on, a couple of men would ride ahead to see what lodgings they could find in the next town or village. The inns of sixteenth-century Spain were a byword for squalor, rough and boisterous conviviality, and often for quarrelling and roguery. Along the roads to Seville, the richest and most populous city in the land and the great entrepôt for the New World, poured a motley crowd of soldiers, merchants, officials, students, beggars and adventurers of every kind, congregating in the inns to drink, eat (if they were lucky), swop travellers' tales and doss down in whatever vermin-infested space the landlord had to offer. The nuns would go straight to the room provided for them, each sister taking her turn to act as 'portress', whilst one of their escort would keep guard at the door – sometimes no more than a blanket slung over an open doorway.

About half-way through their journey, as they were nearing Córdoba, Teresa fell ill with a high fever. The best the inn could provide was a low shed which seemed to have done duty as a pigsty. The sun was still high and streamed in through holes in the roof. The bed on which they laid her 'was so full of ups and downs that I would rather have lain on the floor', she recalls. 'I can't think how I put up with it.' The din made by the shouting and singing of the other guests, the stamping of feet, the twanging of guitars and the rattle of tambourines added to the patient's torment and finally decided them to resume their journey and spend the night under the stars. At another inn, the Venta de Andino, the nuns found themselves in the thick of a fray between soldiers and muleteers – 'Unless we had seen them with our own eyes,' comments María de San José demurely, 'I could never have believed that there were such abominable folk in all Christendom.' The nuns sought refuge with their Mother. The fever had left her and she cheered them with gay laughter. According to another account, she spoke a few words to the rioters which were enough to calm and disperse them. Teresa herself seems to have remembered the incident mainly on account of the appalling heat. Writing to a friend from

Seville, she later remarked: 'The sun has been pretty hot here; but not so unbearable as it was in the Venta de Andino.'

Teresa's companions were not to know that, for all her cheerful serenity, the Foundress had grave preoccupations which she was careful to conceal from them. Shortly before leaving Beas she had learned in confidence that the Inquisition in Valladolid had been asked to trace the whereabouts of her autobiography, which it wished to examine on suspicion of heresy. The demand had come, it seems, not as a result of the delation of the malicious Princess of Eboli, but from the Inquisitors of Córdoba, who were conducting the trial of a group of Juan de Avila's disciples. Through the good offices of her friend Doña Luisa, Teresa had submitted the manuscript to that venerable master, who had read it shortly before his death and, apart from recommending a few minor amendments, pronounced it to be of blameless orthodoxy. But the Apostle of Andalusia had also had brushes with the Inquisition and suffered a term of imprisonment in his youth. Forty years later, suspicion again fastened on the visionaries who found inspiration in his teaching and such works as Teresa's *Life*.

Now, by an irony of fate, Teresa was to see her cavalcade immobilized beneath the very walls of the Alcázar which housed the dread institution. In Córdoba, the travellers needed to recross the Guadalquivir, but found the bridge closed to traffic. Special permission had to be obtained from the Corregidor before they could proceed, and when the wagons at length started to rumble forward again it was found that their axle-poles projected beyond the width of the bridge and had to be sawn off before they could pass. The church on the far side of the river where they paused to hear mass was celebrating its patronal feast, and the nuns' unfamiliar habit aroused the curiosity of the crowds; 'there could not have been more commotion if they had loosed bulls in the place'. Córdoba, in short, proved an altogether unpleasant experience, though Teresa consoled herself with the odd reflection that it must have been the shock of it which cured her fever.

The nuns' arrival in Seville passed, by contrast, almost unnoticed in the bustle of the great city. No one came to regale the travellers with so much as a loaf of bread or a jug of water. The house rented by the unreliable Fray Mariano proved to be a wretched place lacking the barest necessities. The neighbours who lent them a few essentials – a frying-pan, a pail, a candlestick and a table – showed more thrift than charity and soon came to reclaim their possessions. Teresa had wished to found in poverty, and here indeed was poverty in the midst of plenty, indifference in the heart of a city given over to the pursuit of wealth and pleasure and the ostentatious display of devotion. Though the antipathy of the first impact wore off in time, Teresa never felt at home in Andalusia. 'I have always heard it said', she wrote in her *Foundations*, 'that God has given the devils more of a free hand in these parts to tempt mortals, and I certainly never felt so weak and cowardly in my life as I did here. I really scarcely recognized myself.' After some months in Seville she could still write to a friend in Toledo: 'I am happier amongst Castilians, for I get on none too well with the people here.' To her prioress in Valladolid: 'It is amazing what injustices are committed in these parts – what untruthfulness and double-dealing!' And to Fray Mariano, more bluntly still: 'What lies they tell here! They quite make my head spin!'

And the devils, or the insidious climate, seemed to have infected some of her closest companions. María de San José, the once sprightly and adoring maid-of-honour who now at the age of 28 was placed in charge of the fledgling foundation, showed herself sometimes cold and resentful towards the Foundress. Fray Mariano, back from Madrid, proved strangely evasive beneath his Italian warmth. Teresa quickly sensed what the friar was trying to hide. The Archbishop, although well disposed towards the Reform, had not given a licence for any new convent of Discalced nuns and showed no intention of doing so, particularly if it was proposed to found *sin renta*. It was the old battle of St Joseph's of Avila which Teresa now saw herself called upon to fight all over again. Seville, she was told, already had twenty-four convents and eighteen monasteries; why should not her daughters be dispersed amongst existing Carmelite houses where they could exercise their beneficent influence? The Archbishop had sound reasons on his side, but Teresa was confident that once she could speak with him face to face God would put into her mouth arguments that no human reason could withstand. But the prelate kept his distance. He sent friendly messages and offered trifling concessions in token of his good will. Gracián, from Madrid, bombarded him with letters, whilst Mariano, conscious that the nuns had been brought from Beas under false pretences, worked on him zealously in Seville. At last the Archbishop consented to see them. Teresa records the ensuing victory tersely, as if careful to eschew the least traces of Andalusian rhetoric:

> At last it pleased God that he should come to visit us, and I then spoke to him of the trouble he was causing. Eventually he told me I could do just what I liked, and as I liked, and from then on he was helpful and kind to us on every possible occasion.

The Foundress had gained a new ally, but nothing could make good the loss of the one who now frowned upon her from Italy. The General did not even think fit to inform her directly of his displeasure, but had the decisions of the Piacenza Chapter and the Definitors conveyed to her through the Provincials of Castile and Andalusia. Father Angel de Salazar had, as we have seen, always shown an ambivalent and opportunistic attitude towards the Reform. Feeling the cold wind from Rome, he now published a harshly worded decree branding Teresa apostate and excommunicate and ordering her reclusion in a Castilian convent. It was not until she had been in Seville for some months that she learned, through Salazar's Andalusian colleague, of her disgrace and sentence. By this time the dispute between Calced and Discalced had grown fiercer and the struggle over jurisdiction more bitter and embroiled. We must briefly try to disentangle its main threads.

The thunderbolt from Italy had struck Father Gracián as soon as he arrived in Madrid from Beas. He refused to accept the Chapter's decisions or to dissolve the reformed houses in Andalusia. Salazar thereupon excommunicated him and turned him out of the Madrid priory. Ormaneto, the Papal Nuncio, hastened to his defence, rebuked Salazar for daring to punish one who had rightly obeyed the Pope's representative rather than his General, and had him reinstated in the priory. Gracián, though resolved to pursue his reforms, would gladly have renounced his thankless role as Visitor to the Calced, and he addressed a petition to this effect to the Nuncio and the King. But the two latter, determined not to lose face by yielding to pressure from any Order, would not hear of retreat. On the contrary, at the beginning of August 1575, Gracián was expressly confirmed in his powers as 'Provincial Superior' of the Discalced and Visitor to both Calced and Discalced in Andalusia. After three months in Madrid and a personal interview with the King, he resumed his visitation of the Discalced houses in Castile, and then, in October, prepared for the more onerous task of visiting the Andalusian priories. Word reached him that the Calced friars were resolved to resist. Ormaneto made light of the news. He had obtained papal confirmation of the powers vested in Gracián and issued the latter with additional and specific authority to proceed with his visitation in spite of any 'Counter-Brief' from the General.

Watching these dissensions with growing concern, Teresa became convinced that peace could only come through granting a greater measure of administrative autonomy for the Reform. Not, indeed, the establishment of an independent Order (though that was to come about in time) but, as she put it in a letter addressed to the King, 'unless the Discalced are made into a separate Province, and that with all speed, much harm will be done and I deem further progress to be impossible'. As the head of such a Province, she added, none was more suited, on account of his exceptional gifts and virtues, than Father Gracián. To the latter, then still making his visitations of the Discalced houses of Castile, she wrote in optimistic vein. The Calced in Andalusia, she believed, 'were all determined to obey your Paternity, so long as you deal with them gently, as I am sure you will'. Several had paid her friendly visits, including Friar Gaspar Nieto, whose name has not figured in our story since we saw him playing a leading part in the revolt against Father Rossi eight years before. His brother Baltasar, another former ringleader, was already abusing his position as prior of Pastrana to intrigue against Gracián – a foretaste of the troubles to come within the ranks of the Discalced themselves. By some ironic misunderstanding, the Visitor now striving to call the turbulent friars to order had himself fallen into disfavour with the General who had first aroused their hostility for attempting to impose similar reforms. But the issue had not yet been put to the test and Teresa was still hopeful. 'If you treat them mildly at first and avoid making a stir,' she wrote to Gracián, ' I believe you will accomplish a great deal of good, but you must not expect to do it in a day.' In the meantime, he was to take every care of his health and safety, for his life was precious to many souls. Was he wearing enough warm clothes, she inquired with motherly solicitude, now that the weather had turned colder? And he had lately been having so many bad falls from his donkey! If he insisted on covering ten leagues a day, his companions ought at least to see that he was securely strapped on!

Father Gracián reached Seville in mid-November. Even with the authority behind him, he wished to take further soundings before embarking on measures which he knew would provoke violent reactions. He consulted the Archbishop, Teresa, and Friars Antonio, Mariano and Gregorio; all agreed that he had no alternative but to proceed. The fiery Italian urged him to take an uncompromising line with the Calced; the others stressed the need for moderation and conciliation. It was decided to begin with the Calced Priory in Seville. Father Suárez, the Provincial of the Calced, prudently withdrew to Madrid and confined himself to passive resistance. But when Gracián arrived at the priory to read the Nuncio's letter of authority, the friars refused him a hearing. Gracián insisted, the friars shouted and threatened, and finally slammed the doors in his face. Gracián replied by thundering excommunication against them. Teresa deplored their obduracy but thought the Visitor had been too hasty. 'Even if they refuse to obey, Your Reverence should hesitate before issuing letters of excommunication against them', she counselled. 'I should be sorry to see them feel they had been driven into a corner.'

Gracián's arrival in Seville, Teresa soon saw, had only made matters worse. She now had serious fears both for the future of the Reform and for the safety of the man who was its chief pillar. Rumours even reached her that the Visitor had been killed in the fracas at the priory, and for some time afterwards, suspecting that the Calced might try to poison him, she arranged for him to take meals in the convent parlour. But her inner voices still spoke of Father Gracián in words of comfort and assurance. Rapt in contemplation, she heard: 'He is a true son of mine; I shall not fail to help him.' Once at Communion she beheld him in a strange vision, radiantly transformed and garlanded with sparkling gems, and surrounded by angelic maidens carrying palms and singing praises to God. She opened her eyes in an effort to shake off the vision, but it remained with her for more than an hour, infusing a still more ardent love and veneration for him into her heart. Shortly before Gracián's arrival in November, she saw him in another vision coming towards her with a joyful and trans-figured countenance and heard the divine command: 'Tell him to begin at once and without fear, for victory will be his!' A few days later, when the commotion caused by his attempt to read out his Brief to the embattled Calced had so upset Teresa that she found herself unable even to pray, her voices soothed and consoled

her: 'Calm yourself, oh woman of little faith, for all is well!'
It needed faith indeed to believe that all was well. Soon after her
arrival in Seville, Teresa had received two letters from the General
in Rome, written respectively six and nine months before, which
revealed all too clearly his growing disquiet and anger. Her own
letters must have taken equally long to reach him, if they ever
arrived at all. We know that in June she sent him at least three
letters describing the progress of the Reform and defending Gracián
and Mariano from the accusations which were discrediting them in
the General's eyes. The only one of these to have survived is a
masterly blend of filial submission, persuasive argument and
eloquent apologia, with undertones of reproach and even
admonition, as when she reminds Father Rossi that Gracián's
brother is one of the King's confidential secretaries. She begins by
assuring his Reverence of her continuing affection and obedience
and justifies her foundation at Beas on the rather enigmatic
grounds that the town was 'not Andalusia, but a province of
Andalusia' (i.e. it was outside the political, though not the
ecclesiastical, jurisdiction of Andalusia). She goes on to say that she
is now in Seville on instructions from Father Gracián, whose
authority she felt bound to recognize. If only his Reverence knew
him, she exclaims, she was sure he would value him as a most
dutiful son who has only the interests of the Order at heart and
'behaves like an angel'! Friar Mariano, she admits, tends to act
hastily, and may have unwittingly caused offence, though he too
was virtuous and thoroughly loyal. She fears the General must
have been misinformed about them both. As for her own activities,
Teresa reminds him that the last patent he sent authorized her to
make foundations anywhere; that at least was the opinion of the
learned men she had consulted. She herself was now old and tired
and would like nothing better than to stay quietly in her convent.
She only drove herself to continue her work as a foundress because
she believed it to be God's will and the General's wish. The friars
who had joined the Reform were leading exemplary lives, in

marked contrast to most of their Andalusian brethren; why, only the other day, two Calced friars brought disgrace on the Order when they were found by the police in a brothel and hauled off to gaol in broad daylight. If the virtuous Discalced were now to be persecuted and driven out of the Reform, it could not possibly be for the good of the Order, 'nor will Our Lord be served thereby'.

The General turned a deaf ear to Teresa's pleas. He was now nearing seventy and the direction of affairs was passing to others who knew little of Spain and showed no desire for reconciliation. Early the next year (1576), in one of the most remarkable of all her letters, Teresa made a new attempt to regain Father Rossi's favour for the Reform and to intercede for Gracián and Mariano. The two friars, she assures him again, are his loyal sons – no less so, she ventures to add, than others who would persuade him to the contrary. She implores him to forgive them the displeasure they have caused him and to believe what she writes. She has nothing to gain from misrepresenting the truth, and indeed would consider it a grave sin to do so. Moreover, she adds with a touch of irony, 'although we women are not much use as counsellors, we are sometimes right all the same'. Then, with an assurance which only a diaphanously pure conscience could claim without presumption, she tells him: 'When we both stand before the judgement seat of God, Your Reverence will see what you owe to your loyal daughter Teresa de Jesús.' She recalls the new foundations she has made in Andalusia, all with the required licences and on instructions from Gracián, the Visitor vested with the Nuncio's powers for this purpose; the loyalty and veneration he still feels for the General (as does Mariano, too, though 'he cannot express himself properly' and so may have caused offence); her affectionate submission to the General's commands, despite her grief at having angered him and at the harsh things said about her by Father Salazar; the mortified life of the Discalced nuns ('they subsist on nothing but bread') and the distress they suffer on account of the turmoil within the Order. Finally, she expresses her fear that the General will cease to write to her, will forget her, and will deny her the joy of reconciliation until – and again that shaft loosed heavenwards from the bow of a saint – 'until that endless eternity in which your Reverence will discover how much you owe to me. May the Lord in his mercy grant I may merit it.'

Teresa wished to leave Seville in obedience to the General's orders as soon as she received Father Salazar's harsh notification. She disliked Andalusia, and the sentence of reclusion in a Castilian convent, though intended as a punishment, promised her the calm and solitude which her soul craved. But whom was she to obey – the General, unjust in his anger and misinformed, or the Visitor who held the Nuncio's commission, and to whom she had furthermore made a vow of personal obedience? Gracián was firm: the Foundress was not yet free to leave Seville. The establishment of the convent was still precarious. No permanent building had been acquired for it, and recruits were proving disappointing in number and quality. Convent life was not made easier by the incompatibility of temperament between the Andalusians and the nucleus of Castilian nuns whom Teresa had brought with her. Nor were matters helped by the differences with the Calced and also with the Franciscans, who resented the Discalced's claims on the charity of the faithful. Finally, unfamiliar brands of contemplatives had become suspect on account of a recrudescence of *alumbrismo* in Estremadura and in Seville itself. A certain Doña Catalina had recently been penanced by the Inquisition as a false visionary and publicly flogged.

The first postulant to be accepted by the convent was a young woman of good family called Beatriz de Chávez, whose abnormal childhood and youth Teresa recounts at length in the *Foundations*. Maltreated by her parents, first for allegedly trying to poison a rich aunt and then for refusing to marry, she claimed to have been restored to health by a mysterious visitor whom the credulous identified as the prophet Elijah. Gracián, who had moved her by his sermons, believed her to be an inspired and innocent soul and recommended her acceptance. But Beatriz was to prove unstable and at times extremely troublesome to her sisters. Another postulant of dubious worth was the middle-aged María del Corro, who expected that her reputation as a *beata* would entitle her to special privileges and prestige. Her disenchantment and subsequent attempt to put the blame on the convent came near to bringing it to ruin. Nor were all of Teresa's own nuns wholly reliable. Isabel de San Jerónimo, once suspected of diabolic possession and rescued from a nervous breakdown by St John of the Cross, seemed to be getting more neurotic again under the hot Andalusian sun. Affecting an extravagance of mortified humility (she signed herself 'Isabel the Dungheap'), she was much given to purported visions and revelations, which the Foundress firmly forbade her to commit to writing. Teresa never forgot that the watchful eye of the Inquisition was upon them, and that the Reform had many enemies.

Gracián, too, was made aware of this new danger soon after his arrival in Seville. A friend, who was a functionary of the Inquisition, warned him that there was trouble ahead and took him sharply to task for sponsoring such a dubious visionary as Teresa de Jesús. When he passed on the disturbing news to Teresa, Gracián was amazed to see that she seemed to take a positive delight in it, laughing and rubbing her hands together as if relishing the prospect of a great treat. The Holy Office, she reminded him, had been divinely appointed to protect the Faith, and she was ready to die a thousand times over rather than deny a single one of its articles. Neither she nor her daughters would be found wanting, God be praised, on that score. But when María de San José shrewdly observed that the Inquisitors might take her departure from Seville as an attempt to escape their jurisdiction, she readily agreed that the Prioress was right, and that she ought to stay.

One day in February, as Gracián was on his way to the convent, he was dumbfounded to see a number of horses and mules tethered at the doorway. The Inquisitors had come to interrogate the nuns.

The official account of their proceedings does not survive, but we can deduce its gist from a letter sent to their colleagues in Madrid with a request to forward the book said to contain the suspect's revelations and teachings – the same book that the Inquisitors of Córdoba had been anxious to lay hands on, and which was to remain in the possession of one branch or another of the Holy Office for a dozen years – Teresa's *Life*. The delation received by the Seville Inquisitors had emanated from the disaffected *beata* María del Corro and from another unsatisfactory recruit to the convent, both of whom had soon left it. It was aimed specially against Teresa and the convent's Achilles heel, the weak-minded Isabel de San Jerónimo. The Foundress was charged with teaching 'new and superstitious doctrines resembling those of the *alumbrados* of Estremadura . . . full of frauds and deceits, and most harmful to the Christian commonwealth'. To judge from allusions in Teresa's letters and the reminiscences of María de San José, the charges on which the Inquisitors proceeded to cross-examine the suspects seem unbelievably far-fetched. 'They said we used to tie the nuns hand and foot and then beat them', writes Teresa. 'Because we were poor and had not enough veils, or sometimes because we forgot them and borrowed each other's before attending Communion, they accused us of practising "ceremonies" of some sort', recalls María. And again: 'We used to attend Communion in a little patio where the sunshine was so strong that, in order to shade ourselves a little and become more recollected after communicating, we would turn our faces to the wall; and this too they construed in a sinister way and blamed on our holy Mother.'

The interrogations lasted for two days. Teresa has little to say about them, but several accounts testify to her cheerful and unruffled serenity, the prudence and sincerity with which she replied to the absurdest of questions. Three Censors, all Jesuits, were appointed to go into her case, and Gracián says that 'they probed her spirit very deeply, as if expecting to find the most dangerous things'. It was on their orders, it seems, that she wrote two notable Accounts of Conscience, giving a full and frank description of her spiritual development. These, and the impression made by the nuns themselves under cross-examination, finally convinced the Inquisitors that the delation was little more than a pack of absurdities and malicious lies. We hear no more of the embittered *beata* who had brought the trouble upon them, except that Teresa would never allow an ill word to be spoken of her. Her companion entered another convent but fared no better there, for we learn from a letter of Teresa's that she was later found to be insane.

One event afforded Teresa some consolation for all these tribulations. Her brother Lorenzo de Cepeda, whom she had not seen for nearly thirty-five years but had kept in affectionate touch with by letter, returned from America. He was a widower and had three children to educate – two boys in their teens and a lively, eight-year-old daughter, Teresita. Don Lorenzo, like his father, was a grave, upright and charitable man, who had given loyal service to the Viceroy of Peru and been rewarded with wealth and a position of some importance in Quito. Like his father, too, he strove uneasily to reconcile a love of ostentation with a somewhat awkward itch for ascetic devotion. His affection for his sister, four years his senior, was tinged with veneration, and he submissively took her as his spiritual mentor. With him came another widowed brother, the touchy hypochondriac Pedro, who had failed to make good in the New World and was to remain a disgruntled and troublesome dependant. Another brother, Jerónimo, to whom Teresa was much attached, had died whilst awaiting embarkation.

Lorenzo's arrival was providential. Once before, when Teresa was struggling to make her first foundation, he had come to her rescue with a timely gift of Peruvian gold. Now he again generously opened his purse to support her nuns and help them acquire a permanent home – a fine house with a view of picturesque towers and tall masts which enchanted Teresa. Still greater was the delight she took in her small niece and namesake. The Foundress adored children and had always been happy to have them round her, if possible in her own cell – first her younger sister Juana, then a succession of nieces and novices, and now this reincarnation of her childhood self, all the more bewitching for the exotic traits added by the Indian strains in the little girl's ancestry and upbringing. The Council of Trent forbade the profession of novices before the age of twelve, but there was no objection to children being brought up in a convent and dressed like their elders. 'Here she is, clad in her habit and going about the house like a little fairy', Teresa delightedly wrote to Gracián. 'Her father is in raptures and everyone is charmed by her. She has an angelic nature and keeps us amused at recreation time with stories about the Indians and the voyage which she tells much better than I could do.' At times Teresa anxiously asked herself whether the affection she felt for Teresita, and indeed for all her family, was not incompatible with the detachment required of those who aspired to follow the way of perfection. Was it not laid down in her own Constitutions that the Discalced should have as little as possible to do with their kinsfolk? She wrestled with these scruples in prayer, until her voices bade her have no fear. She could help guide their footsteps along the selfsame path.

By the end of May 1576, one year after their arrival in Seville, the new house was ready to receive the nuns. Juan de la Miseria had been summoned to decorate the chapel, and Gracián also ordered him to seize the opportunity of painting a portrait of the Foundress. Teresa protested indignantly, almost forgetting her vow of obedience. Why should anyone want to have her picture? Was it not vainglory and a waste of time? She sat reluctantly whilst the artist made a rapid sketch, leaving the details to be filled in later. 'God forgive you, Friar John', she exclaimed, half in jest and half in vexation, when he showed her his handiwork. 'You have made me look ugly and blear-eyed!' The portrait is indeed an uninspired work, suggesting nothing of the mobility of expression, the blend of human warmth, charm and saintliness which held its fascination even in old age. Gracián, who knew her best, speaks slightingly of it, though others found it a tolerable likeness. It is, at all events, the only authentic portrait from life that we have of her. About the same time that it was painted there arrived in Toledo, where she was to spend the next year, the enigmatic genius whom the Spaniards called El Greco. It is curious to reflect that he was there conjuring from his imagination those incomparable saints and mystics in ecstasy, yet ignorant of the presence of two great living exemplars (for St John of the Cross came to Toledo too, in the harrowing circumstances we shall shortly see). But this was certainly as Teresa would have wished it. If her features were to be recorded for posterity, then let it not be through the inspired vision of a master, but in the rough brush-strokes of a poor artist-friar, 'simple in the things of this world'.

The nuns moved into their new home on 3 June, the Sunday before Whitsun. Teresa would have preferred to keep the ceremony simple, but she yielded to the persuasions of those who argued that now was the time to show the whole city that the convent had emerged triumphant from all its trials. The Sevillans welcomed any excuse for a fiesta, and this was to be one after their own heart. The Archbishop, accompanied by a great train of clergy and confraternities, carried the Holy Sacrament to the newly decorated chapel. The crowded streets were gay with flowers and rich hangings and re-echoed to the playing of bands, the singing of ministrels, and the discharge of cannon and fireworks. A stray rocket started a blaze which sent a sheet of flame shooting up to the vaults of the cloisters, blackening its arches but miraculously failing to set the silk hangings alight. Teresa had no doubt that 'the Devil must have been so furious at the solemnities and the sight of yet another house of God that he wanted to get his own back, but the Almighty prevented him'. At the end of the service, she knelt before the Archbishop and received his blessing. Then, to the general amazement, the Archbishop in turn fell on his knees before the Foundress and asked for hers. 'Just imagine how I felt', she exclaimed in a letter to Ana de Jesús, her prioress at Beas, 'when I saw such a great prelate kneeling before this wretched old woman and refusing to get up until I gave him my blessing, and in the presence of all the Orders and Confraternities of Seville too!' The ceremony signalled the completion of her work in Andalusia. Neither Gracián nor the Inquisitors nor the pleas of her daughters could now prevent her from obeying the General's order of reclusion. She completed her preparations to leave the same night, and by two o'clock the next morning Teresa de Jesús was on her way back to Castile.

14

Work Suspended

The journey north was uneventful. Don Lorenzo insisted that his sister should travel by coach rather than covered wagon. He and his family accompanied her, Teresita beguiling the tedium of the road with her childish prattle. Their only misadventure occurred when — as the Foundress vividly described in a letter to Father Gracián —

> a great salamander or lizard ran up my arm, between the tunic and the flesh; by the mercy of God it got no further or else — to judge from my sensations — I think I should have died. My brother quickly snatched it up and threw it from me, but it struck Antonio Ruiz on the mouth.

Their immediate destination was Malagón, where the condition of the convent was causing disquiet. The house provided by Doña Luisa de la Cerda had proved damp and unsatisfactory and the prioress was ill. Teresa wanted to see things for herself before going on to Toledo to press the benefactress for something more suitable. Matters were settled without much difficulty, but Teresa remained in Toledo far longer than she had first intended — for over one-third of her three years' reclusion. But though she was forced to remain physically inactive, it was to prove a period of intense literary and spiritual creativity. The ecstatic seizures, from which she had been relatively immune for some time, now returned in all their alarming intensity. They would come upon her at Matins and on other public occasions, leaving her 'as if drunk' and causing her such shame and distress that she felt like slinking away and finding somewhere to hide. She writes of them to Lorenzo as if reporting the recurrence of some troublesome disease, saying that she was praying to be delivered from them and asking for his prayers too. She also mentions that she had been thinking of writing some account of her spiritual life since the point where she left off at the end of the autobiography now with the Inquisition. That manuscript, denounced by the malice of her enemies, was being read by the Grand Inquisitor in person. He seemed well disposed and had confided to their mutual friend Doña Luisa that he had found nothing blameworthy in it. This was reassuring news indeed, which she asked Lorenzo to keep to himself and commend earnestly to God.

At Gracián's urging, Teresa used her period of reclusion to bring her *Book of the Foundations* up to date. She asked Lorenzo to send her the draft of the first nine chapters and other papers left in Avila, and in October she got down to work, writing with such speed that in less than six weeks she had composed eighteen more chapters, thus completing the whole book except for the final chapters added in the last years of her life.

Not content with this, Teresa embarked on an entirely new work – *The Mansions of the Interior Castle*. Once again it was Gracián who pressed her to undertake it. One day, whilst they were discussing a point which she had treated at some length in her *Life* and regretted being unable to refer to, Gracián urged her to start work on a fresh account of this and other matters for the guidance of those aspiring to practise mental prayer. She demurred at first; then, true to her vow of obedience, started work on Trinity Sunday, 2 June 1577, nearly one year after her arrival in Toledo. The central idea for the book, a description of the soul's progress along the Mystic Way through seven successive stages or 'mansions' to the inmost chamber where 'the most secret things pass between God and the soul', came to her in a vision of a beautiful crystal globe in the likeness of a castle. The words flowed so swiftly from her pen that, despite poor health, the time taken up by her correspondence, and some three months' interruption when she was fully occupied with the practical business of the Order, it was completed in Avila by the end of November. Some claimed that she composed it by a sort of automatic writing whilst in a trance-like condition. A nun who often saw her at work declares that she commonly wrote after receiving Communion: 'She looked most radiant and wrote with great rapidity; she was generally so absorbed that even if we made a noise she would not stop, or even say we were disturbing her.' It seems astonishing that Teresa should have composed the sublimest of her mystical works at a time when she was beset with so many personal and administrative anxieties, and the Reform for which she had striven was persecuted and threatened with extinction.

Teresa's care for her convents did not cease with their foundation. She followed their fortunes with close and affectionate attention, watching over the material and spiritual progress of each with shrewd, motherly solicitude, and keeping up a tireless correspondence with her prioresses, with the protectors and protagonists of the Reform, and with her own family. Toledo was excellently placed for this demanding work by virtue of its position as the old hub of the peninsular communications system (though this role was now passing to Madrid) and by the excellent relations she enjoyed with the chief courier there. It also meant – as she frankly declares in her letters – that she would be more closely in touch with her dear Gracián, and through him with the successive twists and turns in the struggle between Calced and Discalced, the General with his allies in Rome and the party of King and Nuncio in Spain.

Neither side showed any real disposition to yield. After their defiance of the previous November, the Calced friars of Seville had been forced to make a show of submission. Gracián sent Friar Antonio de Jesús and the sub-prior Juan Evangelista (who had come over to the Reform) from cell to cell impounding possessions acquired in disregard of the Rule, and making sure that the friars were keeping within the monastery walls at night. Some degree of discipline was outwardly restored. But two emissaries were secretly dispatched to put the case for the Calced in Rome, and though they returned with nothing definite achieved they brought news of the new offensive which the General was preparing. It envisaged the dispatch of a Vicar-General to Spain, who was to secure the revocation of Gracián's powers and enforce the dissolution of all the Discalced priories in Andalusia. The man chosen to carry out the General's mandate was Jerónimo de Tostado, an astute and tenacious Portuguese friar who had ably carried out several commissions for him before. Tostado appeared in Madrid some weeks after Teresa's arrival in Toledo. The Nuncio informed him that the Royal Council would not recognize his functions in Castile and advised him to go on to Portugal and carry out his visitations there. 'God has delivered us from Tostado!' Teresa jubilantly informed one of her correspondents. But her optimism proved premature.

Gracián was in a delicate position, which any shift in the balance of power might quickly render untenable. He asked once more to be relieved of his responsibilities towards the Calced – Teresa favoured this course too – but was again firmly told that he must carry on. A royal decree was issued enjoining the secular authorities to give him whatever help he might need in carrying out his visitations. Knowing the furious animosity his personal intervention provoked amongst the Calced, he thought it prudent to use his powers sparingly. This was interpreted as a sign of weakness by his enemies, who were encouraged by news of Tostado's commission to regain the initiative. Father Suárez, the Provincial of the Andalusian Calced, emerged from his passivity to hold a Chapter at Ecija which deposed Juan Evangelista and other friars whom Gracián had put in as priors. Salazar, his colleague in Castile, also summoned a Chapter, which took care to endorse the Piacenza anti-Reform resolutions before the Discalced delegates arrived. The King declared the decisions of the Castilian Chapter null and void, and Gracián summoned all the Discalced priors in Castile and Andalusia to a meeting at Almodóvar. This was virtually a Chapter of the Reform, for its avowed purpose was the establishment of a separate Province, with its own Provincial and Definitors – the *de facto* creation, without reference to the General, of an autonomous branch of the Carmelite Order.

The next months – the winter of 1576 and the spring of 1577 – saw a lull in hostilities. Some of the Discalced priors passed through Toledo on their way from the Almodóvar Chapter and gave Teresa an enthusiastic account of it. 'It is all your handiwork, though – as you say – our prayers may have had a good deal to do with it', she wrote to congratulate Gracián, adding with perhaps excessive optimism: 'I was delighted to hear that all possible efforts are being made to induce our Father General to set up a separate Province and are making headway. To be at odds with one's Superior is the most intolerable of feuds.' But the feud continues to echo through her correspondence, though camouflaged with a picturesque cypher of her own devising. The Calced friars appear as 'owls' or 'cats', the Calced nuns as 'night-birds', the Discalced friars 'eagles' and the nuns 'doves' or 'butterflies'. The Inquisitors are 'angels' and the Grand Inquisitor 'the Arch-angel'. The Nuncio Ormaneto is 'Matusalem', Tostado 'Peralta' and Salazar 'Melchisadeck'. Our Lord figures as 'Joseph', the Devil as 'Patillas' ('Hoofy'). She refers to Gracián as 'Paul' or 'Eliseo', to herself as 'Laurencia' or 'Angela'. Even though the chief courier was a close relative of one of her nuns and absolutely trustworthy, the loss or interception of correspondence was a constant danger and might do much harm to the cause. Besides, this private language, these allusions which none but dedicated fellow fighters could understand, appealed to Teresa's sense of drama and added a delicious note of conspiratorial intimacy to the friendship which meant more to her than any other.

The nature of this friendship was the object of much malicious gossip in her day, and it remains as difficult for us to grasp as the whole concept of sanctity of which it is an ingredient. For Teresa's enemies, as perhaps for the cynical observer today, it was no more than the infatuation of an elderly spinster with an ambitious young charmer. The frustrations of a cloistered celibacy and the yearnings of a motherly but childless woman seemed to have found vent in a relationship which also offered the masochistic satisfactions of a will and intellect surrendered to one who combined in himself the roles of spiritual director and co-partner in the great enterprise of her life. There are passages in Teresa's letters which might bear this facile interpretation. We note the almost pathetic insistence with which she assures him of her affection and the pain caused by his absence:

> Since she first saw Paul, her soul had found relief and happiness with no one else . . . After parting from her Paul, nothing she has done has given her satisfaction, she has never seemed to succeed in anything, and even when she wished to submit to somebody else she has been unable to do so.

There is a fierce possessiveness in the claims she makes on his affection. Which, she asks him, does he cherish most – his mother or herself? Paul's mother has a husband and other children, whereas 'poor Laurencia has nobody in the world to love except this Father'. And can we detect almost a hint of feminine jealousy in her admonition that other, younger nuns must not become too fond of their Father? 'There are many reasons why it is permissible for me to feel great affection for you and to show it in our relations with each other', she tells him, but adds that others must not think they have the right to take the same liberties. 'When the sisters observe me doing and saying things which are allowed me on account of my age and of my knowing with whom I have to deal, they quite naturally think they can do the same.' To María de San José, her prioress in Seville, she artlessly exclaims how she envies them seeing so much of her Gracián and enjoying his beautiful sermons! Then, true to her generous nature, envy is swallowed up in an outburst of gratitude; she can never thank them enough for looking after him so well, and for feeding him up in the convent parlour when he might otherwise risk being poisoned by the Calced. They must be sure to write to her fully and often about him, as his Paternity is too busy to send her more than the scrappiest news about himself.

The key to Teresa's attitude towards Gracián is to be sought less in the contradictions of the human heart than in her clear integrity of soul. She believed that God had called the two of them to the same holy mission. It was therefore his will that they should be perfectly of one heart and one mind. 'Joseph' had assured her of this more than once in her locutions. Since God first began to guide her steps along the Way of Perfection, she tells us in her *Life*, 'I have never been able to form a deep friendship, nor find true solace in others, or any particular love for them, unless I deem them to love God and to be striving to serve him.' In Gracián she believed she had found one who was doing this in the highest possible degree, and her affection for him was consequently boundless. In the friendship which quickly developed between them the needs of Teresa the woman and Teresa the saint were perfectly blended and fulfilled.

And Gracián? Though the friar's image emerges from her letters less vividly than their writer's there seems no reason to believe that Teresa was far wrong in her high assessment of his qualities. Brilliantly gifted and utterly dedicated to his vocation, gentle yet firm, a man of peace yet energetic and courageous when he thought strong measures called for, his chief fault appears to have been a certain naivety which Teresa's shrewd admonitions never cured. He seemed unable to imagine the guile of which others, even of his own profession, were capable. Would he *please*, she implored him, cease reading aloud the letters which were meant for his eyes alone?

There is all the difference in the way I treat your Paternity in private and the way I talk of you to others, even to my own sister. Just as I would not like other people to eavesdrop on my conversations with God, or disturb me when I am alone with him, so it is with 'Paul'!

Many years later, Gracián described the nature of their relationship and of his feelings for the great Foundress in words which answer the question she had playfully put to him in one of her letters:

She loved me most tenderly, and I loved her more than any other mortal creature, even more than my own mother. But this great love which I felt for Mother Teresa, and she for me, is of a far different kind from what commonly passes for love in this world, for that is fraught with danger and gives rise to unholy thoughts and temptations which bring no solace but rather weaken spiritual fervour and arouse sensuality. But this love of mine for Mother Teresa, and hers for me, engendered in me purity, spirituality and love of God, and brought her consolation and relief in her trials, as she often told me herself, and so she would not have my own mother love me more than she did.

On the daughters who shared most closely in her labours, Teresa lavished a no less overflowing affection and hungered for it to be as unstintedly returned. 'I must tell you that I enjoy your letters so much that I am always wanting more of them', she assured María de San José, to whom nearly seventy of the extant letters written in the last six years of Teresa's life are addressed. 'I don't know why I have such a special love for your house and for all who live in it unless it is that I have gone through so much there. . . . I sometimes get such a longing to see you that I cannot think of anything else – that is the truth.' A letter saying how much the Prioress and her nuns were missing their Foundress was enough to make amends for the occasional coldness which had wounded Teresa in the past.

I was so delighted and touched to get it that I forgave you on the spot. So long as you love me as much as I love you I forgive you everything, be it past or future. . . . Believe me, I love you very dearly, and when I see you feel the same for me anything else seems a mere trifle and of no account, though in Seville, where we had to go through one thing after another and I was treating you as one of my dearest daughters, I was deeply hurt not to find the same love and openness in you. But this letter of yours has made me quite forget all that.

Another favourite correspondent was María Bautista, whose father was a son of that uncle who used to live opposite Teresa's home in Avila and had once galloped off in pursuit of his little niece and nephew on their way to the Moors and martyrdom. It was the same María who, as a boarder in the Incarnation, had first light-heartedly suggested the foundation of a house where the nuns could follow the Rule in all its pristine strictness. Now she was governing just such a house in Valladolid and had grown into a brisk administrator with a good grasp of money matters and a tendency to be rather too sure of herself and free with her advice:

Your Reverence must not be so sharp [Teresa enjoined her]. It is quite wrong of you to think you know everything and then to say you are humble. You do not look beyond the walls of your own little house instead of to the general good. That way can only lead to strife and bring everything we have built up to the ground . . . No other prioress – or indeed anyone else – has ever taken such a line with me. It puts our whole friendship at risk.

Teresa's words have an ominously prophetic ring.

Of her immediate family Teresa was most intimate with Lorenzo, four years her junior, and Juana, whom she had brought up in the Incarnation after the loss of their mother. Juana had a quiet and gentle nature – 'the soul of an angel', her sister affectionately declared – and showed herself a long-suffering wife to the touchy, self-important, improvident but well-meaning Juan de Ovalle. The latter was torn between resentment on account of the place Lorenzo occupied in Teresa's affections and the need to keep on good terms with a brother-in-law who gave him generous help. 'I am sure he is jealous by nature', Teresa wrote consolingly to her brother. 'In some ways he is a perfect baby. But he acted well in Seville and showed you great affection, so try for the love of God to bear with him.' A still sorer trial was the neurotic Pedro, the brother who failed to make good in America and was left sourly dependent on Lorenzo. A prey to hypochondria and religious melancholy, he wandered aimlessly around haunting churches and talking of becoming a friar. Teresa sent him a *bolilla*, a small metal hand-warmer to take the chill off his church-going, and exhorted Lorenzo to be patient with him and make him a regular allowance.

Lorenzo, like many a *conquistador*, had returned to Spain with a fair fortune and an inordinate desire for social recognition. Fernández de Oviedo, the historian of the Indies, cites the Cepeda brothers as examples of those adventurers with dubious credentials as hidalgos and 'Old Christians' who passed themselves off in the Indies for nobles. Returning with gold to reinforce their claims, the *Indianos* affected a lavish life-style. Lorenzo liked to see himself and his children splendidly attired and to hear themselves addressed as 'Don'. Teresa tactfully advised him to keep the lads to their studies and let them go around on foot like others of their age; 'you are prone to think too much of your social standing'. She also urged him to reduce the number of his servants and was pleased when he settled down as a country gentleman on an estate near Avila.

Like his father, Lorenzo combined a certain love of ostentation with a sincere if somewhat incongruous religious zeal. He had followed with deepening veneration his sister's pursuit of perfection and assisted her work as a foundress with timely gifts. On his return to Spain he looked submissively to her for spiritual, and often for temporal, guidance. He felt the urge to become a friar, to sell up his carpets and silver, to give himself wholly to a life of prayer and ascetic mortification. 'God prefers your health and your obedience to your penances', she had to admonish him. 'It is important not to go without sleep. . . . Time well spent in looking after your children does not injure prayer. . . . I cannot agree to your taking the discipline more than I said.' She made him limit the time he spent wearing the hair-shirt he begged her to send him. Then the humour of the situation struck her: 'I can't help laughing! You send me preserved fruits, cakes and money, and here am I sending you hair-shirts!' She also sent him other trifles – quinces which his housekeeper could make into jam, and sweet-smelling lozenges which were good for colds and headaches when thrown into a brazier. Above all, she sent him guidance about the trials and graces Lorenzo began to experience as he started to practise contemplative prayer, and she berated him at times with sisterly frankness: 'Why do you make vows [of greater perfection] without first consulting me? A fine kind of obedience that is! Remember what God said to Saul, and don't do anything I tell you not to!'

The number and diversity of Teresa's correspondents is astonishing. There survive more than 450 of her letters – a fraction probably of her total output – written to about 120 different recipients ranging from great personages like the Duchess of Alba, Cardinal Quiroga and the King himself, to unknown teenage postulants. The friends and acquaintances addressed or referred to in this vast portrait-gallery must number not less than 800, and some are most vividly depicted. We note the tact with which she handles men of difficult temperament like Fray Mariano – 'I am afraid you are being careless, since you are so outspoken. Once the Archbishop has given you an order, be very careful not to argue with him . . . What we need just now is prudence' – or Friar Antonio – 'I am sorry to hear he is not doing well in his office . . . Make him see that he will have to give an account of his stewardship, like anyone else . . . I am told he is much upset to hear

how many letters I write, but how seldom to him!' Her niece
Teresita and Gracián's little sister Bella are constant sources of
delight. The latter 'says the funniest things, and she is so happy and
gentle in disposition, just like my Father . . . The only trouble I
have is what to do with her mouth, which is very hard, and her
laugh is very harsh too, and she is always laughing.'

Gifts are sometimes exchanged as well as letters. From Seville
come sweets, oranges, fish kept fresh between slices of bread,
scented orange-flower water and petals preserved in syrup, and
exotic produce from the Indies like coconuts – 'presents fit for a
Queen', Teresa exclaims gratefully to the generous María de San
José, though she passes them on to her friends and seldom touches a
thing herself. She is vexed to find so little in Toledo to send in
return; often she must make do with enclosing a recipe or a cure
for toothache. If a purge is needed, she recommends a potent one
called The King of the Medes. Unassuming verses are sometimes
exchanged – *villancicos* or carols composed (often hurriedly, 'with
neither head nor feet') for some church occasion. Teresa enjoys
making up verses, though she claims no great poetic gifts. Once
she sends Lorenzo a poem beginning

> O Loveliness that exceeds
> All other loveliness we know . .

which she wrote down on coming out of an ecstasy.
Unfortunately she has forgotten it all except for the first three
verses – 'What a head for a Foundress!'

Another curious item is a letter to Bishop Mendoza of Avila in
the form of a *Vejamen* – a *jeu d'esprit* once popular in the
universities, when a newly fledged Doctor was facetiously
examined on some set theme. Teresa had received a locution, the
phrasing of which left her puzzled: 'Seek thyself in me!' Under the
Bishop's chairmanship, the nuns of St Joseph's met together to pool
their thoughts. They sent their answers, together with
contributions from Julián de Avila, Francisco de Salcedo, John of

the Cross and Lorenzo, to Teresa. Some, she says, she found enlightening, and others simply made her laugh. In her mock summary she takes each of the major participants in this sacred quiz to task. Julián 'begins well but ends badly, but his errors are pardoned because he is not long-winded'. The *Caballero santo* she charges with contradicting himself and quoting St Paul in such a way as to imply the saint was talking nonsense; unless this is cleared up, it will have to be reported to the Inquisition! Lorenzo (who was not used to being teased and had to be subsequently mollified) 'spoke more than he understood', but he too is forgiven on account of some good advice he gives and the amusement he provides. St John of the Cross is found to declare that we must seek God when we are dead to the world. But this, Teresa objects, was hardly the case with the Woman of Samaria or Mary Magdalene when they found Christ. So 'God deliver me from people so spiritual that they want to make contemplation perfect, cost what it may'. The world does not often catch such glimpses of saints at play, mixing teasing with theology, banter with high seriousness.

Nearly a quarter of Teresa's extant letters are addressed to Father Gracián. They range in tone from maternal solicitude and affection to admonition and shrewd advice. Gracián must be careful to get enough sleep and not to overwork; he should remember he is not made of iron! She is worried he might fall off his donkey or get poisoned by the Calced. How 'Angela would like to make Paul a good meal!' What majesty she finds in his words! His letters breathe perfection and she is delighted with them, particularly when he signs himself 'your dear son', as indeed he is. How wonderful when two souls understand each other! She blesses God for having brought them together in spirit and for the obedience she pledged to him and which she finds sweeter than all her previous freedom. 'Joseph' has assured her (she confides to María de San José) that 'Paul' is making good progress and is winning more and more merit. But 'Joseph' also warns that 'Paul' has many critics. She admires the calm way he meets his troubles and his gift for turning enemies into friends and helpers; all the same, he must be on his guard. He is often too credulous and trusting, too easily influenced by others, and volatile, now 'up in the air, now in the depths of the sea'. And is he always scrupulous enough, she asks, about 'telling the whole truth'? Later, as age and failing health deepen her need of companionship, a note of reproach creeps more frequently into the letters and she laments his absence and what she feels to be his lukewarm response to her unstinted trust and affection.

In June 1577 the fortunes of the Reform took a turn for the worse. Ormaneto, the Nuncio who had been such a good friend to it, died. Tostado forestalled Gracián at the death-bed and blandly informed him that Ormaneto had verbally revoked all Gracián's powers and that he, as Vicar-General, consequently had supreme authority over all the Carmelites. For some time past the Nuncio's favourable reports had fallen on deaf ears in Rome. Cardinal Buoncampagni, the Pope's nephew and the Protector of the Order, was a whole-hearted supporter of the Calced and had briefed Felipe Sega, the Nuncio designate, in their favour. Sega's arrival in August was to shift the balance of forces in Spain against the Discalced and threaten them with complete destruction.

Sega did not move at once against the leaders of the Reform. After summoning Gracián and examining his commissions, he told him that he might continue his visitations so long as the Nuncio was kept informed. Anxious to avoid exacerbating dissensions within the Order and aware that the Nuncio was only waiting for a favourable opportunity to strike, Gracián would have preferred to lie low. He went to consult the Archbishop of Toledo. The latter, according to Teresa's lively account, told him he had no more courage than a fly and sent him to put his case to the King. Philip, after referring the matter to his advisers, ordered him to proceed with his visitations. But still Gracián demurred, and for some nine months did virtually nothing. He was now in a serious quandary. By this passivity he risked forfeiting his one remaining source of strength – the backing of the King, who wished the Reform to go forward and had no intention of bowing to Rome's emissaries. Tostado was still forbidden by the Council to exercise his functions in Castile, and Philip's representations in Rome produced a papal ruling that the Nuncio was to intervene in the concerns of the Orders only at the royal request. Sega, deeply offended, talked of returning to Italy and blamed this humiliation on the machinations of the Discalced.

Gracián was mistaken in thinking that passivity would mollify his enemies. Withdrawing from the scene of hostilities to Alcalá and on to Guadalajara, where he conducted missions in the surrounding countryside during Lent, he then went to Pastrana and lived for a time in the famous caves which the hermits had once made their home. His enemies redoubled their efforts to discredit him by intensifying their slurs – 'such dreadful things', Teresa exclaimed, 'that I cannot write them'. Instead of defending himself, she would rather he had simply laughed at them for the ridiculous inventions they were. Gracián was accused of misusing his visitations as a cover for improper relations with the nuns, even with the venerable Foundress herself. The most venomous calumnies, stemming from a lay brother whom Gracián had once punished and from the veteran intriguer Baltasar Nieto, Prior of Pastrana, at length prompted Teresa to appeal to the King:

I implore Your Majesty for the love of God not to allow such infamous charges to be brought before the Courts, for the world is such that, however unfounded they are proved, some vestige of suspicion will remain in people's minds which they would seize every opportunity of exploiting. It will be no service to the Reform to discredit what it has so truly achieved. . . . I am deeply moved by the sufferings of this servant of God and by the upright and virtuous way he has borne them throughout, wherefore I beseech Your Majesty to protect him from such dangers. . . . He really seems to me a man sent by God and his blessed Mother.

Gracián's innocence was vindicated by a public retraction from the lay brother and a letter of apology from Fray Baltasar. But the Calced continued their whispering campaign and pressed home their attacks as viciously as ever.

The Reform was weakened by the loss of influential supporters. Don Alvaro de Mendoza, who had backed Teresa so stoutly whilst Bishop of Avila, was translated to Palencia. Teresa decided to leave Toledo and arrange the transfer of St Joseph's from the jursidiction of his successor, who might not prove so friendly, to that of the Order, of which Gracián still remained the Visitor. In September the President of the Royal Council, who had also been well disposed towards the Reform, died and was succeeded by the temporizing President Pazos. The following month the nuns of the Incarnation held their triennial elections and voted by 54 to 34 to have Teresa back as their prioress. Tostado declared the elections invalid, and those who persisted in voting for her were insulted and excommunicated. Not long afterwards, John of the Cross and another Discalced friar, confessors at the Incarnation, were abducted and spirited away by the Calced, none knew whither.

Teresa, confined to her convent of St Joseph's, addressed another anguished appeal to King Philip. The Calced, she declared, seemed to fear neither the King's justice nor God himself. She would rather see the kidnapped friars in the hands of the Moors, who would probably show them more pity. John of the Cross, 'who is such a great servant of God, is so weak from everything he has suffered that I fear for his life. For the love of God I implore Your Majesty to command that he be set free at once.' The Calced had also seized Antonio de Jesús, 'a good old man, the first of all our friars', and they were going around declaring that they would make an end of those worthy men since Tostado had ordered it. The King alone could bring this scandal to an end, and Teresa concludes her letter with an ardent appeal that he should do so. Some biographers believe that she followed it up with a personal interview with King Philip, but the account of the alleged audience seems of doubtful authenticity. She makes no reference elsewhere in her writings to any personal contact with the King.

The end of the year brought no end to hostilities. 'Many legions of devils seem to have joined forces against the Discalced friars and nuns', Teresa wrote to a friend. The Calced had been ordered by the King to lift the excommunication pronounced against the obdurate nuns of the Incarnation, but they continued to harass and bully them. Teresa prayed that she might be spared the ordeal of being sent back there as Prioress, for she had troubles enough already. On Christmas Eve she fell downstairs and broke her left arm. It was still paining her four months later when a *curandera* was called in to apply her dubious remedies. Teresa was deeply worried over the fate of the kidnapped friars and her powerlessness to help them. St John of the Cross, she learned, had been taken to Toledo, where Tostado vainly attempted to force him to abandon the Reform and then had him flogged and confined in a punishment cell. His companion was sent to another monastery from which he managed to escape three months later. 'Things are going from bad to worse', Teresa wrote. 'I fear some disaster.' She was haunted by the thought that the Calced would lay violent hands on her Paul, who was still living in his cave at Pastrana, 'suffering abominably from false witnesses', but praying for his persecutors and 'showing a perfection that astounds me'.

Throughout the early months of 1578 Teresa continued to chafe at her enforced inactivity.

It makes me sad to be here doing nothing but eat, sleep and talk about those Fathers. . . . I am fearfully distressed about Friar John and afraid they may bring some fresh charge against him. God treats his friends in a terrible way, though they have really no reason to complain, for that is how he treated his own

Son. . . . I am suffering agonies at not being free to do what I tell
other people to do. . . . I keep thinking of what they have done
to Friar John of the Cross. I don't know how God can allow such
things. For a good nine months they kept him in a prison-cell so
tiny that, small as he is, it would hardly hold him. The Nuncio
ought to be told about it so that he can see what these people did
to this saintly Friar John, who committed no fault at all. It is a
piteous story.

Yet neither Gracián, nor Fray Antonio de Jesús, who was free
again and had influence with the Duchess of Alba, nor Fray
Mariano, who had the ear of the King, seemed to show much
concern at the plight of the prisoner. The Calced were growing
more and more shameless. 'It never occurs to them that they are
working against God. They care nothing for the King, as they see
that, no matter what they do, he remains silent.' Teresa was more
than ever convinced that the only hope lay in securing the
recognition of the Discalced as a separate Province, and she urged
Gracián, Mariano, Father Roca, the energetic Prior of Mancera,
and others to promote this idea as forcefully as possible. But when
the Discalced, on the initiative of the elderly and sometimes
injudicious Fray Antonio, held a second meeting at Almodóvar in
an attempt to present this separation as a *fait accompli*, Teresa
strongly disapproved. She believed it would only make matters
worse and be taken as a sign of outright rebellion. The correct
course was to petition the General and the Pope, and to convince
the Nuncio and the Calced themselves that separation would be in
the interests of all.

In July Gracián emerged from seclusion and resumed his
visitation of the Discalced convents in Castile. He did so
reluctantly, and only after the President of the Royal Council, on
the King's instructions, had ordered him to do so. Teresa heard the
news with foreboding, for it was clear that it was likely to bring
the conflict with Sega to a head. Before the end of the month the

blow fell – an order or Counter-Brief from the Nuncio annulling all the powers granted by his predecessor to Gracián. Sega now proposed to govern the Discalced himself, or in practice through Tostado, the Vicar-General, and the Calced. Gracián was formally apprised of this decision whilst making his visitation at Valladolid, and a few days later a similar notification, couched in harsh words against her Paul, was served on Teresa. Gracián immediately suspended his visitation and returned to Madrid, stopping briefly to see the Foundress on the way.

I was so overcome on seeing your Paternity [she wrote to him the following day]. All yesterday – Wednesday – I was heavy at heart to see you so worried, as well you might be, scenting danger at every turn and travelling by roundabout ways like some malefactor. But I have not lost one jot of my confidence that all will be for the best.

The Royal Council was stirred into action by Sega's move, which was regarded as a deliberate flouting of the King's authority. The Counter-Brief was itself countermanded by a royal order forbidding the Discalced to obey Sega, banning the circulation of his Briefs, and confirming Gracián in his powers as Visitor. The luckless Paul was caught between the Scylla and Charybdis of conflicting jurisdictions. From Madrid he went to Pastrana to join Friars Antonio and Mariano. There Sega's messengers pursued him, presented their Counter-Brief and demanded his submission. The arguments formerly used by the Discalced that in ecclesiastical matters the Nuncio's authority was paramount, since it represented the Pope's, were now turned against them. Gracián decided that he must yield. After turning over all Ormaneto's commissions to Sega's emissaries he returned to Madrid to report to the Nuncio and the King. But his compliance had angered the latter without placating Sega, who proceeded to excommunicate the Discalced leaders and had each of them detained in a monastery. Father Roca, who had come to Madrid to discuss a proposal for a new priory there, was likewise confined. When he finally secured an interview with the Nuncio, the latter delivered a tirade against the Foundress, describing her as a

> restless, disobedient and contumacious gadabout who, under the guise of devotion, has invented false doctrines and broken her enclosure against the orders of the Council of Trent and her own superiors, teaching as if she were a Master, in disregard of what St Paul said about women not being allowed to teach.

Gracián, he went on, was just as bad. The Discalced themselves were less to blame. Provided Gracián was brought to trial and made to answer for his misdeeds, the Nuncio would hold nothing against them and would even petition Rome to let them be formed into a separate Province.

Was the Nuncio then open to reason after all? Unjust and prejudiced though he was against Teresa and Gracián, would he in fact prove not unfriendly to the Discalced and even promote their best chance of survival – a Province of their own? Shortly after this interview he sent again for Father Roca, who found him in a very different mood. Sega had just learned of the royal rejection of his Counter-Brief and the defiant stance the Discalced had adopted at their second meeting at Almodóvar. Angrily withdrawing his promised concessions, he declared that he would place them under obedience to the Calced Provincials of Castile and Andalusia. Gracián, confined in a priory at Madrid, was brought to trial on charges formulated by the implacable Calced of Andalusia and condemned to detention at the Nuncio's pleasure in Alcalá, where he was made to undergo a harsh regime of fasts and scourging and forbidden to have any contact with the Discalced.

The King, though lukewarm in Gracián's defence after his submission to Sega, now reacted strongly to this new provocation by the Nuncio. Royal instructions were dispatched to the Discalced forbidding them to pay any attention to Sega's orders. The friars were caught in Gracián's quandary: whom should they obey – Nuncio or King? Most opted for the former, since the tide still seemed to be running against the Reform. As a result of the second Almodóvar Chapter, two delegates had been dispatched to Rome, but one quickly defected and their case went by default. Father Padilla, an intermediary on behalf of the Discalced with the King, was denounced to the Inquisition and arrested. Fray Juan de la Miseria disappeared – kidnapped, most probably, Teresa was afraid. After eight months' imprisonment St John of the Cross escaped from Toledo, but his ordeal left him so ill and frail that Teresa feared for his life. She herself did everything she could to mobilize support by writing to her influential friends. The Count of Tendilla showed himself particularly ardent in his defence of the Reform. Thanks largely to his intervention, and that of the President of the Royal Council, Sega at last agreed to consider a compromise. Four assessors were appointed to advise and assist him in the dispute. Two of the men named – the Dominicans Hernando del Castillo and Pedro Fernández, the previous Apostolic Delegate for Castile – were old friends of Teresa and sympathetic to her work. The Foundress, who had been blaming herself for causing all the trouble and almost believed that the storm might be stilled if only, like some latter-day Jonah, she were to be thrown overboard, saw the first break in the clouds. 'As soon as I heard that the King had appointed him [Fernández],' she wrote, 'I deemed the matter as good as settled.'

The climate in Rome was also beginning to change. Father Rossi died at the beginning of September. 'I felt deeply grieved at the news,' Teresa wrote, 'and the day I heard it I did nothing but weep, for I was much distressed by all the trouble we had caused him.' She could never forget that it was the General's early support which had made the whole development of the Reform possible, and she remained convinced that its subsequent troubles would never have arisen if only he had been kept fully and fairly informed. The new General lost little time in writing in a friendly vein to the Discalced friars of Seville, who replied pledging him their obedience. The following May Father Roca and another emissary left for Rome. Their mission proved more successful than the first, though it was not until a year later – on 22 June 1580 – that the longed-for Brief creating a separate Province for the Discalced was issued by the Pope.

Meanwhile, in Spain, the Discalced were still beset by trials. Confusion and persecution had sown discord in their ranks. In Alcalá, where Gracián had been sent to serve his sentence, some of his brethren sought to ingratiate themselves with the Calced by reporting that he was trying to re-establish his authority. The Nuncio, ready to believe anything to his discredit, sent the prisoner a sharp rebuke. In Seville, the Calced carried out a visitation of Teresa's recent foundation and bullied some of the nuns into making statements incriminating her and Gracián. Sister Beatriz, whose harrowing childhood is so sympathetically described in the *Foundations*, took the lead in intriguing against and deposing Teresa's faithful Prioress, María de San José. 'All the furies of hell seem to have been let loose together at Seville', Teresa wrote to Gracián, tormented by the thought of the fresh harm these allegations might do him. 'None of the trials we have gone through has been anything compared with this.' But by the end of April 1579 she was able to give him better news. It seemed likely that María would be restored to office. Best of all, the Calced had been forced to relinquish their hold over the Discalced. Under pressure from his assessors, Sega had agreed that the Discalced should be freed from their jurisdiction and given a superior or Vicar-General of their own. Teresa learned with mixed feelings that Father Angel de Salazar, from whose ambivalence and opportunism she had suffered in the past, had been chosen for the office.

God grant he may not enjoy it for long [she wrote to Gracián, hastening to add]: By this I do not mean I wish him a short life, for after all he is the ablest of the Calced and will treat us with great consideration, specially since he is shrewd enough to see what the outcome of the negotiations [in Rome] is bound to be.

Teresa was not mistaken. By the end of June the new Vicar-General had secured the reinstatement of María de San José. It took much longer, and probably the intervention of the King as well, before the Nuncio could be prevailed upon to free Gracián from confinement. Early in 1580 however we find Father Gracián at liberty in Andalusia and even authorized to act in that Province as Salazar's deputy. By that time, too, Teresa's period of reclusion in Avila had come to an end and she was busy again with new foundations. God's gadabout was once more on the road.

15

The Last Foundations

First, the Foundress was instructed to revisit the Discalced houses at Valladolid, Salamanca and Malagón. There was much there that required her presence and personal intervention. In Salamanca the nuns needed to be rehoused; otherwise, Salazar darkly hinted, it might prove necessary to dissolve the community and disperse its members to other convents. There had been trouble in Malagón, and there was even a suggestion that Teresa should stay on there as Prioress. In any case she wanted to supervise the construction of the new convent promised by Doña Luisa. But the Foundress was too shrewd not to suspect that the Vicar-General had mixed motives for authorizing her journey.

Perhaps the Calced friars would be glad to get me out of the way – there are signs of this – and his Paternity may not be sorry to see me a long way from the Incarnation [she wrote to María Bautista in Valladolid]. Just think of a poor old body like me setting off on on her travels again – and then on to Malagón! I tell you, it quite makes me laugh, though I have courage enough for it, and more too!

Teresa was sixty-five, and increasingly poor health made her feel her age. She now depended heavily on the devotion and skill of a lay sister who was to remain a close companion for the rest of her life. Unlike most of Teresa's novices, who came of good and sometimes distinguished families, Ana de San Bartolomé was of peasant stock. Ardent, selfless and ingenuous, she had the makings

of an eccentric or a saint. 'I feel like doing all sorts of crazy things –
if only I were allowed to!' she used to exclaim. Teresa witnessed
the outcome of one such indiscreet urge. Masons were working on
some repairs to the convent and Ana begged one of them to give
her a lesson in mortification. The fellow complied by thrusting his
fist into her veil. Teresa taught the girl to read, took her to share
her cell, and aroused in her a vocation to tend the sick. A visionary
herself, Ana claims in her autobiography to have witnessed many
of Teresa's most exalted mystical experiences and to have been
granted some herself. After Teresa's death, she too became prioress
and foundress and in due course was accounted worthy of
beatification.

For some time past the Foundress had been receiving reports of a
community of seven *beatas* in the remote township of Villanueva
de la Jara, to the east of Malagón. They were leading a life of
exemplary penance, but subject to no Rule, and they desired to
join the Discalced. With memories of the difficulties she had
encountered when asked to incorporate the community formed by
María de Yepes in Alcalá, Teresa had prudently declined. Besides,
the *beatas* had no endowment nor even a suitable building, and the
place was too small to support them through its alms. Villanueva
was a few miles from La Roda, where the holy transvestite
Catalina de Cardona had once lived in a cave and founded a
monastery. It was there that Fray Antonio had been sent to serve
the sentence of reclusion pronounced against him by the angry
Nuncio. He had taken up the cause of the *beatas*, and whilst Teresa
was in Malagón Fray Gabriel, the Prior of La Roda, came to add
his eloquent pleas on their behalf. But still Teresa demurred. All
reason seemed against the project, and she had little doubt that
Father Salazar, with his realistic outlook and lack of enthusiasm for
the Discalced, would endorse her refusal. But human prudence
was overruled:

After Communion one day, when I was commending the matter

to God [Teresa recounts in the *Foundations*] his Majesty sternly rebuked me, asking what resources I had had when making my previous foundations and telling me to have no hesitation in accepting this house, for it would be greatly to his service and the profit of many souls.

Teresa obeyed at once, and preparations were quickly made. Salazar accepted her change of plans with unwonted good grace, two nuns were selected from Malagón and another two from Toledo, and in the middle of February 1580 the party set off from Malagón on their thirty-leagues' journey. Teresa had been confined to her bed, unable to move her injured left arm. Now, suddenly, she felt imbued with fresh strength. 'It pleased the Lord', she wrote, 'that the weather should be fine, and my health so good that it seemed I had never known a day's sickness.' News of their coming spread through the villages and townships of La Mancha, where the friars escorting them were well known, and several of her own nuns had relations. Folk flocked to catch sight of a real live saint – this nun, old and infirm, miraculously restored to health in order to go about God's business. In one village a rich peasant mustered his whole household, and the cattle as well, to receive her blessing. In another, the throng was so great and persistent that the constables had to clear a way. The night before they arrived at La Roda, the travellers lodged at an inn where Ana and another nun shared a room with Teresa. The lay sister was woken by the strains of strange music and roused her companion to listen whilst the Mother slept. It was of a celestial sweetness quite beyond the power of any earthly musicians to create and could only have come from the harps of angels. So at least it seemed to the two nuns who have left accounts of their rare experience.

The following morning the party reached the monastery of Our Lady of Succour, built eight years before in a wild and beautiful spot outside La Roda. The friars came out in procession and, after kneeling before the Foundress for her blessing, escorted her to their monastery. She herself modestly ascribes the solemnity of the welcome to the friars' joy at the return of their prior, and adds:

> At the sight of their coming out to meet us, barefoot and clad in rough frieze mantles, we were filled with devotion and I felt greatly moved. It was as if I had been transported back to the great days of our holy Fathers. They seemed like white, sweet-smelling flowers blooming in that wilderness.

They entered the chapel, where a Te Deum was sung, through an underground entrance which the ingenious Fray Mariano, giving free vent to his exuberant imagination and engineering skill, had fashioned to represent the cave of the prophet Elijah, the Carmelites' famed predecessor. The saintly Catalina had died three years before, and her tomb was held in fervent veneration. Teresa was seized with a craving to imitate the virtues and sufferings of the hermit, who appeared to her during an ecstasy after Communion. 'She exhorted me not to grow weary, but to strive to go on making new foundations, and although she did not say so explicitly, I understood that she was helping me before God', Teresa writes, adding rather mysteriously: 'She also told me something else which it is not fitting to write down here.'

The entry into Villanueva de la Jara, three leagues further on, was a triumphal procession, very different from the furtive way in which Teresa had often found it prudent to slip into a hostile or indifferent town. Here the Municipal Council and all the inhabitants enthusiastically awaited her coming. The children came out to greet her and receive her blessing, the local confraternities and the friars from a Franciscan monastery which followed the strict Rule of St Peter of Alcántara joined forces with the Carmelites from Our Lady of Succour, and the bells of the parish church pealed out a welcome. After Mass, the nuns intoned a litany and prayed for rain, for the land was suffering from drought. Miracles were in the air, and before nightfall the rain came.

The seven *beatas* shared all work in common and recognized no Superior. They slept little and ate less, supporting themselves through their spinning and the alms they received. Only one could read well, the rest reciting the Office as best they could from cast-off breviaries. 'God will have accepted their good intentions and the pains they took,' Teresa charitably observed, 'though it must all have been chock-full of mistakes.' Such was the strange little community which, after the bestowal of the habit, Teresa's nuns had to transform into a convent of the Discalced. 'For the first few days they told me they found it uphill work,' she writes, 'but once they got to know them and realized their virtue, they were very glad to stay with them and came to love them very much.'

By the end of March Teresa was back in Toledo. Fortune seemed to be smiling once more on the Reform. The negotiations in Rome for the establishment of a separate Province were going well. In Andalusia, Gracián was at liberty again and allowed virtually a free hand. They were both impatient to meet, but Teresa realized the need for caution.

> Although you must not come and see me yet [she wrote to him] it made me happy when you said you would come if I wanted you to. But I fear these brethren of ours would seize on it, and besides it is a long way to travel and would be very tiring for you. I must content myself with the assurance that you cannot fail to come later.

Father Salazar now seemed positively eager for fresh foundations and pressed her to undertake one at Palencia, where her old friend Don Alvaro de Mendoza was Bishop. Teresa would have preferred to see a convent established in the capital, Madrid. For this a licence from the Archbishop of Toledo would be required and the usual objections were sure to be raised. Cardinal Quiroga, who was Inquisitor-General as well as Archbishop, was not ill disposed towards the Reform, but all Teresa's attempts to obtain an interview with him went unheeded.

'I cannot think why it is that Our Lord is putting so many obstacles in the way of my going to see this "Angel"', Teresa wrote, dropping again into their confidential code, to her Paul. Gracián had to pass through Toledo on his way to visit the Discalced houses in Castile, and together they waited upon the Cardinal-Archbishop. The stern old man received his visitors courteously and assured them that a licence would be issued. He also raised a matter which had been weighing heavily on Teresa's mind – the fate of the *Life* which had been denounced to the Inquisition. The book, he declared, had been examined with the greatest care, and he had read it himself. He pronounced it to be 'sound, true and most profitable', and promised it would be returned to her whenever she wished. But in spite of these reassuring words, Teresa never succeeded in getting the licence for her Madrid convent and it was left for others to found it. Nor did the Inquisitors ever return to her the manuscript of her *Life*. Some four years after Teresa's death the resourceful Ana de Jesús at last secured its return. It is now preserved, together with the manuscripts of St Augustine and St John Chrysostom, amongst the most precious treasures of the Escurial.

There were other writings which still lacked the stamp of official approval. The sublimest expression of Teresa's mystical experiences and teaching, and therefore the most vulnerable to attack or misunderstanding, was *The Mansions of the Interior Castle*. Before leaving Toledo, Gracián suggested that they should take with them the manuscript of this work and scrutinize it with the help of a theologian whom he knew in Segovia, Father Diego de Yanguas. The three of them, Teresa behind the double enclosure of veil and parlour grille, spent many hours together in her Segovian convent discussing and amending the text, which has yet miraculously preserved the graceful spontaneity with which it was composed. Teresa's shorter *Meditations on the Song of Songs* fared less happily. Alarmed at the delicate nature of the subject and at Teresa's presumption in flouting the convention forbidding women to teach, Father Yanguas ordered her to burn it at once. She obeyed, not realizing that copies had been made and that its survival was thus assured.

Whilst Teresa and the two priests were poring over *The Mansions* in the parlour of the Segovian convent, great events were occurring in Spain. The empire of the Most Catholic King was nearing its apogee. Two years before, the young King Sebastian of Portugal had perished with the flower of his nobility in an ill-conceived crusade against the Moslems of North Africa, and the aged Cardinal who succeeded him died childless. Philip, as Sebastian's uncle and closely connected by blood and marriage to the royal house of Braganza, had a strong claim to the throne and was determined to enforce it. His troops were already mustering on the Portuguese frontier when fate threatened to thwart his designs. The influenza epidemic which had been sweeping Europe ravaged the army, struck down his young Queen, and put his own life in danger. Teresa too fell sick in Toledo and was to suffer a still more serious bout in Valladolid. The same epidemic cost the lives of her old friends Francisco de Salcedo, the *Caballero santo* of Avila, and her one-time confessor Baltasar Alvarez, and may have hastened the death of her brother Lorenzo. Philip recovered, suppressed his grief at the Queen's death, and pushed on with his plans. To command the enterprise he appointed the Duke of Alba, still the foremost soldier of his day though now elderly and in disgrace. He had beguiled the tedium of his enforced leisure reading Teresa's *Life*, of which the Duchess had had a copy made. Strange to think of this embodiment of Castilian pride and intransigence, this crusader bent on extirpating enemies of the faith with blood and fire, pondering the narrative of a soul enamoured only of humility, sacrifice and love!

Teresa had watched the deepening crisis with foreboding. The year before she had written to Don Teutonio de Braganza, Archbishop of Evora and an uncle of one of the claimants to the throne, imploring him to use his influence to avert the threatened conflict.

If God should permit such a disaster, I hope I may die rather than see it [she wrote]. Everyone here says that our King has right on his side . . . At a time when there are so few Christians, it would be a calamity if they were to start fighting one another!

But once the die was cast for war, she wrote to the Duchess congratulating her on Alba's restoration to favour and assuring her that all the nuns were praying for the success of the expedition. The Duke's ruthlessness and the superior strength of the Spanish army quickly gained the day, and Philip found himself master of Portugal and its vast overseas possessions.

Any satisfaction which Teresa, as a loyal subject of the Most Catholic King, may have felt at this manifestation of divine favour was soon marred by family troubles. At the end of June she learned that Lorenzo had died. Prematurely aged by his exertions in the New World, he had for some time had premonitions of his approaching end. Only a few days before his sudden collapse, Teresa had given him a sisterly scolding:

I can't think how you have got it into your head that you are shortly going to die, or why you have such ridiculous notions and worry about what won't happen! Trust in God who is a true friend and will not fail your children or you.

Lorenzo's eldest son, who had inherited his father's name but not his piety, had indeed given some cause for concern. Packed off at the age of eighteen to Peru, where he eventually made good, he had already begun to sow his wild oats and left a natural daughter in Spain. His brother Francisco had thoughts of becoming a Discalced Carmelite friar, but abruptly changed his mind and followed his brother to America with a penurious fourteen-year-old bride. Another family problem was their uncle Pedro, who had lived at his brother's expense and sorely taxed Lorenzo's patience with his irritability, restlessness and deepening religious melancholia. 'I don't know how anyone could put up with him or do things for him just in the way he fancies', Teresa wrote to console Lorenzo. 'To be of such a humour is terrible both for himself and everyone else.' Lorenzo bequeathed his brother a small annuity, and Teresa, named executrix of his estate, had to make sure he received it. The following winter we find her writing: 'I have been so worn out by my relatives since my brother died!' and nearly a year later: 'If you only knew the trouble I have been having with all these relatives! I spend my whole time trying to avoid getting mixed up with them!'

After a hurried visit to Avila to look into her late brother's affairs, Teresa turned her attention again to her convents. First, she needed to discuss matters with Don Alvaro de Mendoza, who generally resided in Valladolid in preference to the old cathedral city of Palencia, thirty miles distant, where the next foundation was due to be made. But soon after arriving in Valladolid, Teresa suffered a relapse, probably brought on by the exhaustion of constant travelling and the grief of bereavement, which seemed 'so serious that I thought I should die'. It left her exhausted and listless. Her will seemed numb with an unwonted weariness of spirit. Was this the after-effect of illness, or was the Devil behind it? She consulted Father Ripalda, a Jesuit friend, who declared that it was simply the effect of advancing age. Gracián noted the physical deterioration which had set in. Until then, Teresa had carried her sixty-five years with the sprightly grace of youth; now, all at once, she was an old woman, dependent more than ever on the care of her nurse-companion Ana. Father Ripalda's diagnosis did not convince her. 'I am now older still,' she observed when concluding her *Foundations*, 'but that feeling has quite left me.' Everyone was urging her on – Ripalda, Salazar, the Bishop, her own daughters – and not only in Palencia were they clamouring for a foundation, but in Burgos as well. What torment to feel strength of body and soul ebbing, when so much remained to be done in God's service! She wrestled in prayer with her plaints and doubts, and one day after Communion reassurance came: 'What do you fear? When have I ever failed you? I am the same now as always. Do not give up either of these foundations.' The effect of the locution was instantaneous. 'My courage and resolution quickly returned, and no obstacles in the world could now stop me. I set to work at once, and the Lord began to provide me with means.'

The foundation at Palencia proved to be one of the most straightforward ever undertaken by Teresa. There had been some opposition at first from the Town Council, which was at odds with the Bishop, for Palencia was a poor place and had five convents and several monasteries already. But the critics yielded with a good grace. 'It seems that Mother Teresa carries in her bosom some mandate from the Almighty's Royal Council,' one of them wryly remarked when Gracián came to take preliminary soundings, 'and, like it or not, we must do as she wants.' Once again, the Foundress let herself be guided by a locution. Faced with a choice between two houses for her convent, she was on the point of signing a contract for the one which seemed to offer most advantages when she was given to understand that she should choose the other. She resisted at first, unwilling to go back on decisions already taken and to embarrass her helpers. Would it not look like mere feminine caprice, and how could she be sure she was not just imagining things? But the inner voices persisted and left her in no doubt. The confessor whom she consulted proved of the same mind. A way was found to extricate themselves from the undesirable deal – 'It was now clear that the Devil had been blinding us!' – and the new convent was established next to a chapel after which it was quaintly named St Joseph's of Our Lady of the Street.

Though all but submerged by her duties as executrix and foundress, Teresa was serenely borne along by the mighty currents of her spiritual life. For more than twenty years she had striven to plot their course in the Accounts of Conscience drawn up at the behest of her confessors. The last to come from her pen, and one of

the most remarkable, was written in Palencia in May 1581 and
addressed to Dr Velásquez, an old friend and confessor from
Toledo and now the Bishop of Osma and sponsor of her next
foundation. It breathes a spirit of extraordinary calm and detachment. Her soul, she writes, seems utterly secure in God's keeping,
as if in some impregnable castle, though she has not lost her fear of
offending him or her longing to do and suffer for his sake – a
longing now so ardent that her soul seemed to have lost a part of its
very being. She had grown less concerned with bodily
mortification and more with preserving her health and husbanding
her strength so that she could continue to serve God; perhaps there
was some selfishness concealed in this, though she could say in all
truth that her wish to do penance was as strong as ever. 'Imaginary'
visions no longer came to her, but she seemed to be granted –
except in moments of grave illness – a perpetual awareness of the
presence of the Holy Trinity. Her inner voices still spoke to her;
she had indeed been saved by them from going seriously astray in
Palencia. Her greatest misery was to see herself so useless in God's
cause, her keenest desire to love him more fully and to see all men
serve him. Whether she lived or died was now all one to her,
except when she was overcome by a craving to see God. But if, she
concludes, through her intercession she could help a single soul to
love and praise him more, albeit only for a short time, that seemed
to matter more to her than that she should be in glory.

Whilst she was in Palencia, the Bishop of Osma wrote to ask
Teresa to make a foundation in Soria, a city in his diocese where a
pious widow called Doña Beatriz de Beamonte had offered half
her fortune for the endowment of a convent. Though this meant
postponing her plans for Burgos – and the Foundress was still
hoping to obtain the Primate's licence for a convent in Madrid –
Teresa could not refuse. With the Bishop's support things could be
expected to go smoothly in Soria as they had done in Palencia.
Doña Beatriz sent a carriage to fetch her and the journey was made

in some style, though it amused Teresa to learn that some passers-by mistook them for a posse of prisoners under escort to the dungeons of the Inquisition. The Foundress was happy in the knowledge that all the formalities had now been completed for the establishment of a separate Discalced Province. Gracián had been duly elected to head it at a Chapter which met in Alcalá to lay down its constitution and administration. But though more than two months had passed since the Chapter concluded its sessions, Gracián had not returned as promised to assist her with the new foundations. Teresa could not conceal her disappointment. She had been looking forward to making the journey in his company, she told him plaintively, and now that this was denied her she was beginning to feel tired already.

I tell you, my Father, that the flesh, after all, is weak, and what has happened has made me sadder than I could have wished. I have felt it very keenly. At least your Paternity might have postponed your departure [from Palencia] until you had seen us into our new house. A week one way or the other could not have mattered to you very much. I have been very lonely here. . . . I shall have little heart for anything now, for after all the soul suffers from the absence of one who both governs it and brings it solace . . . Oh, how tired poor Laurencia is of everything! She commends herself earnestly to your Reverence, and says her soul can find no peace or quietness in anyone but God and in those who understand her, as your Reverence does. Everything else is such a cross to her that no words can describe it.

In the same letter Teresa thanks Gracián for having sent Father Doria in his place to help with the Soria foundation. The Genoese banker, six years older than Gracián, had come to Spain in 1570 and taken the Carmelite habit seven years later after his brilliant financial and administrative gifts had brought him to the favourable notice of the Archbishop of Seville and the King himself. Teresa too was quick to discern his quality. 'A man of great distinction and perfection', she calls him – 'a sound man, full of humility and penitence'. But she also notes his lack of 'graciousness and serenity'. Later, as she came to know him better, she seems to have sensed – though she never permitted herself to censure – the Italian subtlety and the ruthless drive for power which would inevitably set him at odds with the frank and gentler Gracián.

As the travellers entered Soria and passed in front of the mansion where the Bishop was staying, Teresa pulled back the carriage curtains and asked the driver to stop. The nuns knelt to receive the Bishop's blessing. Everything had been prepared as promised, and Doña Beatriz proved a munificent and understanding patron. Only her nephew Don Carlos, who felt his expectations defrauded by her benefactions, found difficulty in concealing his resentment. Teresa, reading his thoughts, assured him that though he might be materially the poorer, the time would come when he would reap rich spiritual benefits. Many years later, Don Carlos was to present sworn testimony describing how, when prostrate upon a sickbed from which he never thought to rise, he had seen the saint in a vision, been converted and restored to health, and devoted the rest of his days to working for the Order he had once vehemently abused. Others vowed that it was already clear in her lifetime that the Foundress was a saint. Did not the small children of Don Suero de Vega and his wife, her good friends in Palencia, call attention to the delicious odour pervading her habit, which they clung to exclaiming: 'How lovely this lady smells!' And had not Father Yepes, her future biographer, noticed the same mysterious odour of sanctity on administering the sacrament? When she drew back her veil to receive the Host, Teresa's face, care-worn and sallow, was suddenly transfigured with radiant beauty, and though he noticed her teeth were blackened and decayed, her mouth distilled a perfume like musk. The Father was scandalized at first, thinking that this nun whom people said was so holy used scent.

Castile was shimmering in the summer heat when Teresa left
Soria. She travelled to Avila by way of Osma and Segovia,
stopping awhile at the convent there, with only Ana and a
prebendary as travelling companions. The guides they managed to
pick up on the way 'would leave us whenever we reached a bad
part of the road, saying they had business to do elsewhere'. The
driver did not know the way 'and took us along tracks so bad that
we often had to alight and walk, whilst the cart hung suspended
over the brink of steep precipices'. At last they reached Avila, but
it was a cheerless homecoming. Teresa was feverish and suffering
from a painfully sore throat. The absence of Lorenzo, Francisco de
Salcedo and other old friends left a void which could not be filled.
'Here I am in Avila, my Father,' she wrote to Gracián, 'and would
gladly be your daughter again if only you were here, for I feel very
lonely in this place and can turn to no one for solace. The further I
journey in this life – God help me – the less comfort I find.' Was
this craving for human affection and companionship an imperfection in one whose heart should be given to God alone? Her
greatest joy, she confided to María de San José in Seville, was to
receive letters from her friends:

> Your letters always refresh me as much as others tire me. I assure
> you that if you love me dearly I am happy to hear you say so, and
> I love you dearly in return. How deeply rooted in this nature of
> ours is this desire to see our love returned! It cannot be wrong,
> for our Lord wishes it too, though the love we owe him, and
> which he so much deserves, is incomparably greater. But let us
> imitate him even in this.

What distressed Teresa most was the deplorable condition in
which she found St Joseph's. It hardly seemed possible that its
falling-off could be so rapid and so complete. The fault, it grieved
her to see, was partly that of the chaplain, Julián de Avila, who had
faithfully shared the trials of her early foundations but had now
grown easy-going and indulgent towards the nuns. Old age was

probably to blame – 'God deliver us from elderly confessors!' A more general cause was the penury induced by Spain's economic decline and by the death or departure of the convent's principal benefactors. The Bishop had left, Lorenzo had remembered the convent in his will but probate was not yet through, and the *Caballero santo* had likewise bequeathed a legacy, but one 'too small to supply our dinner, and we have not enough for supper either'. The worst of it was that people believed he had provided amply for all their needs and so stopped giving alms themselves. What the nuns could earn from their labour covered only a fraction of expenses, and little could be expected in the way of dowries from fresh novices. Teresa was always ready to take girls without any dowries at all if they seemed to have the makings of good nuns, though she could also be firm in pressing for the maximum if a family was wealthy enough to pay. Her niece Teresita had not yet made up her mind to take the veil, and showed signs of yielding to pressure from her unstable brother Francisco and his astute and unscrupulous mother-in-law Doña Beatriz de Castilla y Mendoza, who were trying to induce her to renounce her share of her father's inheritance in their favour. The Foundress, with her immense authority, experience and powers of persuasion seemed the only person capable of putting the convent back on its feet, and reluctantly – for she felt the task to be now beyond her strength – she yielded to Gracián's insistence that she should resume control. 'They have made me Prioress out of sheer hunger', she complained to María de San José. 'Pray for me to God, all of you, that I may find enough for the nuns to eat, or I don't know what I shall do.'

Yet fresh demands continued to be made on Teresa's time and scanty resources. She was distressed by rumours that her niece Beatriz de Ovalle had been enticing a married man, and she wrote to Alba urging the girl's mother to come to Avila at her expense and discuss what should be done. She wrote too to young Lorenzo, now beginning to prosper in America, on behalf of that insatiable scrounger Juan de Ovalle. Gracián also needed money, and

Teresa managed to contribute four ducats for a project very near to her own heart – the printing of the Revised Constitutions for the Discalced drawn up at the Alcalá Chapter. The letters and memoranda which she had sent him on the subject from Palencia embody the ripe fruit of her experience and meditations. Whilst at Toledo four years before she had already drawn up, at his request, an admirable 52-point memorandum *On the Visitation of Convents*, full of good sense and shrewd insight. The points stressed for the Alcalá Chapter reveal once again Teresa's exceptional knowledge of human nature and her genius for combining firm administration with sensitivity and human warmth. She urges that the Discalced friars should act, wherever possible, as confessors to the nuns, but they should not seek to control their temporal as well as their spiritual affairs. They should claim no monopoly as preachers or in other ways, for 'a soul cannot serve God in a strait-jacket'. They should avoid all occasions for gossip or any kind of intimacy with the nuns, who for their part should be scrupulous in wearing the veil and observing strict enclosure. All excessive rigour should however be avoided; 'it is enough to observe the obligations prescribed by the Church, without adding to them'. The Constitutions should be kept simple and free from exacting detail, prayers should be simplified and innovations resisted. The use of high-sounding modes of address in letters should be avoided. The friars should be allowed more food than they were generally given, and use more clean table- and bed-linen; it would cost more, but it is 'a terrible thing' where this is lacking. The clauses in the Constitutions forbidding any endowment of monasteries should be amended, for most houses were on the way to having some income now. But no Superior has the right to permit friars to have personal possessions. Teresa concludes her advice by urging Gracián to note down her main points and then burn her letters, which might otherwise come into the wrong hands, 'and that would be serious'.

At the end of November Teresa wrote to María de San José: 'After Christmas I am off to make the foundation at Burgos. It is a terribly cold place at this time of the year.' She still hoped to see that convent in Madrid on which she had set her heart, but the Cardinal-Archbishop, for all his previous promises, remained inscrutably silent. Preparations were also far advanced for a foundation in Granada, and Friar John of the Cross made the long journey from Andalusia to induce her to undertake it. It was their first meeting since his imprisonment four years before, and it was to be their last.

John brought with him a letter from Gracián authorizing him to escort the Foundress to Granada 'with the comfort and care due to her person and her age, together with such other nuns as may be required'. No record of their meeting survives beyond a brief reference in one of her letters telling us that it brought her joy. But though she designated the nuns to accompany him, Teresa would not herself go to Granada. Her refusal wounded Friar John's sensitive nature more deeply than he cared to show. Many years before, in her time of need, he had gone at Teresa's bidding to Avila; now that he needed her, the Foundress would not come. Teresa must have told him that God wanted her to make the arduous journey to Burgos. And where it was a question of obeying what she believed to be the divine guidance, Teresa showed all the ruthlessness, as well as the fortitude and patience, of a saint.

For the journey which lay before her Teresa needed this patience and fortitude in full measure. No one could ever remember such a wet winter. Rain fell all the way from Avila to Medina, and from there to Valladolid the downpour became a deluge. In Palencia, the crowds braved the weather and came out into the streets to give the Foundress an enthusiastic welcome, but she would not pause to rest there for more than a couple of days. By now Teresa was seriously ill. The soreness in her throat had become an open wound which made it agony for her to swallow anything except a little liquid or even to speak. She trembled so in every limb that she could hardly walk. The woman who had lived so long in the harsh climate of Avila could now no longer bear the bitter cold. 'Pay no heed to the cold, for I am the true warmth', her locutions reassured her. 'The Devil is exerting all his strength to hinder this foundation. Use all yours to further it, and do not fail to go there in person, for much good will come of it.'

The party which travelled with her was a large one. Besides her nurse-companion Ana, she took Teresita, whom she was anxious to keep out of the clutches of the scheming relatives; Tomasina Bautista, a sensible woman who was the prioress-designate; her sub-prioress Inés de la Cruz; Catalina, a daughter of the lady who was to be their chief benefactress in Burgos; and one or two other nuns and lay sisters. Gracián and a friar from Granada accompanied them on mule-back. The muleteers were mainly young and inexperienced, but they and the servants, aided at times by the friars, performed prodigies of valour hauling the carts through the thick mud and throwing themselves on to the wheels to keep them from slithering down dangerous slopes. The nuns had often to alight and flounder through the water. Rumour spread that Gracián had fallen from his mule and been drowned. He in turn feared the Foundress had come to grief, but the body sprawling in the mire proved to be that of a muleteer who struggled to his feet bedraggled but unharmed. A scout sent on ahead returned with the news that the roads were quite impassable. Teresa ignored his report and the caravan pushed on.

As they neared Burgos, the travellers reached the worst part of the road – a stretch of marshy ground traversed by narrow pontoon bridges. It was dangerous at the best of times and was now completely covered with water. A lurch to one side, and the carts would be carried away. The keeper of a nearby inn took pity on them and volunteered to guide them across. The nuns implored their Mother's blessing, sought absolution from the priests, and kept up their courage by reciting the creed. Even Teresa's heart sank when she saw the expanse of swirling, muddy water. But at once her courage and gaiety returned. 'Come now, my daughters!' she cried, 'What more could you want than to end your lives here as martyrs – should it come to that – for the love of God?' But even in this emergency Teresa's prudence and good sense did not forsake her. She ordered the nuns to let her go first. If she were to be swept away they must not attempt to rescue her but they should return to the inn. They all waded safely across the flooded pontoons, and 'once the danger was over, it was fun to talk about it. It is a great thing to suffer under obedience.' Tradition adds that Teresa complained in prayer about the trials of this journey and was answered by the locution: 'But that is how I treat my friends!' 'Yes, Lord,' she is said to have replied, 'and that is why you have so few of them!'

It was still raining in torrents when the travellers reached Burgos. Their benefactress, Doña Catalina de Tolosa, was a widow of some means and rare piety who already governed her large household, under the direction of Jesuit confessors, like a well-run convent. In due course she and all her children were to join the Discalced Carmelites as nuns or friars. Doña Catalina welcomed the sisters with open arms and dried their habits before a blazing log fire. Gracián went to lodge with Dr Pedro Manso, a friend from his student days and now a canon of Burgos Cathedral. Exhaustion had left Teresa spitting blood and suffering violent attacks of vomiting. She was obliged to keep to the bed which they made up for her behind a curtained grille looking onto a corridor where visitors were received. Gradually she recovered her strength, though she could still take no solid food. Dr Manso, who became her confessor, declared many years later that as he approached the invisible nun his limbs began to tremble and his hair to stand on end, so strong was the impression that he was entering into the presence of a saint. The good canon's reaction was the more remarkable on account of the scepticism with which he had greeted reports of Teresa's sanctity. The respect he soon acquired for her intelligence was no less great. 'God help me,' he is said to have exclaimed after a discussion with her on some business matter, 'I had sooner argue with all the theologians in the world than with this Mother!'

Teresa and her little band had been brought safely to the shelter of this friendly house. They were now to face the opposition of which she had been warned in one of her locutions. From which quarter was it likely to come? The Devil had not yet shown his hand, and all seemed to promise well. The capital of Old Castile, it is true, had lost something of its former prosperity since the wars in Flanders had begun to ruin the once flourishing wool trade. Other Orders were also at the time competing to establish themselves in the city. But the Town Council had raised no objection to the coming of the Carmelites. The latter had every hope too of finding a friend in the Archbishop. His family had been connected with Teresa's in Avila; he was the son of that luckless Viceroy of Peru, Blasco Núñez Vela, by whose side her brothers had fought and one of them lost his life. He was also a friend of Don Alvaro de Mendoza, now his colleague in Soria, who had been singing the praises of the Discalced. So it was in confident mood that Gracián waited on the Archbishop to pay his respects and request formal confirmation of the permission promised for the new foundation.

He returned with disconcerting news. The Archbishop had received him coldly and refused to grant a licence. Inflexible like all his family, he had not been swayed by Gracián's persuasions. The Archbishop could not forget the fuss caused in Avila when Teresa founded the first St Joseph's there *sin renta*, and he had no wish to see similar trouble stirred up in his see. He admitted that he had said Teresa might come to Burgos, but he had meant her only to discuss matters and not to bring so many nuns with her, as if his consent were a foregone conclusion. Unless the nuns could show they had a suitable house and endowment he would never agree to a foundation and they might as well go back home straight away: '– in such nice weather and by such fine roads, too! – ' Teresa comments ironically.

The ailing Foundress prepared to do battle. Canon Manso and other well-wishers intervened with the Archbishop, but all to no avail. He even refused to authorize mass to be said in Doña Catalina's house, though the Jesuits had celebrated it there for ten years before acquiring premises of their own. Teresa mustered her strength for a personal interview but had no more success than her friends. God's great 'gift of pleasing' which had so often turned enemies into friends, won over obdurate prelates, and brought an Archbishop to his knees to ask for her blessing glanced harmlessly off the rock of Vela intransigence. The Foundress told him that she had left her nuns praying with tears in their eyes and the discipline in their hands. The Archbishop replied that they might go on scourging themselves as much as they pleased, for he had no intention of giving his consent.

The Archbishop did, however, grudgingly agree that they might stay on where they were for the time being. When Doña Catalina generously offered her entire fortune to help them find a suitable house and endowment, he sent a message expressing satisfaction and telling them that his Vicar-General would now be able to settle matters with them. But his representative proved even more difficult than the Archbishop himself and raised fresh difficulties which he clearly hoped would induce them to leave. 'The Devil must have been getting at this Vicar-General as well', Teresa comments. Gracián was plunged into dejection and talked of sending the nuns back to their old convents. The Foundress put a brave face on things. Much as she grieved to see him go, she begged Gracián not to delay his visitations any longer on their account, but to leave her and the nuns to continue the battle. The Lord would surely find somewhere else where they could live. He had spoken to her in no uncertain terms: 'Now, Teresa, stand firm!'

From Doña Catalina's house, which the Vicar-General unconvincingly insisted was too damp and noisy for nuns, they moved temporarily into the attics of a large hospital. It was anything but a desirable lodging, though the Foundress seemed quite content with it. The attics were rumoured to be haunted, and the stench and noise penetrating the rat-infested floorboards from the wards below made life almost insupportable. Teresa spent all the time she could with the patients, surreptitiously distributing amongst them the oranges and other titbits which the faithful Doña Catalina continued to bring for her own relief. With quiet resolution she also continued her efforts to find a house and secure the licence. She wrote to the Duchess of Alba, meditated an approach to the Nuncio. Don Alvaro de Mendoza sent her a letter for the Archbishop, but it was so sharply worded that she feared that difficult prelate would take offence and she made the good Bishop redraft it. Her friends continued to scour Burgos for a suitable house, and eventually found one which the agents of the other Orders had somehow overlooked. A contract was hastily drawn up and the grilles and other fittings essential for the nuns' enclosure were installed. Then they moved in.

But still the Archbishop's attitude remained ambivalent. He wanted to see the convent established, he declared; but the licence was still not forthcoming. 'As he is such a good Christian,' Teresa observed, 'he would not tell an untruth; but his actions hardly correspond to what he said.' He objected to the grilles and the 'turn', and said he had never authorized the nuns to install them. Teresa placated him by explaining that this was normal practice in their convents. A protesting tenant had to be ejected from the building, and at this too he took offence. Teresa continued to find excuses for him. 'Even when he gets annoyed, he is a good man, and his anger is soon over.' Their troubles, she added, were due rather to his Vicar-General, who would have gone on harassing them for ever 'had not God in due course converted him and made him another man'.

The patient bearing of the nuns in the face of official hostility and the veneration which many people had come to feel for their Foundress were winning a good deal of sympathy for them in Burgos and corresponding odium for the Archbishop. Canon

Manso told him so to his face. His Grace had no wish to appear a persecutor of virtuous innocence, and on 18 April 1582, nearly four months after their arrival, he at last granted them a licence. Gracián returned from his visitations for the dedication ceremony which the Archbishop graced with his presence. The following day the first postulant, Doña Catalina's young daughter Elenita, was given the habit, and the Archbishop preached a moving sermon. He was now all benevolence. According to Teresita's account, he even asked the nuns' forgiveness for having made them suffer.

There was another reason for the obstruction they had encountered to which Teresa alludes only delicately in her *Foundations*. Doña Catalina's Jesuit confessors were exceedingly displeased by the widow's wish to bequeath to the Discalced the fortune which they counted upon for their own College. 'They are really beginning to show themselves our declared enemies', she wrote some days after the nuns had moved in. 'The Devil is making them blame me for the very thing they ought to be thanking me for.' How sadly things had changed from those days in Avila when, at the outset of her troubled pilgrimage, Teresa had found in the Jesuit Fathers the surest of her guides! Since then, the Society had come to view even the most orthodox manifestations of mysticism with deepening distrust. Those, like Teresa's old confessor Baltasar Alvarez, who were attracted to its practice incurred disfavour and sometimes persecution. An embarrassing episode had occurred not long before when it was rumoured that Father Gaspar de Salazar, a friend of Teresa and a former Rector of the Jesuit College in Avila, was planning to leave the Company to become a Discalced Carmelite friar. Teresa had been bitterly – and unjustly – charged with enticement. Now, in Burgos, the Fathers were trying to discredit the Discalced and stop Catalina de Tolosa from having anything to do with them. After consultation with Gracián, Teresa decided on a bold step. To remove all ground for their hostility she renounced Doña Catalina's promised bequest and signed a formal statement to that effect. This she kept secret from the Archbishop for fear of provoking a fresh outburst of irritability.

Everything was now working out as the Lord had promised, and Teresa's heart was once again overflowing with joy and gratitude. The Devil had done his utmost to prevent the foundation, but God had given her strength to thwart his plots. Critics might object that she had been a trifle disingenuous with the difficult Archbishop. He had authorized the foundation on condition that it had adequate endowment, and as soon as his licence had been obtained she had secretly renounced the promised legacy on the strength of which he had given his consent. But the Lord had expressly said to her: 'Do you mean to hold back on account of money?' She had not held back; in fact, she had thought of a move which would clear her conscience and ought to satisfy the Archbishop should he come to hear of it. Two of Doña Catalina's daughters were making their profession that very month in the Discalced Convent at Palencia and had renounced their property in favour of their mother, as was quite usual. The terms of their renunciation were now modified in favour of the convent at Burgos. Elenita, the young postulant, likewise made over her property to the convent, although the latter could not benefit from it immediately as she was not yet of age to be professed. So, even without Doña Catalina's benefaction, the convent was in effect adequately endowed.

Although she was sure that God would provide for their immediate needs, Teresa would have liked to stay on a little longer with her nuns until the new community found its feet. But one day after Communion, the familiar voice spoke once more, and the old Foundress received her marching orders: 'Why do you still have doubts? Your work here is over. Now you can leave.' Ana, the saint's confidante, speaks of a still more peremptory and disturbing command: 'Go! You have yet to suffer greater things!'

16

Mission Completed

It was midsummer again when Teresa left Burgos for Avila. She was accompanied by Ana and Teresita, who would be sixteen in a few weeks' time and old enough then to take the veil. 'She's a good little thing, but a mere child after all', Teresa confided to María de San José in Seville, anxious to see her settled and worried by the girl's occasional moods of taciturnity and restlessness. The intrigues of Francisco's covetous mother-in-law, who was straining every nerve to secure the novice's dowry, were poisoning the family atmosphere and mounting to a climax. Teresa longed to be back in the peace of St Joseph's, first and dearest of the communities which God had led her to found, where she could help to guide the footsteps of her young niece and namesake along the Way of Perfection whose earthly course she herself had all but run. 'Then I shall not have to go travelling about any more,' she wrote to a friend, 'for I am very old and tired.'

But what of those 'greater things' she understood she must yet suffer? Perhaps they were to do with the proposed foundation in Madrid which the Cardinal-Archbishop kept promising but would never authorize. 'All we can do now is to wait until the Archbishop gives us the licence out of sheer exasperation', she wrote, trusting in her proven tactics of patience and divine persistence. It might well seem that a foundation in Spain's new capital would be a fitting crown for her life's work. But the only crown which Teresa de Jesús was to receive in this life was her master's crown of thorns.

In Burgos she had bidden farewell to Father Gracián, who was leaving for a round of visitations which would take him to Andalusia. They were not to see each other again. Doria, his coadjutor, had been sent to Italy to seek the blessing of the Carmelite General and to assure him of the loyalty of the Discalced. Teresa was delighted to learn that he was succeeding brilliantly. She was not to know that his success would also gain him the ear of Rome as his hostility to the guileless Gracián grew sharper and more open. The Italian's partisans in Spain were already murmuring that he had been sent abroad to rid the Provincial of a dangerous rival. She found the same distressing rumours rife when she reached Valladolid. 'Since coming here', she wrote to Gracián, 'I have been told that your Reverence is notoriously averse to having anyone of weight near you. . . . Be careful about this, for the love of God.' It is long and rather querulous, this last letter penned by the ailing Foundress – the last, at least, that has come down to us – to her dear friend, son and father in God, but a letter still full of concern for family and friends and the multitudinous affairs of the Reform, and illumined by flashes of the old humour and spirit. 'Don't think of turning yourself into an Andalusian', she admonishes. 'You are not really cut out for living amongst them!' But the dominant note is one of anxiety and plaintiveness:

> Your frequent letters are not enough to alleviate my distress. . . . The reasons you give for having decided to go do not seem to me sufficient. . . . I have felt your absence at this time so keenly that I quite lost all desire to write to your Paternity. . . . I don't know what reason your Reverence can have for staying so long in Seville. . . . As for your sermons there, I earnestly implore your Reverence once more to watch your words most carefully . . . Oh my Father, I have felt such a weight on my mind these last days, but it quite went as soon as I heard that all was well with you . . . May the Lord watch